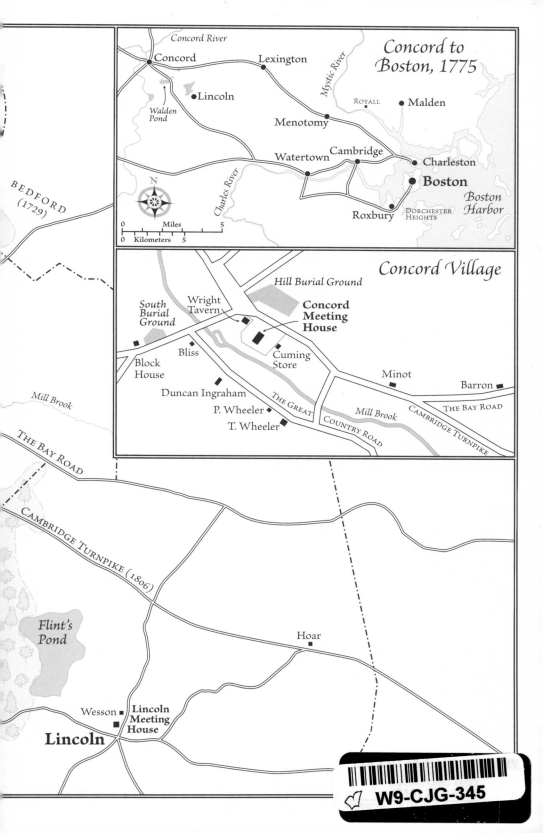

Concord to Boston, 1775

Concord River

Concord
Lexington
Mystic River
Lincoln
ROYALL
Malden
Walden Pond
Menotomy
Cambridge
Charleston
Watertown
Boston
N
Charles River
Roxbury
DORCHESTER HEIGHTS
Boston Harbor

BEDFORD (1729)

0 Miles 5
0 Kilometers 5

Concord Village

Hill Burial Ground

South Burial Ground
Wright Tavern
Concord Meeting House

Block House
Bliss
Cuming Store
Minot
Barron
THE BAY ROAD

Mill Brook
Duncan Ingraham
THE GREAT
CAMBRIDGE TURNPIKE

P. Wheeler
T. Wheeler
COUNTRY ROAD
Mill Brook

THE BAY ROAD

CAMBRIDGE TURNPIKE (1806)

Flint's Pond

Hoar

Wesson
Lincoln Meeting House

Lincoln

W9-CJG-345

Black Walden

Black Walden

Slavery and Its Aftermath in Concord, Massachusetts

Elise Lemire

PENN

UNIVERSITY OF PENNSYLVANIA PRESS

Philadelphia

Published by
University of Pennsylvania Press
Philadelphia, Pennsylvania 19104-4112

Printed in the United States of America on acid-free paper
10 9 8 7 6 5 4 3 2 1

Library of Congress Cataloging-in-Publication Data
Lemire, Elise.
    Black Walden : slavery and its aftermath in Concord, Massachusetts / Elise Lemire.
        p. cm.
    Includes bibliographical references and index.
    ISBN 978-0-8122-4180-8 (alk. paper)
1. Slavery — Massachusetts — Concord — History. 2. Slaves — Massachusetts — Concord —
Social conditions. 3. Concord (Mass.) — Social conditions — 18th century. 4. Thoreau, Henry
David, 1817–1862. Walden I. Title.
    F74.C8L46 2009
    974.4'4--dc22   2009001010

For my parents,
Robert and Virginia Lemire

EAST OF MY BEAN-FIELD, *across the road, lived Cato Ingraham, slave of Duncan Ingraham, Esquire, gentleman of Concord village; who built his slave a house, and gave him permission to live in Walden Woods; —Cato, not Uticensis, but Concordiensis. Some say that he was a Guinea Negro. There are a few who remember his little patch among the walnuts, which he let grow up till he should be old and need them; but a younger and whiter speculator got them at last. He too, however, occupies an equally narrow house at present. Cato's half-obliterated cellar hole still remains, though known to few, being concealed from the traveller by a fringe of pines. It is now filled with the smooth sumach (*Rhus glabra,*) and one of the earliest species of golden-rod (*Solidago stricta*) grows there luxuriantly.*

Here, by the very corner of my field, still nearer to town, Zilpha, a colored woman, had her little house, where she spun linen for the townsfolk, making the Walden Woods ring with her shrill singing, for she had a loud and notable voice. At length, in the war of 1812, her dwelling was set on fire by English soldiers, prisoners on parole, when she was away, and her cat and dog and hens were all burned up together. She led a hard life, and somewhat inhumane. One old frequenter of these woods remembers, that as he passed her house one noon he heard her muttering to herself over her gurgling pot, — "Ye are all bones, bones!" I have seen bricks amid the oak copse there.

Down the road, on the right hand, on Brister's Hill, lived Brister Freeman, "a handy Negro," slave of Squire Cummings once, — there where grow still the apple-trees which Brister planted and tended; large old trees now, but their fruit still wild and ciderish to my taste. Not long since I read his epitaph in the old Lincoln burying-ground, a little on one side, near the unmarked graves of some British grenadiers who fell in the retreat from Concord, — where he is styled "Sippio Brister," — Scipio Africanus he had some title to be called, — "a man of color," as if he were discolored. It also told me, with staring emphasis, when he died; which was but an indirect way of informing me that he ever lived. With him dwelt Fenda, his hospitable wife, who told fortunes, yet pleasantly, — large, round, and black, blacker than any of the children of night, such a dusky orb as never rose on Concord before or since.

—HENRY DAVID THOREAU, *Walden* (1854)

CONTENTS

Introduction	The Memory of These Human Inhabitants	1
Chapter 1	Squire Cuming	15
Chapter 2	The Codman Place	41
Chapter 3	British Grenadiers	70
Chapter 4	The Last of the Race Departed	91
Chapter 5	Permission to Live in Walden Woods	112
Chapter 6	Little Gardens and Dwellings	128
Chapter 7	Concord Keeps Its Ground	151
Epilogue	Brister Freeman's Hill	175
Dramatis Personae		177
Notes		183
Bibliography		211
Index		221
Acknowledgments		233

The Memory of These Human Inhabitants

E ACH YEAR, HALF A MILLION PEOPLE visit Walden Pond in Concord, Massachusetts. Most come to pay homage to Henry David Thoreau, who for two years lived a quiet, contemplative life in a small cabin he built not far from the pond's shores. And yet in *Walden; or, Life in the Woods* (1854), his famous account of his experiment in subsistence living, Thoreau asks us to experience the Walden landscape as a rich repository of a long and complicated human history that began well before his arrival in 1845. He devotes the better part of a chapter to a community of former Concord slaves who lived not far from his cabin during the first four decades of the new nation's existence. Their experiences after emancipation were one reason Thoreau was drawn to live in Walden Woods himself. He regarded the former slaves' persistence in the face of isolation and harassment as heroic, and like them he sought to live independently. He also enjoyed living in a part of town where, because of its past association with former slaves and other outcasts, few of his white contemporaries chose to linger.

Mary Minot was one of those people who avoided Walden Woods when she could. Her story, which Thoreau uses in *Walden*, is a good place to start a book that investigates the long-forgotten connection between Walden Woods and Concord's slave history. Mary was born in Concord six years after her father Ephraim fought the British at Concord's North Bridge in 1775. While her father could say he helped set in motion one of the great political revolutions in western history, Mary led a relatively quiet life. She never married and lived with her younger brother George and her business partner, Elizabeth Potter, in an unpainted, four-room cottage. George Minot, who also never married, spent his days farming and fishing, rarely venturing from the town in which his ancestors had lived since the mid-seventeenth century. Only once did he go as far as Boston, even after tracks were laid in 1844 and the port city became reachable in an hour by train. Mary made a meager living as a seamstress, sewing clothes with Miss Potter's assistance for the town's second-class laboring men. She was rarely asked to make anything for her neighbor, Concord's wealthiest resident, the philosopher Ralph Waldo Emerson, who lived diagonally across the road from her and to whom the Minots regularly sold eggs and cream. Henry David Thoreau, a dear friend of George's and just as eccentric, was a more frequent customer. The Harvard graduate famously shunned the black suits worn by the educated men of his day, requesting of Miss Minot clay-colored corduroy clothes with overly large pockets for his daily walks so he could carry his notebook and spyglass easily and be "less conspicuous in the fields" as he tracked Concord's wildlife. Mary also sewed for her younger sister Lavina Minot Baker who, with her husband Joseph, had five children. Mary would walk two and a half miles to the Baker farm on the Lincoln side of Walden Woods and stay for a day or two. [1]

Years later, George Minot told Thoreau about a particular August day Mary spent in Lincoln sewing for their sister. After hours spent bent over her needle, Mary attempted to carry home what her brother told Thoreau was "the rather onerous present of a watermelon," prompting Thoreau to recall in his journal "the old saying" that a person "cannot carry two melons under one arm" and to note that "it is difficult to carry one far, it is so slippery." Mary was seventy-eight when Thoreau recounted her attempt in an 1859 journal entry. The day she set off through Walden Woods with a heavy watermelon in her arms must have taken place years earlier, probably in the 1820s or 1830s when Lavina's children were growing fast and their wardrobes thus in constant need of attention. Mary, then in her forties or fifties, set out holding the tricky fruit as best she could, eager to share this favorite summer treat with her brother and Miss Potter. Called the Great County Road in its heyday, the road she followed is known today as Walden Street or Route 126. The stagecoach used to rumble along this way, as did numerous farmers' wagons and rich men's chaises, all conveying goods and people either north to New Hampshire or east to Boston via its connection to the mainland at Roxbury Neck. But since the completion of a bridge that connected Charlestown to Boston in 1785, the majority of traffic ran farther to the east along the Lexington road, formerly called the Bay road, which now ran directly into Boston. The Walden road had since become a mere shadow of its former self, used by Concord and Lincoln residents mainly to access their woodlots. [2]

On this particular day, however, the farmers who normally filled the woods with the ringing of their axes must have been celebrating the end of haying season with their annual fishing trip to Dorchester. And although Mary sometimes brought her partner with her to Lincoln, she had made this visit alone. There was no one to help carry the watermelon or any of the other items Mary toted. Nor was there anyone to keep her company as the silence closed in around her. All she could hear were the whispering of the pines Thoreau described as so close to the road they would "scrape both sides of a chaise at once." [3]

As Thoreau well knew and as he points out in his journal on the occasion of reporting what happened next, "Walden Woods . . . had a rather bad reputation for goblins and so on in those days." As a young child, he had heard reports from other children about an Indian doctor living there who "caught small boys and cut out their livers to make medicine." More recently, Mary's brother George had told him of once hearing a "colored woman . . . somewhat witch-like," mutter something like an incantation over the contents of a cauldron she was stirring in a small hut in Walden Woods. "Ye are all bones, bones!" she cackled in what George described as a "shrill" voice. Thoreau had heard too of a "large, round, and black" fortune-teller who had lived just down the road from the witch. Having presumably heard these same stories from her brother or other locals, Mary became anxious as she approached the remnants of the dwellings in which these notorious characters once lived. The watermelon, Thoreau notes, "did not grow any lighter, though frequently shifted from arm to arm." Quickening her pace, Mary failed to keep her grip on the slippery melon. It smashed to pieces "in the middle of the Walden road." Thoreau muses only half seriously that the accident might have been caused by "one of those mischievous goblins." Certainly Mary thought so. Her brother reported to Thoreau that, "trembling," she stopped only to gather the choicest pieces of fruit in her handkerchief before she "flew rather than ran with them to the peaceful streets of Concord." In *Walden*, Thoreau draws on Mary's experience of the Walden road, writing that "women and children who were compelled to go this way to Lincoln alone and on foot did it with fear, and often ran a good part of the distance." [4]

Figure 1. *Herbert Wendell Gleason, Walden from Emerson's Cliff.*
Photographed November 7, 1899. Courtesy of the Concord Free Public Library.

I GREW UP IN LINCOLN, MASSACHUSETTS, in a house two miles from Walden Pond (Figure 1). The Walden Woods I knew in the 1970s and 1980s was not a place one feared. I took swimming lessons at Walden Pond in my childhood, canoed it as a teenager, and returned regularly over the years to hike its perimeter, often alone. I had no idea during my childhood or early adulthood that there had once been former slaves in the area — let alone slaves in Concord — or that Thoreau's experiment in subsistence living was influenced by their lives. The homes of the former slaves had vanished. My white, suburban upbringing had not compelled me to think particularly hard about slavery anyway, much less about how slavery might have shaped the privileged, leafy world I inhabited. In fact, Concord was the last place I thought about when I thought about slavery at all.

All that I knew about Concord was what I had been taught in school: that it gave birth to the nation and the nation's literature. When friends would visit from out of town, I was as eager to show off Concord's many famous sites as they were to tour them. We would begin our walking tour at the Old North Bridge, where the American Revolution began on April 19, 1775, when the colonial militia or minutemen faced down British regulars and sent them fleeing back to Boston. Ralph Waldo Emerson's description of "the embattled farmer" and "the shot heard round the world" is etched on an obelisk at the eastern side of the bridge. On the western side is a statue of a local man leaving behind his plow to take up his musket against his mother country. Since its erection on the one hundredth anniversary of Concord Fight, the Minuteman Statue has become iconographic, a statement that the commitment of the United States to liberty is natural and thus inevitable, having sprung from the very soil, the *Concord* soil, tilled by local farmers. On my twelfth birthday, I received a miniature, sterling silver version of the Minuteman Statue to add to my charm bracelet, a reminder that I was born where American freedom began. [5]

After showing friends the bridge, I would lead them to the nearby house where Emerson's grandfather watched the battle from his backyard. This was where the tour would turn to American literature, which, like the country, was arguably born within sight of the North Bridge, making this part of Concord doubly sacred ground. Emerson was staying here when he drafted his essay *Nature* (1836) before purchasing the house in which he lived across from George and Mary Minot for the rest of his life. A newly married Nathaniel Hawthorne later rented the same house by the bridge. Once called the Manse in honor of the ministers who lived in it, first the Reverend William Emerson and then the Reverend Ezra Ripley, it came to be called by the name Hawthorne gave it in the book he wrote while living there, *Mosses from an Old Manse* (1846). Toward the end of his life, the author of *The Scarlet Letter* (1850) purchased another home in Concord he named the Wayside. This house is located next-door to Orchard House, where Louisa May Alcott wrote *Little Women* (1868), the much-beloved tale of four sisters attempting to make their own way in a world that would have preferred their conformity. American literature has long been celebrated for its deep commitment to the same values the colonial militia fought for in the town that would later produce so many of the nation's most prominent authors: personal freedom and individualism. And first among the American classics written in Concord that celebrates these values is *Walden*. And so after touring the battle site and the Old Manse, my friends and I would head next to Walden Pond.[6]

Like the Minuteman Statue, the site of Thoreau's sojourn has become an internationally recognized symbol of freedom. Thoreau's purpose in building a cabin next to Walden Pond and subsisting on what he could grow nearby was to achieve freedom from capitalism, conformity, and all the other constraints of modern life. It was also, somewhat ironically it now appears, the place where he sought to extricate himself from the politics of slavery. A few weeks after setting up camp in the woods, Thoreau was stopped by Sam Staples, who in his capacity as tax collector asked Thoreau to pay his delinquent poll tax from the past six years. Thoreau refused on the grounds that the Mexican-American War was a plot on behalf of the government to expand slavery. His refusal cost him a night in the Concord jail. In his account of that night, "The Rights and Duties of the Individual in Relation to Government" (1849), Thoreau famously asserts that "Under a government which imprisons any unjustly, the true place for a just man is also a prison." With these words he inspired freedom movements around the globe to use civil disobedience as a means of protesting injustice.

Almost everyone who visited me in Lincoln came to the Walden Pond State Reservation expecting to find unspoiled nature and the story of a man who sought in its bosom the inspiration and strength to fight injustice. They were never disappointed. The Massachusetts Department of Conservation and

Recreation maintains a life-size replica of Thoreau's sparsely furnished cabin next to the parking lot so that visitors can see how serious he was in his determination to live a "primitive and frontier life." There are maps posted that direct tourists to the original "site of Thoreau's hut" and a well-maintained path that takes them there. When they arrive at the granite posts that mark the site, there is a sign quoting Thoreau's assertion in *Walden* that he went to the woods to live "deliberately." Visitors are encouraged to commit themselves to a similarly deliberate life by leaving a stone on the cairn started near the cabin's location shortly after Thoreau's death. Nothing distracts from the sense that one is making a sacred pilgrimage and that the pilgrimage is all about Henry David Thoreau. Clearly the Commonwealth of Massachusetts takes very seriously the terms of the gift that resulted in the creation of the reservation. In 1922, when private citizens granted eighty acres of Walden Woods to the state, they did so with the stipulation that it "preserve the Walden of Emerson and Thoreau." Their version of Walden did not include the ghosts that once troubled Mary Minot. Concord's slaves and former slaves were replaced by a minuteman at one end of town and a dedicated abolitionist at the other. In retrospect, it hardly seems surprising that I knew nothing about Concord's slavery past until years later, after I had moved away. [7]

Because I assumed I knew what lay between the book's covers, I did not actually read *Walden* until I took a graduate course on American literature. I had made so many visits over the years to Walden Woods, I knew by heart each of its signs as well as the pamphlets distributed there by the state. I was thus very familiar with Thoreau's account of why he determined to live for two years in a tiny cabin he built on the fringes of his hometown. "I wished to live deliberately," he explains, "to front only the essential facts of life, and see if I could not learn what it had to teach, and not, when I came to die, discover that I had not lived." I thought I knew, too, what Thoreau discovered during his experiment in subsistence living. My parents had a quotation from *Walden* hanging in our front hall exhorting my brother and me to reach for the proverbial stars: "If one advances confidently in the direction of his dreams, and endeavors to live the life which he has imagined, he will meet with a success unexpected in common hours." [8]

Lifted out of context, as these quotations so often are on coffee mugs, calendars, bumper stickers, signs and posters, they had become platitudes. What I discovered upon reading *Walden* was anything but. Thoreau had a wonderful way of looking at a world he scrutinized carefully. Everything he observed was a metaphor awaiting his unique interpretation. In one example I particularly love, Thoreau describes a bug that "came out of the dry leaf of an old table of apple-tree wood, which had stood in a farmer's kitchen for sixty years." It seems an egg had been "deposited in the living tree many years earlier still, as appeared by counting the annual layers beyond it." "Hatched perchance by the heat of an urn," the bug was heard "gnawing out for several weeks." Thoreau uses the story as an occasion to hope for the transformation of humankind. "Who knows what beautiful and winged life, whose egg has been buried for ages under many concentric layers of woodenness in the dead dry life of society . . . may unexpectedly come forth from amidst society's most trivial and handselled furniture, to enjoy its perfect summer day at last!"⁹

I also discovered that Thoreau was not only an extremely deft writer, but an irreverent one as well. *Walden* is full of puns (over five hundred by one scholar's count). Thoreau jokes at one point that he "enhanced the value of the land by squatting on it." But even as he uses potty humor (he means in part that he fertilized the land by defecating on it), Thoreau is as serious here as he is in his recounting of the bug in the farmer's table. He *did* enhance the value of the land by squatting on it. Better to squat on the land (live on land you do not own) than carry the weight of a mortgage on your back. "The portionless, who struggle with no such unnecessary inherited encumbrances, find it labor enough to subdue and cultivate a few cubic feet of flesh."¹⁰

Although I was surprised and delighted by Thoreau's poetry and his puns, I was completely unprepared for the chapter in *Walden* entitled "Former Inhabitants; and Winter Visitors," in which he describes the outcasts who lived in Walden Woods prior to his arrival. Half of them were former African and African American slaves. Thoreau carefully describes the bean field he planted during his Walden stay as situated in a landscape marked by their presence. To the east of his bean field was a cellar hole where the home of Cato Ingraham used to stand. Formerly the "slave of Duncan Ingraham," Cato was said by some locals to be a "Guinea" or African "Negro." By the corner of Thoreau's bean field, "still nearer to town," "a colored woman" named "Zilpha" lived in a "little house," where she spun linen for the townsfolk. "Down the road, on the right hand," Thoreau continues, lived Brister Freeman and his wife Fenda. Brister was the "slave of Squire Cummings once." It was Zilpah (Thoreau misspells her name as well as Squire Cuming's) whom George Minot heard as she watched over a "gurgling pot" and Fenda who was the fortune-teller. [11]

In the years after graduate school, I put *Walden* aside and wrote a book about the role slavery and abolitionism played in shaping white views on interracial sex and marriage in Massachusetts and other Northern states. At that point, I no longer assumed that all of Concord's history was as white as it and the town of Lincoln once seemed to me. And yet even as slavery in New England became a major field of study, yielding a wealth of new information about the extensive role slavery played in New England's culture and economy, the history of slavery in the nation's birthplace remained unwritten. The new books being published about Concord were still more or less about the town's role as the cradle of liberty and literature. I found myself thinking again about Thoreau's chapter on the former inhabitants. *Walden* seems to offer several clues about the experiences of individual slaves in Concord both before and after slavery. Thoreau's extensive journals, I found out, offer still more. While he was never intent on writing a book about Concord slavery himself, Thoreau nevertheless recorded a plethora of information about area slaves and former slaves gleaned from town and county archives, area graveyards, and local memory, more, it turns out, than anyone before him or since. I decided it was time to finish what Thoreau had started: the history of slavery in the place we both called home. [12]

IN THE COURSE OF MY RESEARCH, I came to learn that Concord, Massachusetts, of all places, was a slave town. From its founding in 1635 until after the Revolution, enslaved men and women helped to build what would become New England's most storied town. To be sure, there was never the same percentage of slaves here as in the South. While I discovered more than twice the number of slaves in Concord than scholars have previously noted (thirty-two on the brink of the Revolution as opposed to the thirteen counted in the often cited 1771 tax valuation list), their numbers never exceeded 2 to 3 percent of the local population. But Concord was a slave town nonetheless. Every inhabitant who was not enslaved, whether a slaveholder or not, agreed to uphold the institution, watching slaves as they went about their masters' business and questioning them if there was any reason to suspect they were intent on running away. On the one known occasion when a Concord slave attempted to run, virtually everyone joined in the chase to hunt him down. It never struck even the most ardent Concord Patriots that their efforts against British authorities were in direct contradiction to their actions as either slaveholders or the co-conspirators of slaveholders. When slavery finally came to a gradual end, by a process that has long confounded historians, it was not because Massachusetts slaveholders somehow became more egalitarian-minded than their southern brethren on account of their early role in fomenting a revolution in the name of liberty. Nor was it because slaveholders "gave" their slave men their liberty in "exchange" for their service in the Continental Army (a common formulation in the history books that credits only the slaveholders with ending slavery). Rather, after the British began to occupy Boston, slaves in Concord and across Massachusetts took stock of the mounting political tensions and threatened to expose their masters to whichever side their respective masters considered the enemy. Many slaveholders decided to abandon their slaves to their freedom rather than suffer the political consequences. But even as these slaves effected a revolution of their own, slavery did not completely end in Massachusetts with the war. Not all slaves were relinquished. Nor did all those who had the option to strike out on their own choose to do so. Some slaves continued to serve their masters in exchange for room and board rather than risk abject poverty. There were men and women still enslaved in the Commonwealth as many as twenty years after the Revolution.[13]

The slaves who managed to take their freedom faced numerous challenges. To begin with, they were forced to stay in the towns where they had been enslaved because of what was known as the warning-out system. Anyone who tried to move to a new town without a means of support was warned or kicked out of that town by its officials and sent back to their hometown in order to ensure that each jurisdiction accepted financial responsibility for all its inhabitants. Unable in most cases to purchase land, the abandoned slaves were permitted by their former owners to squat locally, but only on the most out-of-the-way, infertile places. Walden Woods was one of those sites. The first European settlers had given up attempts to till what Henry David Thoreau calls Walden's "sterile" soil, leaving the area forested as a source of fuel and timber. The swampy edge of the town's Great Field, no longer the centerpiece of the town's agricultural system, was another similarly infertile place. Those who had been enslaved at what is now called the Codman estate chose to settle in Walden Woods on account of its proximity to their former home and the community they had cultivated there, while those who had been enslaved on estates on the other side of town settled by the Great Field. A former slave from Virginia raised his large family on arid land he purchased near the Old Marlborough Road, which became Concord's third area of black inhabitation. Here on the fringes of Concord, without adequate and fertile land to squat on and typically with no means to purchase more of a better quality, it was impossible for the former slaves to rise out of poverty. After forty years of struggling and largely failing to adequately feed their families, the black community in Walden Woods ceased to exist. The black communities on the Old Marlborough Road and the edge of the Great Field fared somewhat better, lasting almost one hundred years in the latter case, but they too vanished. The children of these black enclaves who did not die of malnutrition left town, leaving Concord the predominately white suburb I knew in my childhood.[14]

The segregation imposed in slavery's wake set the stage for Henry David Thoreau's experiment in independent living. In seeking to escape capitalism, war making, and other evils of modern life, Thoreau sought what he called a "wild" place where he could escape into nature and himself. By "wild," he meant a place with relatively few people and little or no cultivation of the land. Walden Woods, the edge of the Great Field, and the Old Marlborough Road were three of the four "wild" tracts he identified in Concord. These places had remained uncultivated and uninhabited because the soil there was poor and because whites like Mary Minot avoided lingering, let alone building and living, in what they perceived as an impoverished and later haunted part of town. But for Thoreau, it was the marks left on the landscape by the former slaves and other outcasts as much as the plants and animals that made these areas so interesting and he thus devotes a section of *Walden* to their memory. That chapter, "Former Inhabitants; and Winter Visitors," makes the case that the green spaces cherished in Concord today are not solely products of nature. They are the result of a highly stratified social order in which the highest echelon was comprised of Concord's wealthiest residents, more than half of whom were slaveholders, and the bottom echelon of slaves who were shunted by their former owners onto Concord's margins and left there to make a life for themselves as best they could. To put it more concisely, the history of slavery and its aftermath reveals that at least some of our nation's cherished green spaces began as black spaces, with Walden Woods a particularly striking case in point. [15]

In what follows, I have reconstructed the life stories of several of Concord's former slaves, both before and after their freedom, with a particular focus on the former slave who made the most lasting impact on the Walden landscape. Brister Freeman, as he named himself upon taking his freedom, seems to have been born at the Chambers-Russell estate, now called the Codman estate. (I say seems to have been because what little evidence survives about his childhood is largely, although not entirely, circumstantial.) But while relatively little is known of his early life, bits and pieces of his life after thirty-five years of slavery were widely known during his day and remembered long afterward. Stitching them back together reveals an exceptionally ambitious man. Understanding full well that social acceptance, economic prosperity, and even civil rights required property, he was the second former slave in Concord to purchase land there. He spent the rest of his life defending his right to own that land and to bequeath it to whom he pleased. It was a constant battle against town officials and other white men, one of whom almost cost Brister his life. The story of that life is told here for the first time.

By necessity, however, *Black Walden* is also the story of Concord's slave owners. Their needs, real and imagined, fueled and shaped slavery and ultimately the Walden landscape. As such, the first half of this book is mainly concerned with the many intimate details of their lives that made slavery seem imperative to them. This part of the book is centered on John Cuming, one of the wealthy gentlemen whose vast estates dotted the landscape and whose large, opulent mansion houses presided over it. He and the town's other gentlemen residents were afforded the time to practice their professions and rule the town's and eventually the nation's civic affairs by the slaves, servants, and hired hands who did the necessary work of raising food for their owners. John Cuming was wealthier and more prominent than most. Long after his death, the town went so far as to declare holidays in his honor. John Cuming was also Brister Freeman's master for a quarter of a century. It seems more than coincidental that the town's leading patriarch was also the owner of the slave who cut the widest swath in Concord. Left to manage John Cuming's estate during his master's many absences, Brister Freeman learned a wide array of farming and other survival skills. And in watching his owner rule a town, he learned what it takes to navigate local politics.

Unlike Brister Freeman, whose name survives in *Walden* the book and at Walden the place, where a hill bears his name, John Cuming has been largely forgotten. His reputation was first eclipsed when Ralph Waldo Emerson moved to Concord in 1835. It was buried soon thereafter when the minutemen became the nation's symbol of all that was independent and good in the United States. John Cuming was not the sort of independent farmer memorialized in the Minuteman Statue. His vast estate was tilled by slaves and hired men. Broken up long ago, it is now the site of a state prison and his mansion house the site of a prison office building. The Cuming name survives locally only on a medical building, a small tribute to John's career as a doctor. But until his story and those of his gentlemen contemporaries are fully told, Walden Woods will continue to appear wholly separate from the estates, or plantations, whose slaves seeded its black enclave. This is especially true insofar as the largest Concord slave estate, the Chambers-Russell-Codman estate, has been separated from Walden Woods since 1754 by a redrawn town boundary line that has long obfuscated the deep ties between the two.

The intertwined lives of John Cuming and Brister Freeman shape the narrative arc of this book, but theirs are just two of the stories I tell here. In order to reveal the larger history of slavery in Concord as well as the biography of a green space very much related to that history, I have cast my net wider than these two men's individual lives and wider even than Concord's geographical limits. The slaveholders of Concord considered themselves part of a culture of gentility that extended from Concord to Cambridge, Charlestown, Boston, and London. In the pages that follow, you will meet members of the elite and very wealthy Royall, Vassall, Chambers, and Russell families, not all of whom lived in Concord but whose alliance with one another brought new slaves to the Concord area. The slaves of Concord also considered themselves part of a larger community of slaves that stretched well beyond the town limits. When children were sold or given away to new owners in distant locales, as so often happened, other slaves stepped in to care for these orphaned children and to relay information about their whereabouts and welfare back to their parents. The last names slaves took upon achieving their freedom are testaments to how important these networks were. And thus the story of what I am calling black Walden is the story of slaves and slave owners from across Massachusetts. (See the Dramatis Personae at the back of the book for a complete listing.)

IN HOMAGE TO THE GROUNDWORK Henry David Thoreau laid for this book when he recorded as many stories as he did about Concord's slavery and postslavery days, each of *Black Walden*'s section titles is taken from the phrases he used in *Walden* to describe Concord slavery and the landscape the former slaves made in its wake. The sole exception is the Epilogue, which I have entitled "Brister Freeman's Hill." Like his townsmen, the author of *Walden* referred to the hill on which Brister Freeman owned land in Walden Woods as Brister's Hill. Brister's Spring, Peter's Field, Peter's Path, Peter's Spring, and Caesar's Woods were similarly labeled with the first names of the former slaves who lived nearby. Every site in Concord named after a white person, however, is designated by the person's last name. Emerson's Cliff, Flint's Pond, Heywood's Meadow, and Thoreau Street are just some examples. In an effort to give Brister Freeman the same due, I have added his last name to the hill where he once lived. Conversely, throughout the rest of the book, I refer to the author of *Walden* not as "Thoreau" but as "Henry" or where clarity requires it "Henry David Thoreau," so as not to continue to accord him more authority and respect than the men and women who preceded him on the shores of Walden Pond.

CHAPTER ONE

Squire Cuming

I
N THE TOWN OF LINCOLN, much of which was a part of Concord until 1754, a story has been passed down through the generations about a local white woman who, shortly before Lincoln's incorporation, journeyed to Cambridge to sell produce from her husband's farm and came home with something besides currency in her saddlebags. Although little is said in the story about anyone besides the local woman, who told her descendants only what she herself endured, the details indicate that the events of that day most likely began in one of the many lavish mansion houses that formed a distinct Cambridge neighborhood along Brattle Street. Surrounded by elegant gardens, these homes were comprised of large rooms appointed with goods from around the globe. Here was where wealthy merchants, lawyers, and owners of West Indian plantations enjoyed their fine mahogany furniture, looking glasses, and Turkish carpets, while their every need was attended to by slaves bustling to and fro.[1]

One of the women enslaved in Cambridge, a new mother, had recently grown anxious. Her baby boy was beginning to reach for solid food and no longer needed her breast to thrive. She knew her master was aware that her child would soon be weaned and that it was only a matter of time before he determined to give away the child or sell him. Already a well-established gentleman, her master did not need to raise an additional slave who, in the years before he could contribute to the immense job of running a large estate, would distract his mother and take up precious space in the already crowded garret. Aspirants to the rank of gentleman, in contrast, would be eager to invest in a more prosperous future by purchasing a slave child, they being less expensive than their adult counterparts, or by accepting one as a gift. Once the boy was sufficiently grown, he could be put to work farming or performing other tasks that would free his new owner to leave his fields and pursue professional or civic goals, such as a prestigious position in town or county government, or better yet a Crown appointment. At a time when only the wealthiest, most educated men were thought fit to govern, owning a slave was a sign that his owner was able to invest his energy in other activities besides his own self-sufficiency. It was thus entirely likely the slave mother would never see her son again. The same ambition that led a man to buy or accept her slave child might very well lead him to move far away. Britain's empire was a vast one and its greatest opportunities required its population to be mobile. Not a few slave women chose infanticide over the inevitable separation from their children. [2]

After what must have been many sleepless hours pondering these realities, the slave mother rose from her pallet before dawn. Stopping only to gather a few articles of clothing, she took her son in her arms and quietly left the house. She made her way to the road that ran westward to Watertown, Concord, and beyond, alongside of which impoverished people were allowed to squat in makeshift huts. Leaving her son inside one of these tiny dwellings, she scanned the travelers coming into town. At this time of day, farmers from the surrounding countryside were en route to the Cambridge market, where the town's wealthy residents could be counted on to purchase their produce. She did not have to wait long before her eyes alighted on the young white woman of Lincoln lore riding into town on a horse weighted down with panniers and baskets filled with produce for sale. The woman appeared to be experienced caring for young children, having with her a girl around the age of two. She also appeared to be well off. As the slave mother knew, few in colonial Massachusetts were able to afford a horse. The story goes that the slave mother stepped boldly into the road and "begged" the white mother on horseback to "take her baby for she feared that if she kept him with her, he would be sold as a slave."

According to her descendants, Elizabeth Hoar stopped when she heard the slave mother's plea and considered the offer seriously. She and her young daughter Sarah, Elizabeth's first child, lived in precisely the circumstances the slave mother seems to have anticipated. John Hoar, Elizabeth's husband, owned a good deal of land fifteen miles west of Cambridge as well as a large house he and his wife hoped to fill with children. But concerned it would be difficult if not impossible to carry another child when her panniers and saddlebags were

already full, she informed the slave mother she would take the child on her return trip if the slave mother had not found someone else to take him in the
meantime. Even as the slave mother knew she would pay dearly for her absence
from her master's house, she apparently waited in the hut by the road for the
hours to pass. Finally, in the afternoon, she began to watch for Elizabeth's return. Again, she stepped into the road, this time with her son and his small
bundle of clothes in her arms. Elizabeth helped tuck the child into one of the
now empty saddlebags, mounted her horse, and turned toward home. Years
later, she would recall how she obliged the slave mother by making "a most
difficult decision . . . on the spur of the moment." The story concludes by informing us that the boy, who "spent the rest of his life" with the Hoar family,
"was the playmate of the Hoar children."

But rather than adopt the young boy into their family, as the story implies,
John and Elizabeth Hoar were careful to give the boy a name that made clear he
was their property before he was a person. They gave him only a first name,
which effectively excluded him from both their family and civil society, and
they chose it from the four main categories of slave names used in New England:
place names, classical names, biblical slave names, and diminutive forms of these
and common English names. Names drawn from these categories were intended
to advertise a slave owner's values and characteristics, whether his classical education, his religiosity, or his cosmopolitanism. Popular place names, including
London, Cuba, and Boston, were usually major ports in England or its colonies
and thereby made clear an owner's intimate knowledge of the empire. The name
the Hoars settled on was one of the more popular slave names in Massachusetts.
Brister was a diminutive form of Bristol, England's gateway to Africa and the
West Indies and its largest slave port. A port in Rhode Island had already been
named after Bristol, England, in the hopes of garnering similar riches and had
since become a major slave port itself.[3]

When the Hoars acquired and named Brister, John Hoar, for all his property, was not at the top of colonial society. Having to devote all his time to
farming, John was not able to pursue the prestigious civic posts that cemented
a man's ranking among the region's gentlemen. If the story about John's wife
and the slave mother is essentially true, Elizabeth must have thought about
how frustrating John's position was for him as she looked down at the slave
woman pleading with her. No doubt she thought too about all the slavehold-

ers she knew and the power and prestige they enjoyed. Virtually all of the slave-holders in the Concord area and beyond had a title, whether Reverend, Doctor, Colonel, or Captain, which signaled they had a profession or were a military officer. Men freed from farm labor were more likely to earn these honorifics. And men with titles were the most likely to be elected by their townsmen to serve in local government or be appointed by the Crown to the General Assembly or to serve as justices of the peace, the latter of which earned them the particularly coveted title of Squire. Elizabeth's formerly untitled neighbor Timothy Wesson had recently accepted the gift of a slave child from Concord's most esteemed landowner, Squire Chambers Russell, whose 275-acre estate was one of Concord's largest. Indeed, if Elizabeth considered the slave mother's offer as dispassionately as her family later recalled, that was undoubtedly because she was accustomed to seeing enslaved children bought and sold or given away. After becoming a slave owner, Timothy Wesson garnered town appointments and began to be referred to as Mr. Wesson, an honorific bestowed only on those men who were not justices of the peace but who were considered local leaders all the same. Elizabeth Hoar was undoubtedly tempted to take the slave mother's child because she wanted the same status or better for her husband and she knew a slave was the means to get there. The slave boy Timothy Wesson had received from Squire Russell was himself named Brister, and the Hoars clearly hoped that in emulating Mr. Wesson on this front their fortunes would rise in the same way his had.[4]

Those in Lincoln who passed down the story of little Brister's arrival in Lincoln wanted to believe that slavery was not so much enforced servitude as a form of adoption. After slavery ended in Massachusetts and particularly during the Civil War period when Massachusetts fought to abolish slavery, it was easier to imagine that Brister was the Hoars' "playmate" rather than a slave torn from his mother to serve John and Elizabeth Hoar's ambition. And thus over time the story evolved into one about two mothers conferring by the road as to how to make the best of a bad situation. Of course, Brister's mother would have known from the beginning that the Hoars would take her son to be their slave, but this must have seemed a better alternative to her than allowing her master to sell or give her son away to someone who might leave the area, if in fact she did manage to give her son to the Hoars. With her son enslaved within a day's walk of Cambridge, she could at least hope to get word of him from other slaves in the area and perhaps even visit him if her master did not sell her away on account of what would have been considered reckless disregard for his property.

FOR THE SAME REASON Elizabeth and John Hoar acquired the boy they called Brister, Timothy Wesson determined not to keep his. His daughter Abigail was to be married in the first weeks of 1753 to John Cuming, an ambitious young Concord man with the education and land that should allow him to work, govern, and socialize alongside the colony's most elite gentlemen. But in Concord's pre-industrial economy, someone was going to have to grow the Cuming family's food and harvest its fuel supply. If that person was John, he would have no time to do anything else. With cheap land readily available to the north and west, hired male labor was going to continue to be difficult to find. Timothy's solution was to give his Brister to his future son-in-law as a wedding gift. [5]

Initially, Timothy's slave would only be able to attend to simple chores for John. The brown-skinned boy with tightly curled hair his townsmen referred to as "wool" was just nine years old and probably small compared to white boys his age. Slaves were typically not fed adequate amounts of protein until they were old enough to perform a considerable amount of labor. At that point, they were fed more and a late growth spurt usually resulted. If all went well, Brister would soon be able to handle a good deal of the farm labor on John's estate, which would make him an extremely valuable piece of property. When Concord cordwainer and farmer Benjamin Barron died within months of John Cuming and Abigail Wesson's marriage, John Jack, the forty-one-year-old slave man Benjamin seems to have purchased from John's aunt, was worth the equivalent of four acres of plow land in Concord's Great Field. At that time the field was the town's largest expanse of its most prized tillage land; only Benjamin's house and four larger parcels of tillage land were valued at greater amounts. Other than the building in which he lived and his very best parcels of land, a grown slave man was often one of his owner's most valuable possessions. [6]

Before giving his Brister to John Cuming, Timothy made sure to give John a means of controlling his human property. He had Brister baptized on January 4, 1753. Lincoln was in the process of splitting off from Concord and Brister's was the first baptism in the new Lincoln church, built not far from the Wesson and Hoar homesteads. The Reverend Cotton Mather and other church leaders had been encouraging slave baptism on the grounds that slave owners were "the Elect of God" who must thus treat their slaves as "rational creatures whom God has made your servants." But the Reverend Mather had also regarded Christian training as a key means by which "the Elect" could elicit compliance from their slaves on earth. Since 1729, when the royal attorney general assured English colonists that baptism did not enfranchise slaves, slave children had often been baptized before being given away or sold so that their new owners could urge them to seek the spiritual rewards spelled out by Mather in his 1706 essay on "the Instruction of Negro Servants in Christianity," namely "rest from their labors" and "a mansion in Heaven." The Reverend carefully explained the way to these rewards, changing such commandments as "Honor thy mother and father" to "I must show all due respect onto everyone; and if I have a master or a mistress, I must be very dutiful onto them." In the rules he created for his Society of Negroes, which he founded in 1693, Cotton Mather also asked slave members to pledge to help police not only themselves but others: "We will set ourselves . . . to do all the good we can, to the other negro-servants in the town; and if any of them should, at unfit hours, be abroad, much more, if any of them should run away from their masters, we will afford them no shelter; But we will do what in us lies, that they may be discovered, and punished." Slaves were taken to church every Sabbath, and separate galleries were partitioned off for their use so that they could hear the word of God and have their behavior shaped accordingly without thinking themselves the equal of the other Christians in attendance. The Lincoln and Concord churches were no exception to this rule. Timothy gave John a child his son-in-law could govern with promises of Heaven or, when need be, threats of Hell.[7]

Brister was not the only valuable gift John Cuming received when he married. In what had become a rite of passage for the young elite in Massachusetts, his father, Robert Cuming, gave him a mahogany desk. Fifteen years before, the wealthiest man in the colony, Isaac Royall, had given his own son an expensive desk. Isaac Sr. lived on a vast, five-hundred-acre estate in Charlestown and presided over two other extensive New England farms and a sugar plantation in Antigua. He had thirty-nine slaves in Charlestown alone. His fine mansion house there was the most luxurious in all of New England. Isaac ruled his empire from a black walnut desk in the front room, and thus when it came time for his only son to marry, he knew Isaac Jr. would also need a desk in order to take over his father's affairs. Wanting him to have the finest desk money could buy, Isaac spent £26 for a mahogany one, more than he paid for a horse the same month.[8]

Robert Cuming wanted to emulate the Royalls as best he could. He had worked long and hard to rise in colonial society without being rewarded with a civic post. And thus while he could have purchased a handsome desk made in part from cheaper wood, he instead chose a desk for his son John made almost entirely out of mahogany, the finely figured grains of which had become popular in the past few decades after regular trade routes were opened between the mainland and the tropical forests of the West Indies. Polished to a high shine with linseed oil and brick dust, mahogany furniture literally reflected the refinement of a man with the good taste and financial wherewithal to own such a piece. John Singleton Copley would soon depict John Hancock, Paul Revere, and other prominent Massachusetts residents sitting in elegant mahogany chairs or reflected in mahogany tabletops. Robert knew his son would look very refined indeed seated at his own lustrous desk. Cut from a single board an astounding eleven inches wide, the writing surface, when painstakingly polished, reflected the confident demeanor of a gentleman whose father had given him every advantage and who could therefore expect to rise in the ranks of colonial society. Like the slave he received from his father-in-law, the desk John received from his father was also a status symbol, signaling to others that John had the excellent taste expected of the elite. It was also, like Brister, a critical tool for his future success. Its many drawers and pigeonholes were designed to store the vast amount of paperwork that should engross a man with many agricultural, business, and political interests (Figure 2).[9]

Both of the wedding gifts John Cuming received, the slave boy and the mahogany desk, were commodities brought to New England through the so-called triangle trade, that great piston driving New England's colonial economy. Ships embarked from New England with salted pork and cod, iron, and other local products on board. They traded these goods for sugar from the plantations in the West Indies that arose in the wake of cleared hardwood forests and, once back in New England, made it into rum. The rum was traded for human cargo along what the English colloquially called the Guinea Coast

Figure 2. *John Cuming's desk (circa 1750s). Concord Museum, Concord, Mass., www.concordmuseum.org. Photograph by David Bohl.*

of Africa. The New England ships then returned to the West Indies and sold the newly enslaved to the plantation owners there. They eventually arrived back in New England with West Indian mahogany and sugar as well as African slaves for the local market. For John, the desk and the slave boy were thus wholly equivalent to one another for all that one was made of dead wood and the other of flesh and blood. John's ownership of a Brister would, like his ownership of a mahogany piece of furniture, put him on a par with those men who knew and wanted to associate themselves publicly with the British Empire's wealth and global reach. Timothy Wesson, who was not above wrenching a child from his parents and then passing him on to yet someone else, and Robert Cuming, who had failed to achieve the rank of gentleman, gave John the tools he would need if he was going to surpass his and Abigail's parents in the ranks of colonial society. But as helpful as the gifts John Cuming received on the occasion of his wedding would prove, it was the father's thwarted ambition that first set the stage for the son's rise.[10]

ROBERT AND HELEN CUMING were born in Scotland. Like so many others, they left the country in 1717. Some sought to escape anti-Scottish sentiment after the Jacobite Rising of 1715. Others determined to leave when it became clear that the English were not going to honor their promise under the 1707 Union to give Scottish merchants access to English and colonial markets. Robert was already a successful merchant, but he was frustrated by his inability to invest the profits of trade in the one thing that was associated with ancient powers and responsibilities and that thus accorded a man the most prestige: land. In Scotland, land was rarely on the market. It was typically obtained through marriage and inheritance, hence its association with the past and bygone glories. Helen, herself a Cuming, was the daughter of a baronet with lands in Aberdeenshire, but these would one day be passed, along with the title, to her brother. The newly married couple decided to sail to a British colony where new markets were opening up in the wake of the great religious migrations of the seventeenth century and where land was readily available: Massachusetts.[11]

Finding the small, provincial town of Boston already crowded with shops, Robert and Helen quickly moved on to Roxbury, one of the original seven coastal villages founded in Massachusetts Bay and the only town connecting Boston to the mainland. Unless they took the ferry at Charlestown, everyone had to pass across Roxbury Neck on their way to and from the seat of provincial government, making it a good site for trade. Settling into his business, Robert began to inquire about investment opportunities. His first purchase was over seventy acres of wild land in Littleton, a town thirty miles to the west that had been incorporated just four years before Robert's 1719 acquisition. He also began to make smaller purchases of improved land closer to the coast. He had already purchased ten acres of land in Concord, the colony's oldest inland settlement, when smallpox arrived in Boston from Barbados in 1721 and quickly became an epidemic. People fled Boston and its surrounding towns, the Cumings among them. In search of a healthier place to settle where he might thrive in trade, Robert noted that Concord did not yet have a shop where residents could purchase the spoils of England's growing empire. To visit the panoply of shops lining Boston's wharves, Concord's wealthier residents faced a half day of hard riding. Stepping nimbly into this gap and hoping to avoid the reach of a disease that infected half of Boston's ten thousand residents and claimed the lives of over eight hundred, Robert, with Helen and their two young children, Isabella and Alexander, moved west. In 1722, Robert purchased a small workshop on Concord's church green, transforming it into the town's first store.[12]

Concord was already eighty-seven years old when Robert and Helen arrived. It was incorporated in 1635 after Massachusetts's coastal towns became so densely settled that officials organized inland riverine settlements. Five years after the incorporation of Boston, the General Court had passed an order that "there shall be a plantation at Musketaquid . . . the name of the place . . . henceforth to be called Concord." The Indian name for the area meant grass-grown plain, a reference to the miles of lowlands bordering Concord's two rivers. These areas flooded each spring, the rising river water bringing fertilizer in the form of silt and muck to the native grasses that grew there. The English determined that this naturally growing and nutritious hay source could replace the salt hay they carefully harvested along the coast for winter animal fodder. There was also a large tillage field at Musketaquid that had been established long before by the native inhabitants and acres of forestland on upland glacial till that could be harvested for fuel and timber.[13]

Like all of the early English settlements in North America, Concord was laid out around a church. Located near a glacial ridge under whose shelter the first houses were erected and not far from the native tillage field or Great Field as the colonists came to call it, the meeting house became the axis point of a radial road system meant to ensure that all of Concord's residents could make it to mandatory Sabbath services. Because of Concord's early settlement, this road system soon anchored the interior of Massachusetts Bay. After Robert's arrival, the roads that intersected at Concord converged not only at the meeting house, but also at Robert's store. The goods he sold were accessible to local residents and to travelers moving in and out of and up and down the colony.[14]

Religion may have been literally at the center of Concord life, but Robert had moved to a town that, like every other one in the colony, began as a land corporation. Its charter provided the proprietors with the authority to acquire, divide, and manage a grant of six square miles. Governance was set up as the shared responsibility of the town's landowners, who met regularly at town meetings to address any of the issues that arose around questions about land and its management. It was imperative for their survival that each settler owned and had access to sufficient acreage of the different kinds of land that together made a working farm: tillage, meadow, pasture, and forestland. At the time of Concord's incorporation and later, in 1653, when the remaining portions of the town were divided, the proprietors worked hard to ensure land was distributed as equitably as possible. Each family was allotted acreage within the commonly fenced Great Field, as well as acreage within the commonly managed Great Meadows, as they termed the two-mile stretch of meadowland behind the Great Field, in addition to one or more lots within the two-thousand-acre forest that surrounded Walden Pond a mile to the south of the meeting house. Concord farms were thus typically made up of dozens of parcels scattered across the landscape. It was not a convenient situation for the farmers, who had to travel great distances to visit the far-flung corners of their farms, but it was a sustainable one. Farmers foddered their animals with naturally renewable grasses from their meadow lots. They collected the animals' manure from their barnyards and pastureland and carefully spread it on their tillage lots, where it fertilized their grain crops. With careful management of these precious resources, a Concord man was able to put meat and bread on the table year after year.[15]

And yet for all that the grant at Musketaquid was generally divided carefully and equitably into a complex mix of lots, there were a few exceptions that pointed to the strictly hierarchical nature of the town Robert Cuming was joining. Founding, incorporating, and dividing the town had been a monumental effort requiring a number of prominent men whose social and financial position assured potential settlers the endeavor would be a successful one. These men were rewarded with large estates of contiguous acreage, a mode of living and farming in sharp contrast to all of the other farmers whose various parcels of land were scattered hither and yon. The largest investor had been the Reverend Peter Bulkeley, who was rewarded for his efforts with a one-thousand-acre farm in southeastern Concord. As the town's first minister, Peter was the leader of a church whose physical layout reflected the importance of landownership in determining a person's social and political status. Men were given the right to pick the location of their pew on the basis of their landed wealth. Although most men had farms that were roughly the same size, the few men like Peter who owned large, contiguous estates were given first choice in selecting the location of their family pews. Their land gave them prominence and the authority to lead everyone else in matters religious, civic, and social.[16]

By the time Robert arrived in Concord and set up shop in the shadow of the meeting house, Peter Bulkeley had died and his estate had been broken up and sold in parcels. A large section of it was now in the possession of Charlestown merchant Charles Chambers, who not so long after Robert Cuming arrived in town expanded one of the houses there into a fine mansion house for the purposes of entertaining in the country (today's Codman estate in Lincoln). Charles never lived on his Concord property year round, but used his house there for lavish rural retreats. It was situated two miles from the meeting house on a gentle rise with its back toward Walden Woods. At a time when most residents still lived in one- or two-room houses, the wide, two-story façade of the Chambers mansion spoke of large and numerous rooms, each with a distinctive purpose. And whereas most of the front doors in Concord opened directly into a room in which everything from sleeping to eating to working was conducted with little regard to privacy, visitors to the Chambers mansion entered a large front hall off of which were rooms used exclusively for socializing, including a wood-paneled parlor devoted to the new social rituals developed around the spoils of empire. The taking of tea, chocolate, or punch required foodstuffs and an extensive equipage of manufactured goods from around the world, as well as the knowledge of how to properly prepare and imbibe these new stimulants in their various specialized containers. Charles's guests gathered around mahogany tea tables while carefully using silver spoons to add sugar from the West Indies to Staffordshire teacups from England filled with tea brewed from leaves imported from Asia.[17]

Like Peter Bulkeley and Concord's other prominent citizens, Charles Chambers had slaves. Following local practice, he used the names of his slaves to say something about himself and his relationship to the world. Charles named one of his slave men Caesar after Julius Caesar, the great Roman leader who transformed the Roman Republic into the Roman Empire. Caesar was one of the most popular slave names in colonial New England. A man who owned a Caesar said to the world he believed in republican government and knew of the horrors of its opposite. But he also made a joke at his slave's expense. Slaves were the opposite of political leaders, being the lowest on the political spectrum. A slave was no Caesar, nor was he a Cato, Mark, or Scipio, also popular slave names after other great statesmen of the Roman Republic. Charles named another of his slaves Chloris, a name that appears repeatedly in Greek mythology and the use of which thus further showed his classical education, and another Lincoln, after Charles's birthplace in England. He put his slaves to work on his farm, raising his family's food, and in his two houses caring for his wigs, fine clothing, silver plate, and elegant furnishings, among which was a desk of such value it was one of only four items he listed separately in his will. In this way, his slaves allowed Charles to appear on the public stage as a gentleman on a par with the elite of London or anywhere else and thus helped make it possible for him to ascend to the various prestigious political posts bestowed on someone of his wealth and status. Over the course of his civic career, Charles was a selectman, a representative to the General Court, and a justice of the peace.[18]

On one occasion, in 1706, two years before he acquired his Concord estate, Charles took the rare step of permitting two of his slaves to purchase themselves. He made a legal agreement with his slave Jack that allowed Jack to purchase himself and Chloris, to whom Jack had been married since 1697, for £60 paid in quarterly installments over the next four years. The agreement stipulated that the couple must indemnify Charles from "all and every matter contained in the act relating to Mulatto and Negro slavery." This was a reference to the 1703 law requiring owners to post £50 bonds for every slave manumitted so officials would have the means of paying for their poor support should they become a public liability. The legal agreement Charles drew up allowed him to avoid posting those bonds as well as any future financial obligations should Jack and Chloris end up on a poor list somewhere. To further ensure he would not be responsible for them at some future date, Charles banished Jack and Chloris from Charlestown forever. He thereby managed to abandon them entirely while getting from them a good deal of money. In other words, even as he was freeing two of his slaves, Charles was not taking a stand against slavery. Rather, his aim was to off-load two people who, for whatever reason, had made themselves undesirable to him. How Jack and Chloris were ever going to come up with £4 per quarter and support themselves at the same time was a matter of no concern to their former owner. Even if Charles never held them to the payment plan and drew up the legal document merely to avoid paying the bond, he was sending two of his slaves into an uncertain future, abandoning them to their freedom in a town where they would be strangers, rather than reimbursing them for their service or otherwise taking responsibility for slavery's impact on their lives. Charles could now in theory purchase more tractable slaves with the money he ostensibly took from Jack.[19]

Many folks in and traveling through Concord sought to emulate the lifestyle Charles Chambers's many obedient slaves allowed him to enjoy, whether they had slaves or not. One means of doing so was purchasing the goods available for sale in Robert Cuming's shop. Robert did such a brisk business he had money to invest in land in eight different towns. Optimistic about the financial future he was thereby building for his family, he raised his children to one day be ladies and gentlemen on a par with Charles Chambers and his ilk. Helen had given birth to five more children since arriving in Concord: Robert, who died in infancy, James, John, Amy, and Elizabeth. While the majority of Concord's sons were required to farm alongside their fathers for most of the year, Robert and his brother Alexander, a surgeon who had also emigrated from Scotland, were wealthy enough they had indentured servants and slaves to carry out the requisite farm work. This freed the next generation of Cuming men to focus on reading, writing, ciphering, and learning classical languages and literature. Robert's sons most likely studied Greek and Latin with the brother of George and Mary Minot's great-grandfather, local schoolmaster and Harvard graduate Timothy Minot. Nor were the Cuming daughters expected to perform what Elizabeth, or Betsy as she was nicknamed, called "hard labor." They focused instead on fine sewing, embroidery, and penmanship, while the family's young servant girls did the cooking, cleaning, and other household chores. Indeed, Robert's ambitions for himself and his children were such that, like Charles Chambers, he could be quite merciless in extracting value from slaves and servants. After one of his servant girls became pregnant at the age of eighteen in 1725, Robert sued her "debaucher" on the grounds that he had lost three years of her labor, valued, according to Robert, at £60. Unable for years to win reparations and facing inflation, Robert was asking for £200 in damages by 1738.[20]

And yet despite managing to accumulate a great deal of land, Robert Cuming never earned the right to be referred to by a title. Nor was he asked to serve in town government. The problem was Robert's growing reputation for ruthlessness in pursuing his debtors. Enthralled with the worldly goods Robert spread before them, not a few Concord residents found themselves in trouble. Year after year Robert did not hesitate to haul into county court debtors from Concord's oldest families in an attempt to extract restitution. The low purchase prices of some of his land holdings indicate sellers were sometimes pressed into handing over acreage in lieu of currency. Robert may have become landed, but the town was well aware of how he had accomplished this feat: namely by capitalizing on their inability to resist the items with which he so sorely tempted them. Accordingly, he was not regarded as the right kind of man for positions of leadership.[21]

Another Scotsman who set up shop in Concord after Robert fared better. John Beatton also accumulated a considerable amount of wealth but, in contrast to Robert, had a reputation for being so honest he made change down to a split farthing paid in the form of common pins. The town revered him for this and for the monetary gifts it anticipated he would bestow on Concord in his will. John and his wife were childless and had no other heirs. Robert, on the other hand, had a number of children who must be settled on the land he had purchased. When the Cumings' eldest daughter, Isabella, married mariner James Nevin, Robert had given the couple the Littleton property he had purchased upon first arriving in Massachusetts and to which he had added over the years. He would have to make similar gifts to his other children, and his townsmen thus felt less inclined to overlook his rapacious business methods. Not similarly burdened, Robert's rival shopkeeper was appointed to various town posts, as well as to the Court of General Sessions, thereby becoming Squire Beatton, for which the town was amply rewarded, as expected, in his will.[22]

Realizing he would never similarly rise to the rank of a gentleman, Robert did what any ambitious father would do: he became all the more determined to achieve for his sons what he would have liked to obtain for himself. Two of his sons, Alexander and James, had gone to sea as mariners, inspired if not by their brother-in-law then by the success of Charles Chambers and other wealthy Massachusetts merchants. But while appearing to grow smaller every year through the ever quickening pace of trade, the Atlantic was still large enough to separate families for years, if not forever. James decided never to return to Concord, settling three thousand miles from home in London, the hub of the Atlantic world, and later moving to the Isle of Man, where he lived out the rest of his days, still in contact with his siblings but only as sporadically as transatlantic mail would allow. Alexander did not fare as well. He apparently was lost at sea. And so it happened that Robert became bound and determined it would be John, his fourth and last son, born on March 1, 1728, who would have to achieve the life Robert had craved for himself: that of a Concord squire.[23]

That John bore the name of Scotland's most storied men must have made his father's focus on the rise of his youngest son seem the work of fate. Led first by one John and then another, the Comyns had been a powerful Scottish clan before and during the war for Scottish independence. After the death of Margaret, queen of Scots, in 1290, John Balliol was able to become king of Scotland on the strength of the support lent him by the elder John Comyn, known as the Black Comyn. Six years later, when England invaded Scotland, John's son, known as the Red Comyn, supported William Wallace, the folk hero of Scottish legend known as Braveheart, who led a resistance movement against the English occupation. After Wallace died, the Red Comyn appeared to be moving against England's King Edward in alliance with Robert Bruce, who claimed the throne as a descendant of David I of Scotland, when the Red Comyn's life and the reign of his clan came to an end. In 1306, this second of the famous John Comyns was murdered, stabbed to death by Bruce in front of the high altar at Greyfriars Kirk in Dumfries, near the English border. Having dispatched a man he viewed as his competitor, Bruce went on to be crowned King Robert. The Comyns were thereafter forced to become associated with the Montrose branch of the Graham clan, whose shield Robert Cuming should have used for his coat of arms. Choosing instead to use the three sheaves of wheat that constituted the Comyn shield, Robert kept alive his connection to the storied clan of old and to their role in keeping Scotland independent prior to the more recent union with England. Isaac Royall and his son used the same motif for their crest because wheat sheaves were first and foremost a symbol of agriculture and land, a fact that would not have been lost on Robert, who also wanted to stake his claim to the authority born of landedness. Robert's crest constantly reminded John of his father's ambition as well as the pride his father took in his ties to Scotland and especially in the Comyns' prominence there. Over the years, John would strive to live up to his famous name.[24]

His first step was to acquire an education befitting a gentleman. In Massachusetts, that meant Harvard, where John enrolled at the age of fifteen. But while a Harvard education immediately set him apart from his townsmen, only two others of whom enrolled with him in 1743, John still had to contend with his father's reputation. Those who constituted the class of 1747 were "placed" by the faculty, as the College overseers put it, "according to the supposed dignity of the families whereto they . . . belong." The top 10 percent were the sons of squires, men who served as justices of the peace, if not as governors and high-ranking magistrates. If a boy was from this tier of society, he received the best rooms and was permitted to help himself first at meals, be seated first at chapel, and so forth. He was also expected to bring the most honor to Harvard after graduation. The 20 percent below them were the sons of College graduates, most of whom entered the clergy and were also considered part of the gentry. The remaining 70 percent were the sons of men without titles, namely shopkeepers, farmers, mariners, and artisans. The sons of wealthy merchants who had been refused public office were typically placed anywhere from the bottom of the top group to the middle of the lowest group. Entering freshmen were examined by the president in Latin and Greek, but their proficiency influenced their placement only within each of the three tiers.[25]

John was ranked eighteenth in the class of thirty students, two places below his teacher's son and four below another of his townsmen, Benjamin Prescott, the son of Dr. Jonathan Prescott. Of the three Concord boys who entered the class of 1747, Benjamin took precedence in the rankings because of his family's wealth and the fact of having two brothers who preceded him at Harvard. His elder brother John had studied medicine and returned to Concord to serve as a doctor alongside his father. However, he soon left to fight in the West Indies and died of smallpox during Benjamin's first winter in Cambridge, leaving behind a considerable estate that included two slaves. Peter Prescott had studied law at Harvard and settled in Boston to practice. But Benjamin did not stay to enjoy the advantages his brothers and his family's wealth gave him. He appeared before the faculty in March 1744 "to resign up his chamber" because he was going to Nova Scotia to fight "in the expedition against the French at Louisbourg." He was killed there by Indians soon after.[26]

After graduating from Harvard, where he studied religion, the father of the second highest ranking Concord student had failed to secure a pulpit and his son was placed accordingly. Timothy Minot Sr. served Concord as its schoolmaster. His reputation was a good one; boys from surrounding towns came to prepare with him for college, John Cuming and the Prescott boys most certainly among them. Master Minot, as his profession entitled him to be called, became a fairly wealthy man. He was able to have his portrait painted and kept a slave woman, Rose, to help with all of the domestic matters at his home. But without claim to the title of Reverend, Timothy's son ranked below Dr. Prescott's boys. While young Timothy and Benjamin were not fortunate enough to be placed in the first or second tier of Harvard students, at least they were securely in the top half of the lowest group.[27]

John Cuming, in contrast, just managed to escape being placed in the lowest half of the third group. He was placed at the very bottom of the possible rankings for the sons of non-office-holding merchants. His father had gotten him as far as Harvard but his inability to secure public office became a hurdle his son would have to overcome. To reach the heights of a gentleman, John still had a long way to climb.

Robert knew one way he could help John was by providing him with extensive lands. Over the years, he had concentrated his Concord purchases along the town's border with Acton to the west. By localizing his purchases in this one area, John's father was eventually able to create a 240-acre parcel of largely contiguous acreage, which he rented to tenants in the form of two farms until his sons were grown. In 1748, Robert deeded the property to John and Alexander, the latter of whom was not yet known to be lost at sea. It was a significant gift at a time when those men who could afford to educate their sons at Harvard often could not give them land as well, much less the sixty acres scattered across town that constituted the average farm. As would later become all too apparent, Robert was willing to sacrifice the future of his two youngest daughters so that John might rival the man who had replaced Charles Chambers at the top of Concord society and who had thus become the new standard by which Robert gauged local success: Charles Chambers's heir, his grandson and namesake Chambers Russell.[28]

Chambers Russell had already lived in Concord for a short while, serving as a Concord selectman and representative to the General Court in 1739 and 1740. After that, he had moved back to Charlestown, representing that town to the General Court after his grandfather died in 1743. But in 1746, two years after John started at Harvard, Chambers Russell moved his family to Concord for good, along with his chaise, a coach, ten horses, and his slaves, many of whom were born of the same alliance between the Chamberses and the Russells that resulted in a Russell inheriting the Chambers estate. Fourteen years after Charles Chambers's only child, Rebecca, wed Chambers Russell's father, Daniel Russell, in 1711, Charles's slave man Lincoln married Daniel's slave woman Zilpah. The enslaved couple had three children while they were still living in Charlestown. Bilhah, Peter, and Ishmael were baptized there in 1726, 1728, and 1732, respectively. Peter and most likely his siblings as well came with Lincoln and Zilpah when they were moved to Concord with Chambers Russell. Subsequent events indicate that Lincoln and Zilpah had a fourth and fifth child once they arrived, a daughter named Zilpah after her mother, who was born sometime around 1738, and a son Brister. Born in 1744 and like his father named after a city in England, this appears to be the same child Timothy Wesson would later give to John Cuming.[29]

Timothy Wesson had very recently come to be regarded as a local leader after helping spearhead the separation of southeastern Concord into its own church precinct and, later, town. The decision to separate was driven in large part by the difficulty of getting to church from so great a distance in the winter months. The residents of southeastern Concord, an area which included the Chambers-Russell estate, lived as many as two and three miles from the

Concord meeting house and complained that "we and our families are in great measure deprived of the benefit of the public worship." During the winter they were "at the expense of maintaining the preaching of the word of God at a private house amongst ourselves." Residents of those parts of the neighboring towns of Lexington and Weston that abutted them also complained of the respective distances to their local meeting houses. Others wanted to separate due to religious differences with Daniel Bliss, Concord's minister since 1739. Daniel was the kind of minister who could break into a flood of tears, especially when worshipping with George Whitefield, the leader of the religious revival sweeping the colonies. New members were attracted to the church in droves but others got upset when Daniel extemporized from the pulpit and became what they perceived as hysterical. Eventually, a fifth of the town broke off from Daniel's church and formed the West Church, also called the Black Horse Church for the tavern in which they were forced to meet after being denied permission from the General Court to erect their own meeting house. Those in southeastern Concord who had long been seeking to separate on account of the distance, Timothy Wesson among them, now had additional fodder for their case. At last, in 1746, their many petitions to the General Court were successful and a new parish was formed. Soon thereafter, a committee was called to approach the General Court with a proposal to allow the precinct to incorporate as a town. Timothy Wesson served on this committee with Chambers Russell and two other men. Their efforts were rewarded in 1754 when Concord's second precinct was incorporated as Lincoln, named by Chambers Russell for his grandfather's hometown in England, just as his grandfather had earlier named one of his slaves Lincoln.[30]

The separation of Lincoln from Concord propelled Timothy into the upper ranks of his new town. In Concord, he had not been among the twenty residents with the highest real-estate assessments. In the town of Lincoln, however, Timothy was the owner of the precinct's eighth largest estate and thus eighth in line to select the site for his pew in the new meeting house. His role in the separation from Concord and his status in the new town that resulted did not go unnoticed by Chambers Russell, who, when he married in 1738, had been insulted when he received permission to build a pew in the Concord meeting house but only in the women's section of the church. It seems his role in petitioning for southeastern Concord to become a separate precinct had not been appreciated. No doubt grateful to be spared the humiliation of sitting among the women and pleased to now reside at the head of a town whose very name acknowledged his roots as having precedence before all others, Chambers Russell gave Timothy the gift of Lincoln and Zilpah's youngest son. Soon thereafter, in 1758, Timothy's newly magnified status was such that he was elected a Lincoln selectman, an office he held again from 1760 to 1763.[31]

If John Cuming was going to be a Chambers Russell and join the elite club of gentlemen who ruled Massachusetts, he would also have to have a profession in addition to his land and his Harvard education. In the prior century, College graduates had become the leaders of their respective communities by going into the ministry. Peter Bulkeley sent two of his sons to Harvard and both followed his footsteps into the church. Increasingly, however, as the careers of the two eldest Prescott sons made clear, the law and medicine were considered equally prestigious, a development that did not go unnoticed by Robert Cuming. The life of a gentleman doctor, which came with a professional title, coupled with John's land holdings, would provide the perfect platform for John's advancement in colonial Massachusetts. The best medical schools were located in Scotland, where Robert still had family, and so he made arrangements for John to return to the Cumings' homeland, become Doctor Cuming, and thereafter take his place beside Chambers Russell and any other of the colony's most prominent gentlemen of his generation.

As there were no entrance requirements for medical school, John did not stay to finish his Harvard degree. In 1746, before leaving the country, he taught school for nine weeks in Concord. This was a common and usually temporary occupation for local Harvard men. (One hundred years later, Henry David Thoreau would also teach school briefly in Concord upon graduating from Harvard.) Living at home and, on Sundays, attending Sabbath services, John often found himself in the company of Timothy Wesson's daughter in her final months as a Concord resident before the division of the Wessons' part of Concord into Lincoln. John had known Abigail all his life, seeing her if not at Robert's store, once the only one in town, then at the all-day church services, during the breaks of which the town's young folk liked to stroll to the top of the glacial ridge that ran along the Bay road at the center of town and that served as one of the town's two burial grounds. Burial Hill provided sweeping views of the town, from the church green below to land that would soon be John's almost three miles away on the southwestern border of town.[32]

As much as Timothy Wesson's social position had improved, his daughter's admirer was clearly poised to land even higher up the social ladder. And yet there is little evidence that Abigail was purposefully climbing that ladder in rewarding John's attentions to her. The couple's enduring love was amply evident in the letters John would send Abigail from abroad. He wrote in one letter that just as he "spent the greater part of my time with you while at Concord," so when he was parted from her did he spend his time "in thinking of the singular favors I received from you, and reflecting on my misfortune in being at so great a distance from a person who I so much admire and delight in." He called his "Dear Nabby" (a common nickname for Abigail) "the height of perfection and ... the sole easer of my grief and promoter of my happiness and welfare." In one letter, he closed by insisting he was her "faithful and most constant friend and lover till death." Even as he may have wanted to show off his Harvard gentility with his fine phrasings, the feeling of being in love with Abigail and the fact of her returning his affection came through loudly and clearly.[33]

And yet so long as Robert was still alive, John would not be encouraged to put love before ambition. John left Abigail and Concord behind to seek his professional training, setting sail from Boston to London and from there traveling by coach to Edinburgh, where Concord tradition has it that he attended the University of Edinburgh, the best medical school in the English-speaking world. As many as four hundred young men from England and its colonies in North America and the Caribbean were in town in any given year to study anatomy, physiology, wounds, and tumors in the form of one hundred or so public lectures given between early November and early May. Most students stayed for a period of two to three years, living in one of the walled city's many apartment buildings and frequenting its taverns. Only a very few bothered to pay the substantial fee required for graduation. Like the majority of his classmates, John simply left when he felt sufficiently schooled in medicine to return home and set up a practice.[34]

He did not, however, immediately return to Abigail, who had been waiting for him all this time. Instead, John heeded the Crown's call to the young men of New England to shore up its interests in North America against the French. Enlisting in the provincial army, John journeyed to Nova Scotia. Military experience was considered a patriotic duty, but it also provided a chance to survey the full scope of opportunities available to enterprising Englishmen. Many of the New England soldiers who built the new city of Halifax while John was there stayed to farm North America's most fertile soil and to ply its teeming fishing grounds. John might have had a thriving medical practice there, but his brother Alexander's failure to appear and claim his farm in Concord, as well as their father's declining health, drove John back to Concord. Then too, he was concerned that Abigail was getting tired of waiting for him. In one of his letters from Nova Scotia, John expressed dismay at not having heard from Abigail, whom he clearly regarded as his future wife: "I can scarce allow myself to harbor a thought of you being inconstant especially after repeated protestations of sincerity in your regard for me." For his part, he offered assurance "of my sincere love and constancy . . . during my absence." He closes this letter as Abigail's "constant lover in prosperity and adversity."[35]

Once back in Massachusetts, John took over his brother's share of their estate. He either immediately built a home on the property or took possession of a home already there and expanded it considerably. With nine large plate-glass windows reflecting the light on its south-facing façade, the two-story mansion house (Figure 3) dominated the surrounding landscape, especially after John had two rows of trees planted to flank a half mile of the road on the approach to his front door. Visitors nearing the house knew to expect a homeowner powerful enough that he could bend nature itself to gratify their need for shade or anything else. Inside was a main entry hall off of which was a parlor on one side and another large room on the other, one of the first in Concord that would be devoted to dining. Two bedrooms on the second floor formed the house's private space and were reached by a central staircase that circled around the house's large central chimney. There were enough windows in each room that the occupants and their visitors did not need to crowd around the fireplace or a candle in order to see. This was a house in which people could spread out on an ample collection of chairs clustered around tea and dining tables. John also purchased large pictures, looking glasses, and sconces for the walls. The looking glasses reflected the light and thereby gave the illusion that John could turn night into endless day. After his marriage, his mahogany desk would take pride of place in the parlor, polished to a high shine by Brister, the slave boy John would receive from his father-in-law on the occasion of his marriage.[36]

Figure 3. *The John and Abigail Cuming house. The side porch and the window shutters were later additions and the large central chimney has been replaced with a smaller one. Photograph by George Shepard (circa 1936). Courtesy of the Concord Free Public Library.*

On February 8, 1753, after a courtship that spanned more than five years, John Cuming and Abigail Wesson were married by the Reverend Daniel Bliss. Although the Wessons had separated from Daniel's church, Abigail and her family deferred to the Cuming family's religious affiliation. Abigail had every expectation John would provide her with a breadth of experience and level of luxurious living well beyond what her father had achieved. John was already a man of the world, having traveled to London and lived in or traveled to Boston, Edinburgh, and Halifax, some of England's most important provincial outposts. Indeed, there were few in Concord who could claim to have had the kind of launching John had received from his father. His Harvard education, his professional training abroad, his extensive estate, and now the slave he received from Timothy Wesson were meant to place him at the forefront of Concord society. Unlike his title-less father, John could hope to be called one day not merely Dr. Cuming but John Cuming, Esquire.

Robert did not live to see his son married. He died a few weeks before the wedding, hoping, as his gift of the mahogany desk indicated, that John would make the family's name into one to be reckoned with in Concord. As for himself, he must have known he would be consigned to oblivion. While the families of men of his financial means generally erected large tombstones engraved with the deceased's many feats, Robert's family chose not to purchase a headstone because having it carved would have been a considerable expense at a time when his widow needed to save for the futures of her two unmarried daughters. And then there was the embarrassing issue of what could be said in the epitaph. Most families were happy to have their patriarch's title etched in stone for eternity. Robert could claim no title and thus by Concord's standards he had failed to rise above the common lot. And by Robert's own standards, he had thus failed to achieve what he had come to North America to acquire: power and prestige. While John's grief at his father's passing was tempered by his marriage to his dear Nabby after so many years of separation, he was now under inordinate pressure to achieve all that his father had desired and ultimately failed to secure.[37]

No records survive that indicate what Brister was thinking and feeling on the occasion of being given as a wedding gift. Even the story of how the Hoars acquired their Brister only reveals how Elizabeth Hoar felt that day in Cambridge, not how that Brister's mother, much less that Brister, felt. Certainly, John and Abigail's marriage was hardly the happy occasion for their new slave boy that it was for the couple and their families. Having been wrenched from his family at the Chambers-Russell estate, Brister was now forced to once again adjust to new people and a new home. While one white Concord resident would remember him only as "somber" and rather stupid or "dim," later events proved the grave boy who arrived at the Cuming mansion house was thinking very seriously about how he might be able to reunite with his family and improve their situation. Well before that revelation, however, there would be indication enough of just how deeply the local slave population resented the pain suffered when families were broken up by owners concerned only with their own economic and social stature.[38]

CHAPTER TWO

The Codman Place

I N JULY 1755, TWO YEARS AFTER HIS WEDDING to Abigail Wesson, John Cuming was at home in Concord when shocking news broke from Charlestown and spread like wildfire across the countryside. As far as twenty-two miles inland, in Westborough, the Reverend Ebenezer Parkman interrupted his usual journal entries about his family, his farm, and his congregation to report the story on everybody's lips: "Captain Codman of Charlestown was poisoned lately by a Negro." Ebenezer Parkman may not have known who exactly Captain Codman was, but he knew he was a gentleman, as indicated by the title that made his murder at the hands of a slave worth reporting. John Cuming, however, knew exactly who Captain Codman was. Orphaned as a child, John Codman had become the ward of Concord's own Charles Chambers. At the time of his death, the wealthy fifty-eight-year-old was a good friend and business associate of his former guardian's grandson and heir, Chambers Russell. (The two families would remain close. In 1790, John Codman's grandson inherited the Chambers-Russell estate, which has since been known as the Codman estate.) Despite or perhaps because of the connections between the two families, Chambers Russell was one of the four justices who presided over the trial of the Codman slaves. But John Codman's ties to Concord were not the only reasons John Cuming stayed at home for the duration of the summer to follow news of the trial. Like the murdered man, John Cuming had slaves, having acquired a slave man he called Jem, a diminutive for James, and perhaps a slave woman or two, in addition to Brister. Intended to be the key to his rise, as John Codman's slaves had been for him, John Cuming's slaves now had to be regarded as potential murderers. [1]

The first question posed at the trial of the accused slaves was for John Codman's slave woman Phyllis: "Was Mr. John Codman late of Charlestown deceased your master?" When she replied, "Yes he was," she was then asked for how long she had served him. Her reply, that he purchased her when she was a little girl, elicited no comment other than whether Phyllis knew "of what sickness" John died. The separation of children from their enslaved parents was a common practice throughout Massachusetts and certainly in the Concord area where John Cuming was following the trial. In April 1740, for instance, William Wilson of Concord sold to Sarah Melvin, also of Concord, a two-year-old "Negro girl" named Nancy. More recently, in April 1752, Henry Spring, a farmer in Weston, sold to Concord farmer Peter Hubbard "a slave named Cato, being about six years old and something more." Judge Russell had himself given away one of his slave women's children to Timothy Wesson, who in turn had given Brister to John Cuming. In the judges' minds, such separations, being commonplace, required no comment, much less an investigation. Indeed, the issue of motivation took up very little of the trial because no excuse would have justified the slaves' actions. When Phyllis was finally asked "what reason" John Codman's slave man Mark gave "for poisoning his master," she replied that "he was uneasy and wanted to have another master" and that "he was concerned" for her safety and that of Phoebe, John's other slave woman. Judges did not follow up with further questions on this front, as it was widely considered a white man's prerogative to own African, Indian, and West Indian people as slaves and to treat his property however he saw fit. Uninterested in what the Codman slaves had suffered, judges spent the trial of the Codman slaves attempting to determine how Mark and Phyllis had carried out their murderous plans and wondering why they had not been checked by the various mechanisms popularly used to control slaves. John's slaves were asked what poison was used, how and from whom the poison was procured, and how it was administered and by whom. And because Mark and Phyllis were intent on implicating one another, the judges were able to learn much of what had transpired, including, had they cared to listen more attentively than they did, what drove the Codman slaves to murder their master.[2]

ON THE NIGHT OF SATURDAY, JUNE 21, 1755, two slave men had met under the cover of darkness in a barn in Boston's North End. Mark had come by ferry across the Charles River from Charlestown to confer with a slave widely known for his daring attempt three years earlier to escape the prison house of slavery. While still the property of Henry Vassall, a wealthy resident of Cambridge, Robin, along with one of Colonel Vassall's indentured servants, had broken into the mansion house next door, owned by Colonel William Brattle, a wealthy lawyer and doctor whose elegant estate had extensive gardens and a private mall extending all the way to the Charles River. Like so many others in the spring of 1752, the Brattle family had fled town in an attempt to escape a raging smallpox epidemic. Colonel Brattle's slave Dick informed Robin that hidden in the closet of his master's abandoned bedchamber was a chest packed with money and silver plate that would soon be given to the Brattles' daughter and her fiancé on the occasion of their wedding. Robin and his accomplice ventured next door in the middle of the night, retrieved a ladder from Colonel Brattle's barn, climbed into a back window, and stole the iron chest. Taking the chest into a cornfield next to the Vassalls' garden, the servant broke it open with an axe while Robin cowered at a distance, fearful that he might catch the smallpox when the chest was open. After finally summoning the courage to approach, Robin saw more than six hundred Spanish silver dollars, as well as nine porringers, three tankards, twelve teaspoons, four salt salvers, two candlesticks, and numerous other dishes made out of silver. Robin may not have contracted smallpox that night, but officials eventually caught him and threw him in the Concord jail, where he awaited trial. At a hearing of His Majesty's Superior Court of Judicature in Concord, during which it was estimated that the total value of the contents of the chest was £350, Robin testified that he planned to use the money to purchase clothes so that, once disguised, he could escape to Nova Scotia and from there sail to France. Instead, Robin was sentenced to twenty "stripes upon his naked back" and Colonel Brattle was awarded the right to "dispose" of Colonel Vassall's slave "for the term of his natural life." Enslaved now to Doctor William Clarke, Robin still believed in trying to escape the tyranny of slavery and he was prepared to help Mark take his future into his own hands.[3]

Mark had come to the North End seeking Robin's advice regarding an increasingly intolerable situation. Like the two Bristers in Concord, John Cuming's and John Hoar's, he was experiencing the agony of being separated from loved ones. In recent, happier times, John Codman had allowed Mark to live in

Boston with his wife and children as long as he hired himself out for work and gave his master his wages. But when city officials warned Mark out of Boston on February 28, 1755, John Codman called him back to Charlestown without making arrangements for Mark's family to follow. Nor was this the first time Mark's family ties had been severed. He well remembered the terrible sense of dislocation he suffered after being stolen from his home country and brought to New England as a slave. [4]

One of the motivations behind Robin's attempt to escape the country and his desire to help Mark better his situation was that his own family had been ripped apart by slavery. Born to slaves on the Royall estate in Charlestown, Robin, his mother, Abba, and his five siblings were inherited by Penelope Royall when her father, Isaac, died in 1739. Three years later Penelope's eight slaves moved with their mistress to Cambridge when she married Henry Vassall, the son of a Jamaican planter. Robin and this part of his family left behind the eighteen slaves inherited by Penelope's brother, Isaac Jr., among them Robin's father. [5]

Other Royall slaves suffered similarly. When one former Royall slave, a woman named Belinda, appeared before the General Court in 1783 to request a pension for her old age, she related through a spokesman how the separation from her family she endured at age twelve produced an "agony, which many of her country's children have felt, but which none hath ever described," mainly because no one ever asked them. She recounted how she lived "on the banks of the Rio de Valta" (the Volta River in contemporary Ghana) with her parents. Here, where "mountains covered the spicy forests" and valleys were "loaded with the richest fruits," she enjoyed "the most complete felicity," until one day while making her devotions with her parents in a "sacred grove," "an armed band of white men" burst into "the hallowed shade" wielding "bows and arrows . . . like the thunder and the lightning of the clouds." The intruders' interest was solely in Belinda, not her parents, whose "advanced age" made them "unfit for servitude." Her parents' paroxysms of grief on having their child wrenched from them were so intense that Belinda was still surprised seventy years later that the white men were unmoved. "Could the tears, the sighs and supplications, bursting from tortured parental affection, have blunted the keen edge of avarice, she might have been rescued from agony." Instead, "she was ravished from the bosom of her country," taken "from the arms of her friends," and "cruelly separated" from her parents. From a time she recalls as one of perfect plenitude, represented in her account not only by parental love but by a beautiful landscape, an abundance of food, and spiritual wholeness, Belinda was left isolated with no hope of ever finding happiness again. She may have been assisted in the crafting of her account by former slaves active in the cause of emancipation, but her statement still captures the wound that defined slavery. What happened to her in that sacred grove would affect her, Belinda insisted, "forever." She was speaking for herself, but she might as well have been speaking for Robin, Mark, both Bristers, and all of the other slaves ripped from the embrace of their respective families. [6]

Mark had little hope he would ever be reunited with his loved ones. He knew that on account of the 1703 law requiring slave owners to post a £50 bond for each slave they freed, his master was not likely to set him free. Nor was it likely that John Codman would ever sell him. Mark was said to have reported that the captain "had been offered £400" for him "but would not take it." Even if he could sufficiently disguise himself, as Robin had hoped to do, he risked being stopped and asked for emancipation papers. Those who could not account for themselves were eventually returned to slavery. Their captors either reaped a financial reward from returning lost property or sold their captives themselves. If Mark somehow managed to escape being caught, he could expect to be warned out of whatever town he tried to settle in, if not out of concern that he might appear on that town's poor list, then because white residents did not want free blacks in the vicinity of their slaves. Like Robin, Mark knew that if he attempted to escape from his owner, he would have to flee far away across the ocean. But insofar as this would utterly defeat the purpose of being with his family, Mark, like the mother of the Hoars' Brister, was going to have to resort to desperate measures. [7]

One means slaves used to try to effect a change in their situation was making themselves such a nuisance their owners felt compelled to sell them. Charles Chambers's slaves Jack and Chloris appear to have used this tactic. More recently, on March 25, 1755, an ad for a slave had appeared in the *Boston Gazette* that seemed to speak to another such case: "To Be Sold: An honest, likely, cleanly, surly young Negro fellow, that with very little drubbing will make a good servant." The man for sale had not been performing as a "good servant" and presumably this proved an effective means of resistance insofar as it resulted in his master's attempt to offload him. Mark knew that somehow forcing his sale to a new, and he hoped, more kindly master was his only hope of spending more time with his family.

At least one slave in Concord had made himself free by being a nuisance if not a danger to his new owners after his healthy master suddenly died intestate. At the age of sixty-nine, an otherwise robust Benjamin Barron had begun to decline rapidly. He had just enough time to convey to two friends that his property should be divided equally among his children before he died. The children determined, however, that dividing the estate among themselves would not leave enough for the one remaining unmarried daughter, Susanna, to support herself and their mother, Elizabeth (or Betty), and so the other children declined to accept their portions. Susanna and Betty proceeded to pay off Benjamin's many debts by selling off large portions of the estate, including most of Benjamin's land. They did not, however, sell their father's slave man Jack, or John Jack as he came to call himself, who at £120 was worth the equivalent of some of the choicest lots Benjamin owned in Concord's Great Field. The Barron family had not suddenly changed their minds on the subject of slavery. Betty was the daughter of a slaveholder, the Reverend Samuel Parris, formerly of Salem Village. The Reverend Parris had owned two slaves during Betty's youth, including a young woman named Tituba whom he had brought from his former home in Barbados. When she was nine, Betty and her cousin had mysterious "fits" they blamed on Tituba, thereby helping to instigate what became the Salem witch trials. After Tituba confessed to witchcraft and named others as being in conversation with the devil, Samuel Parris was forced to leave Salem Village. He purchased part of the Bulkeley grant in Concord but after financial difficulties sold it to Charles Chambers in 1708 and moved to Sudbury. His daughter married Benjamin Barron there the following year. Long accustomed to slaves, Betty kept her slave woman Violet long after her husband's death. But Jack, who at forty-one was still physically able, seems to have had a long-standing reputation for being difficult that made him unsaleable. When his prior owner, John Cuming's uncle Alexander, was away during most of 1736, he was unwilling to leave Jack with his wife, perhaps concerned that Jack would somehow jeopardize her safety. Having been granted power of attorney by her husband, Anne rented him out to a prosperous farmer for the year. Later, however, John's aunt and uncle risked exposing themselves to further bad behavior when they gave Jack's son away after baptizing him. Like Mark, Jack had thus suffered two wrenching separations, first from his family in Africa, where he was born, and then from his own child. With little land left to farm, the Barron women took a page from John Codman. Rather than expose themselves to Jack's ire, they let him hire himself out for money.[8]

By 1758, Jack had managed to get himself taken out of the Barron estate inventory. And soon thereafter he used his earnings to begin purchasing land in the Great Field, some from a farmer living in Stow and some from Susanna Barron, including a parcel worth exactly what Jack was worth in the initial inventory of the estate. Having made himself sufficiently difficult and having, like Charles Chambers's Jack, provided his owner with a form of financial recompense for his loss, Jack had transformed himself into what his land deeds referred to as "a free Negro man."[9]

Mark had already made one attempt to get a new master. Six years earlier, he had decided that if he could destroy some of John Codman's property, he could force his master to sell the slaves who labored in it, Mark among them. Joining forces with some of the other Codman slaves, Mark determined to burn down both the blacksmith shop and the workhouse John owned next door. The punishment for arson, should they be discovered, was death by hanging. But so desperate were the Codman slaves to change their situation that after Mark placed a pile of wood shavings between the shop and the workhouse, Phyllis ignited the tinder by throwing a lit coal on it. Phoebe helped carry out the scheme. She and Phyllis were driven to participate by the same family deprivation Mark suffered. Phoebe was able to see her spouse, who was owned by someone else, only on the one night per week that slaves were allowed to visit other households. And like the two Bristers, Phyllis was separated from her mother when she was, as she later explained, "a little girl." The kindled tinder went up in flames and several of John's buildings were lost. But while Captain Codman was forced to claim extensive losses, he managed to rebuild without having to part with any of his six slaves. He did think it prudent, however, to make one change. Although not sure if Mark or any of his other slaves played a role in the fire, John allowed Mark to live and work for wages in Boston, thereby granting Mark the respite for which he had been willing to risk his life. For six years, Mark was able to live with or near his wife and their family. But then disaster struck. When Mark was warned out of Boston and forced to return to the Codman mansion house in Charlestown, John sold or gave his child to someone in the country. His family broken, Mark came to Robin hoping to find a way to better his situation permanently. He was willing to do whatever it took. [10]

Robin had access to the powerful medicinal substances in his master's apothecary, including arsenic. An extremely toxic substance, it was used to treat syphilis, but as little as half an ounce of the white powder would induce vomiting, acute diarrhea, convulsions, and eventually death. Anticipating Mark's visit, Robin had recently stolen from Doctor Clarke an ounce of the poison, which he folded up in a white piece of paper and tied with some twine. Now, under the cover of the barn, he gave Mark the tiny parcel and an iron measuring device, instructing him to put a small bit of the arsenic into an empty glass medicine vial to which he should add some water. The toxic water could be mixed with food and administered to the victim. Robin thought that two separate doses would be enough "to kill the strongest man living." And he assured Mark that no one would be the wiser, noting of the arsenic that "there was no more taste in it than in cold water." The proof was that seven slaves belonging to Boston merchant John Salmon had successfully poisoned their master using the same means the previous year without getting caught. (The possibility that the Barrons' two slaves, Jack and Violet, were inspired, as were the Codman slaves, by the actions of Salmon's slaves was never raised, at least through official channels, even though Benjamin Barron sickened and died unexpectedly. Then again, poison was not considered the cause of Salmon's death until the Codman slaves said as much during their trial. Jack later willed his estate to Violet, his fellow sufferer and perhaps co-conspirator.) Robin never said if it was he who supplied the Salmon slaves with arsenic, but he was clearly willing to risk his life to help slaves when others were not. The previous winter, when Mark had attempted to procure arsenic from a slave man who belonged to another doctor, the slave had denied his request upon the advice of Phoebe's husband, who was afraid that anyone who got involved in such a risky plan would be "brought into trouble." [11]

Upon returning to the Codman mansion in Charlestown, Mark discovered that he had lost the iron implement Robin had given him for measuring out the arsenic doses. He went out to his owner's rebuilt blacksmith shop and quickly made another one under the guise of performing another task. He gave the implement to Phyllis and instructed her to give it to Phoebe when the two were alone in the kitchen. Since the death of John's wife Parnell in 1752, Phyllis and Phoebe had again determined to join forces with Mark to improve a situation that was quickly becoming unbearable. For despite the obvious interest of numerous widows, John had not remarried, choosing instead to allow his daughters Elizabeth and Mary, then thirty-one and twenty-nine, to run the domestic affairs of his Charlestown mansion house. Without a wife, John was free to indulge his darkest moods. Her death most likely stirred up memories of the death of his parents within two years of each other before his thirteenth birthday and the loss of his remaining brother at sea five years after that. John had been left all alone in the world save for an older married sister and the man appointed to be his legal guardian, his father's friend and associate Charles Chambers. Abandoned yet again when his wife died, John had recently struck his slave man Tom full in the face and so severely that one of Tom's eyes was seriously injured. [12]

It was the rare owner who could check the absolute power that was his by legal right. As Thomas Jefferson noted, "The man must be a prodigy who can retain his manners and morals" when given carte blanche by slavery to do as he pleases. In his 1798 autobiography, Venture Smith recounted several severe beatings he and his wife received at the hands of their Connecticut slave owners. On one occasion, Venture was beaten by his master's son with a pitchfork. On another, he entered the house to find his mistress beating his wife. When he entreated his wife to beg the woman's pardon for whatever had upset her, the mistress "took down her horsewhip" and began "glutting her fury with it" on Venture. Venture was later punished for taking the whip from his mistress and throwing it into the fire. A few days later, his master came up behind him seeking retribution and gave him what Venture described as "a violent stroke on the crown of my head with a club two feet long and as large around as a chair post. This blow very badly wounded my head, and the scar," Venture reported, "remains to this day." The initial cause of his mistress's ire, he added, was "a small affair that I forbear to put my mistress to the shame of having it known." [13]

The trigger for most slave owners was not having their orders carried out expediently and correctly. On March 18, 1756, a year after the Codman trial, John Cuming's friend the Reverend Ebenezer Bridge of Chelmsford admitted in his journal of his recently deceased slave Venus that she "hath gone through a great deal of hard service, one that hath provoked me and my wife a multitude of times to rash and unjustifiable expressions and hard treatment of her." Like John

Codman's slave women, Venus was named for a character in classical literature and mythology. But while the Codman slave women's names were meant to signify their owner's love of the pastoral (the name Phoebe appears frequently in classical poetry) and nature more generally (Phyllis comes from *phylla* for foliage), the slave name Venus was meant to demonstrate her owner's appreciation of the Roman goddess of love. And yet when given absolute control over another person, Ebenezer demonstrated anything but loving behavior. Only Venus's death prompted him to examine his inability to check his temper when his orders were not carried out exactly as he wished.[14]

Nor was Ebenezer the only minister who became a tyrant on account of the awesome power slavery placed in his hands. After purchasing a slave in Boston in 1728 with his father's financial assistance, the Reverend Ebenezer Parkman, who hoped to now have more time to devote to his profession, changed the slave's name from Barrow to Maro and proceeded to make his way homeward to Westborough, stopping at various towns along the way to rest: "I rode to Cambridge, Barrow, alias Maro, running on foot. Though somewhat rainy, it cleared away after noon." By changing his slave's name, Ebenezer had immediately asserted control over the slave's entire identity and helped break the slave's ties to his past life, while also managing to advertise his own education at Harvard in the classics. Although known in English as Virgil, the author of the *Aeneid*'s full name was Publius Vergilius Maro. The name Barrow would not have meant anything to the colony's other educated men or, worse, would be mistaken for a white last name being used as a first name, as Chambers was in the case of Charles Chambers's namesake, Chambers Russell. The name Maro, in contrast, would have been immediately recognized for its classical roots, thereby making clear the man's status as a slave while reflecting well on Maro's owner. Ebenezer's choice of this particular classical name was quite clever. The change he imposed was not as drastic as it might have been phonetically because of the rhyme of Barrow and Maro. But that Ebenezer felt entitled to make the change to suit his own purposes speaks to his complete usurpation of his slave's personhood and his interest in imposing a name that branded Maro a slave. From there, it did not seem much to ask that Maro run from one town to the other. Four months after being forced to travel by foot in the rain from Boston to Cambridge, Maro was dead. For the Reverend Bridge, his slave man was no more than a beast of burden and he was physically treated as such. Disease could strike down even the hardiest of men in colonial America, but being forced to run long distances in the rain hardly improved the chances of survival. [15]

Having seen what John Codman did to Tom and no doubt aware of similar injuries sustained throughout the New England slave population, Phoebe was unable to tolerate such treatment any longer. She hid the iron measuring device in a hollow over the window in the third-floor garret, which she shared with Mark, Phyllis, and on Saturday nights when slaves were allowed to be at large, her husband. Mark hid the arsenic there as well. On Sunday morning, June 22, Phoebe and Phyllis mixed some of the arsenic into a vial of water and hid the vial in a corner of the kitchen closet behind a black jug. As they did all the work of cooking for the large Codman family, no one else would be apt to discover it.

As desperate as they were, the Codman slaves were governed in these actions by a strong sense of morality. Mandatory attendance in the slave section of the Charlestown meeting house had done at least some of the policing the Reverend Cotton Mather had hoped for when he encouraged slave baptism and religious education. Mark was determined not to break any commandments. He told Phyllis and Phoebe the Bible stipulated "it was no sin to kill" John "if they did not lay violent hands on him . . . by sticking or stabbing or cutting his throat." The threesome also determined not to harm anyone else in their crowded household except the man directly responsible for their situation. During the first twenty years of John and Parnell's marriage, Parnell had given birth to a child every other year, her last in 1739 when she was forty-three years old. The ten of the couple's eleven children who survived infancy lingered at home into their twenties and thirties, enjoying their father's significant wealth and the ease of life in a mansion house attended by five slaves. But the Codman slaves determined that neither Miss Betty nor Miss Molly, their names for the two Codman women under whose direction they were forced to labor, nor the rest of the large Codman family would be harmed. And so Phoebe and Phyllis proceeded to add the arsenic only to those dishes consumed solely by their master. That first Sunday, when the rest of the family was taking tea, they added the poison to what they called the master's "infusion," a tisane of various herbs and spices. Later that same evening, they introduced some arsenic to their master's elaborately prepared chocolate drink.

First, they ground some imported cocoa beans, a luxury favored by wealthy men for cocoa's stimulating properties. Then they added some arsenic to the boiling water they poured over the grounds. Next, Phoebe and Phyllis milled the liquid, sweetened it, and then boiled it again before leaving it to stand overnight. In the morning, they milled, boiled, and milled the chocolate again, finally serving the poisoned beverage to the master in his silver chocolate pot. John sat at a small mahogany table in the kitchen, enjoying a breakfast served in opulent dishes while his daughters hovered in the background ready to order his slaves to tend to his every need, a setting designed very much to remind John of his financial standing and his position at the head of the family. Unbeknownst to him, however, his silver dishes held more than the luxurious energy boost he so enjoyed from his chocolate. [16]

That Tuesday, Mark had to pick up some earthenware pots for his master at the workhouse of potter John Harris. He used the opportunity to purchase a mug so he could buy Robin a drink as compensation for his assistance and to procure additional poison. Not wanting to be recognized, Robin used his old trick for getting around incognito. He came over the river disguised as a gentleman in a black wig and a fancy blue coat with a yellow lining that showed on the turned-up cuffs. Still needing to be cautious, however, Mark and Robin left the potter's separately. They caught up with one another at a local Charlestown slaughterhouse and proceeded together along one of Charlestown's back lanes to a shop owned by the widow Mrs. Sherman near the long wharf where the ferry launched for Boston. Robin lingered in the lane, out of sight of most of the traffic, while Mark went in and had his new mug filled with toddy, which he brought outside to share in the lane after paying for it with some of his Boston earnings. John Codman, who was still well enough to be out and about attending the launching of one of his ships that day, was informed by passersby who observed Mark and Robin that Mark was enjoying an alcoholic beverage. Robin later saw the captain enter Mrs. Sherman's shop, where, as Mark soon learned, he instructed the proprietor not to sell any more drinks to his slaves. Still unaware that John knew Mark had been drinking, the men finished the toddy and took the back way to the ferry. Mark turned off into his master's yard, carrying the pots he had picked up at John Harris's. Captain Codman thought Mark's only infraction that day was drinking and fraternizing, but Mark had also managed to acquire galena, or lead sulfide, used by potters as a glaze. It seems a slave working for John Harris stole some of this highly toxic material from the potter's workhouse and gave it to Mark, who secreted it in his master's blacksmith shop. [17]

The next day, a Wednesday, Phyllis and Phoebe again poisoned John's morning chocolate with arsenic, using up almost all their supply in the process. But as John continued to feel fine, Mark, who was afraid to administer the lead on account of its telltale gritty texture, determined to request more arsenic of Robin in Boston. On Thursday, he took the ferry across the Charles River and secured a promise from Robin to bring him more of the poison the following night. Robin appeared in the yard behind the Codman mansion house after dark on Friday, again in a disguise. Phyllis thought she recognized the visitor, who denied he was Robin Vassall when she pressed him, insisting instead he was a "country negro" come to bring Mark news of his child. Phyllis was prevented from speaking any further with Robin by someone in the Codman family calling for her. John was finally beginning to experience stomach problems and her help was needed. In any event, Mark was not at the Codman house, having gone to Boston seeking Robin. Returning to Charlestown, he was frustrated at having failed to cross paths with him. Mark remarked with disgust to Phyllis that he and Robin had been playing "blind-man's bluff." Each had been over the ferry twice that night and missed each other both times. [18]

The following morning, Saturday, June 28, the Codman daughters instructed Phyllis to prepare John a porringer of water gruel instead of his usual breakfast. Feeling increasingly worse, the captain took water gruel for dinner as well. Phyllis took this opportunity to mix the little remaining arsenic with it. John did not, however, seem sick enough that his death was assured. Mark headed back to Boston to try to procure the second paper of arsenic Robin had promised him. He found Robin out in the street in front of Doctor Clarke's house in the North End. Robin told Mark he could not get the arsenic for him at that moment but would have some more for him "on the Sabbath night after candle light." Mark stayed in Boston Saturday and Sunday night, finally procuring the arsenic from Robin, and returned to the Codman mansion on Monday morning. [19]

That morning, John was feeling steadily worse and suffering from vomiting and acute diarrhea. His daughters requested that his slave women make him a porringer of sago, a gruel made of a powdery starch imported from the

East Indies. Mark found himself alone in the kitchen while the sago was boiling in an iron skillet on the fire. Not yet having had an opportunity to get the arsenic into the vial hidden in the kitchen closet, Mark added some of the lead to the sago, hoping this would finally spell the end of John Codman. His master complained of the gritty texture, as Mark had feared he would. Nor did he die that night. So when John's daughters requested more sago for their father, his slaves laced it with the arsenic from the second paper. Within hours, after being administered arsenic seven times, John began to convulse. The next day, Tuesday, July 1, he died.

RATHER THAN CONSIDER WAYS OF AMELIORATING or even abolishing the institution that had caused Mark, Phyllis, and Phoebe to commit murder, judges sought a means of punishing all three of them that would be severe enough to deter other slaves from copying them. There were ample precedents to consider. In 1739, forty-four slaves were killed and beheaded in South Carolina after obtaining weapons and killing twenty whites in the Stono Rebellion, also called Cato's Conspiracy. Their heads were spiked on posts placed every mile between the Stono Bridge and Charleston. Two years later, in New York City, thirteen slave men were burned at the stake, seventeen slave men hanged, and eighty-four slave men and women sold away to the Caribbean after whites began to suspect that as many as two hundred slaves were conspiring to burn down the city. Massachusetts officials were even more familiar with the outcome of a plot in Antigua in the late 1730s that caused the Royall, Vassall, and other English families to flee for Massachusetts, where their lives of splendor were financed by the West Indian plantations they continued to own and manage from afar. According to one report, "while the Gentlemen and Ladies" of Antigua "were diverting themselves at the [King's Coronation Day] Ball," the slaves planned "to convey a great quantity of gun-powder into the cellar and blow the house up." Thirty-seven slaves implicated in the rebellion were banished from the island. The rest received death sentences that entailed considerable public displays of torture as both a punishment and a warning against future rebellions. The two men deemed the principal actors were stretched on a wagon wheel after which a hammer was used to break all of their bones. The wheel was then hoisted onto a tall pole where it could be displayed. If they were not finished off by birds and animals picking away at their flesh, the victims died of shock and dehydration. Seventy-seven more slaves in Antigua were burned at the stake. The remaining six slaves implicated in the rebellion were gibbeted alive, a form of execution often called being hanged "in irons" or "in chains." Used only for the most heinous of crimes, a gibbet is a human form made of iron for the purpose of displaying a body either alive or dead (Figure 4). If the latter, the iron form held the rotting corpse together for several weeks. If the body was tarred first, the corpse lasted even longer. Two of the seventeen men hanged in New York had been gibbeted. Hanged and left to rot on the common land that ran alongside highways, a gibbeted corpse was a warning to all who passed it not to upset the colonial order of things. [20]

Terrified the recent events in Charlestown might mushroom into something worse, the judges of Middlesex County determined to apply the same means used in New York and Antigua to put the fear of eternal damnation into the minds of the area's slave population. On September 26, Ebenezer Parkman again interrupted his usual accounting of his day to record their decision: "The Negro man and Negro woman who murdered Captain Codman of Charlestown, were executed last Thursday, at Cambridge." Referring to Mark and Phyllis, he noted that "The man was hanged, and was afterwards to be hanged in irons on Charlestown Neck: the woman was burnt to death." (Phoebe was deported to the West Indies and Robin escaped punishment altogether.) Ebenezer was as impressed as colonial officials intended him and everybody else to be. The pyre reminded him of the eternal fires of Hell, the mere thought of which was "a frightful spectacle!" Chambers Russell and his fellow judges had made a decisive statement aimed expressly at the local slave and servant population. Broadsides circulated among the large crowds attending the executions on September 8, 1755, asserted that slaves and servants should "their masters serve with fear." [21]

AT THE TIME OF THE CODMAN TRIAL, Britain and France were on the brink of war, battling for imperial control of the North American continent. Thousands of New England's men were in Canada shoring up Britain's position at the Canadian border. John Cuming, however, was lingering at home even as the prestige of a military title awaited him. Educated men with professions and thus high-ranking social status were ensured officers' positions because it was assumed that troops would defer to them. But after two years of marriage, John and his wife finally had a child and John wanted to see Abigail and their baby

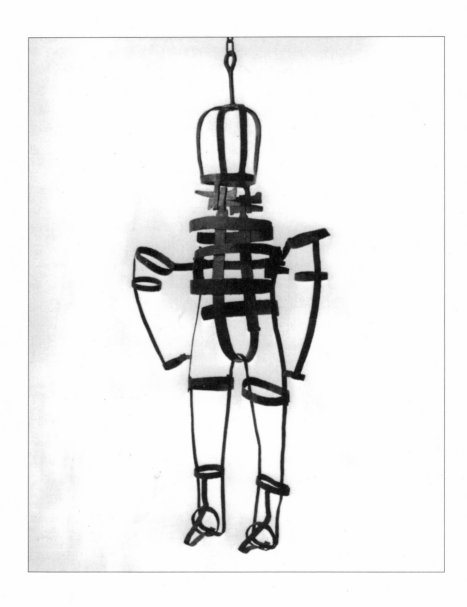

Figure 4. *Eighteenth-century gibbet. Courtesy of the Atwater Kent Museum of Philadelphia.*

through the first critical months after delivery. Little Helen's birth on May 18, 1755, was John's first inkling that he might not be quite as committed to rising into the ranks of the colonial elite as Robert had intended him to be. Having experienced the loss of two of his brothers and his father, John decided that family was the one thing he would allow to come before his father's ambitions.

Whether or not John stayed on in Concord longer than he intended in order to follow the trial, he did not enlist in the French and Indian War until two days after the warrant for Mark's and Phyllis's executions was issued. Once it was clear their respective punishments would send a clear message to area slaves, John must have felt it safe to leave his own slaves unattended. His delay saved him from participating in the Battle at Lake George, a bloody routing that left some two hundred dead on each side. When John finally did enlist, he was made a lieutenant colonel and put in charge of a company of forty-three provincial soldiers. Lieutenant colonels were paid over £16 per month, whereas doctors were only paid £10 per month. But John's real impetus in eschewing the job of army surgeon was no doubt the status conferred on officers. Again, only the most elite men were so appointed, as it was assumed in a very status-conscious society that they would best be able to ensure the obedience required for skillful military maneuvers. John was listed as "Esquire" on the list of men under his command in deference to his preeminence over his townsmen, won on account of being Harvard-educated and a large landowner. Although not yet a justice of the peace, he had finally achieved not just one of the titles that eluded his father but two others besides. For the rest of his life, he would be known in Concord as Colonel John Cuming even as he had the right to be called John Cuming Esquire or Doctor John Cuming as well. (John was never officially promoted from lieutenant colonel to colonel but the use of the latter title for the former position was and remains customary in the military.) An acknowledgment of John's earned position at the very top of the local aristocracy, colonel was such a prestigious title it trumped the other two. In December 1765, when the Reverend Ebenezer Bridge's daughter became ill and John journeyed to Chelmsford to administer "vomits" or emetics, Ebenezer did not refer to John as Dr. Cuming, even though the context was solely a medical one: "Last night my Daughter Sally was so bad that I was obliged to send for Col. Cuming in the night." Others were also careful to refer to John as Colonel once they learned of his position in the Concord hierarchy. When the Reverend William Emerson first came to

Figure 5. *Phoebe Bliss [Emerson Ripley], Sampler (1749). Concord Museum, Concord, Mass. www.concordmuseum.org. Photograph by David Bohl.*

Concord as a prospective preacher, he was careful to use the honorific, writing on December 17, 1764, that he "visited Col. Cuming." Formality prevailed in Massachusetts even in the privacy of a diary. [22]

John Cuming's first tour in the French and Indian War proved to be of relatively short duration. After directing his men in the building of Fort William Henry at the southern end of Lake George, Colonel Cuming was discharged on December 16, 1755. Within weeks if not days of his return, John would have had to journey to Boston to report to his superior officers, renew his medical supplies, and learn the news of the day at the taverns and coffeehouses there. To get to the city, he had to pass over Charlestown Neck and through the peninsular town of Charlestown to reach the ferry that would carry him across the Charles River to Boston. Like another one of his medical colleagues, he might have stopped at the Neck to examine Mark's gibbeted body. The colleague was on his way to Ticonderoga in 1758 when he noted in his journal of Mark that "his skin was but very little broken, although he had hung there near three or four years." It seems officials had coated Mark's body with tar to ensure it would last as a warning to slaves that they had better toe the line or suffer similar consequences. Twenty years later, when Paul Revere rode westward to warn local militias of the impending arrival of British regulars, Mark's corpse was still hanging on Charlestown Neck. [23]

OVER THE COURSE OF THE NEXT FOUR YEARS, as the French and Indian War raged, little Helen Cuming and the slave Brister, eleven years her senior, spent their time in close proximity but in entirely dissimilar ways. Helen passed her days in the Cuming family parlor being schooled in all of the arts considered requisite for a future lady, first among them fine needlework and the ability to read and write, both of which were taught through the sewing of a sampler. Another Concord daughter, the eldest of minister Daniel Bliss, born three years before Brister, had recently inscribed her effort with her name and age: "Phebe BLISS aGeD 8Y" (Figure 5). Perfect stitchery, patience, and gentility were valued as highly in women as literacy, if not more, as Phoebe's erratic use of uppercase and lowercase letters attests. As important as the ability to form the alphabet (four of which compose the body of Phoebe's sampler) was the demonstration of an appreciation for beauty, which Phoebe amply displayed in the flowers, hillocks, and geometric shapes she used to form the border. Taken together, a sampler made clear a girl's leisure time and her good sense in using it to cultivate literacy and artistic sensibilities. Once she was old enough to sit still and grasp a needle, Helen began to prepare for the day when she could complete a sampler that would similarly advertise her family's wealth and her attractiveness as a future wife.[24]

When she was not sewing under her mother's tutelage, Helen would have been allowed up on her father's lap to peruse one of the books in his growing library and to practice wielding a quill at his mahogany desk. As Phoebe Bliss's sampler attests, literacy was a means of claiming ownership of oneself. Phoebe used the occasion of making the alphabet to inscribe her name and thereby through language write herself into existence outside of space and time. Other young, white Concordians were meant to follow suit. Still in school at age twenty-two, Concord resident Stephen Barrett wrote in the margins of his school copy book: "Stephen Barrett is my name and a very good rightor is my fame." But as Stephen well understood, literacy was also the means by which one claimed ownership of another person in a slave society. In one school exercise dated February 10, 1772, Stephen would draw up a mock deed stipulating that his father, Colonel James Barrett, was selling to Francis Moore of Cambridge, then a young man in Cambridge about Stephen's age, "a negro boy named Philop, seven years of age." Stephen's father did, in fact, own a slave boy named Philip of about that age, but his will stipulated that, rather than be sold, Philip was to be bequeathed to Stephen's youngest brother, Peter, then seventeen. Nevertheless, Stephen had every reason to expect that he might one day produce the paperwork that would make him a slaveholder and so he practiced writing a bill of sale in anticipation of that day. Once Helen married, any slaves she inherited from her father would belong to her husband. But she might, like John's aunt, have occasion to take on her husband's power of attorney, provided she could read and write. John's sisters were prolific letter writers their entire lives, using their letters to convey news of the day and to advertise their business interests in the paper. John had every intention of his daughter joining literate society so that she might also wield the extensive powers literacy provided.[25]

John did not, however, teach Brister to read or write. While one of Brister's first jobs was most likely to polish John's mahogany desk, he was never permitted to sit there, much less peruse books or attempt to write. Like most slave owners, John determined to keep his slaves illiterate so they could not forge documents that would allow them to move about freely if not escape. And thus years later, when Brister finally had cause to sign legal documents, he could make only an "X" for a signature. [26]

The two children also lived in different versions of the same house. While Helen slept upstairs in a room used exclusively for sleeping, Brister slept on a pallet on the floor, most likely placed in the barn during the summer and in the kitchen during the winter. His bedding was then rolled up in the morning and stored out of sight. But as the Codman slaves well knew, a barn and a deserted kitchen were a means of crafting a separate community from slaveholders. Brister had Jem and no doubt other slaves and servants as well with whom to talk and empathize. Nor were his brother and sister so far away that he lost touch with them. What they said to one another when slaves were allowed to visit each other on Saturday nights is lost, but Brister's later actions make clear that, like Mark and his fellow Codman slaves, he was keeping a careful watch on white society, dreaming of how he might escape its clutches, and plotting with others what he would do once he did.

Life at the Cuming mansion was otherwise punctuated by John's frequent absences. Brister and Jem's labor allowed him to attend to patients across the county and to serve additional tours in the French and Indian War. When Helen was four, John again left for the war front. This time, however, the luck he had enjoyed in earlier tours ran out and he was shot in the hip and taken captive by Indians on the French side. Finding himself at the mercy of people who did not dress, speak, or act like him, John had every reason to fear he would never see his Nabby and his beloved Helen again, much less resume his comfortable position at the forefront of Concord society. Certainly he knew of men and women who had survived their capture, either by being ransomed, running away, or killing their captors. No less a famous captive during Metacom's (King Philip's) War than Mary Rowlandson had her ransom brokered in 1676 on the Massachusetts frontier by Concord's John Hoar (one of the ancestors of John Hoar, the owner of the other Brister). He brought her back to Concord where she was finally safe in the Garrison or Block House, to use the name by which that house was known in John Cuming's day, by which point it was the Reverend Daniel Bliss's home. Hannah Emerson Dustan, in contrast, had eluded her Indian captors in 1697 by tomahawking them while they slept. She was careful to scalp each of her victims for the bounty she knew to expect from the General Court before making her way down the Merrimack River to safety. But escape by these or other means was not inevitable for a man with a bullet lodged in his side. [27]

Indians across North America had long regarded male captives as a means of replacing their waning physical and spiritual powers in the face of decimation from the diseases and warfare that arrived with the Europeans. Had he been captured by nonconverted Indians, John would have been adopted into their tribe as a means of replacing a fallen Indian. Many such adopted white captives chose never to leave, enamored of the way of life to which the Indians introduced them and thus living out their days as Indians in all but birth. Catholic Indians, however, regarded captives as slaves to be subdued, worked, and then sold or ransomed. John's experience seems to have been of the latter type. Whether or not he was made to run the gauntlet naked as was the brother of his friend Ebenezer Bridge, he was most likely tied up at night for days, if not weeks, during the march northward. What John experienced was the same total loss of autonomy Brister and Jem had to contend with daily. [28]

While John was suffering enslavement, the English began to take the lead in the race for North America. When word reached Boston in late October 1759 that Quebec had fallen, bells tolled, sermons were read, and artillery was fired throughout the region in a massive salute. But while people across Massachusetts rejoiced that the English were wresting control of Canada from the French, Abigail Cuming was experiencing the darkest period of her life. Less than two weeks after that battle, while her doctor husband was still lost on the frontier, little Helen Cuming sickened and died four months after her fourth birthday. For all that Abigail knew, John was dead as well, dispatched by savages in the wilderness while she was left in Concord the sole survivor of their family.

Of course the death of a child was not uncommon in colonial Massachusetts. William Emerson, who replaced Daniel Bliss as Concord's minister after Daniel died, recorded the deaths of many children in his journal and usually in the same very matter-of-fact way he reported the work performed on his farm. On November 10, 1766, for example, he wrote "Wood-Day 27 loads. Mr. Flint's child buried, and Mr. Champney's." Two weeks later, he recorded the death of "Mrs. O. Wood's child." At the end of that year, he noted that there had been twenty-eight deaths in all, "14 of which were children under 8 years of age." But for all that children succumbed at a discouraging rate, the loss of each one was still deeply felt. On January 17, 1727, the Reverend Ebenezer Parkman recorded one of many occasions when he was asked to visit a sick child in Westborough and ended up comforting a bereft family. Finding the child "but alive," Ebenezer prayed with the family for his survival, but "the child changed and expired," leaving the minister to "instruct, exhort and support the heavy and sorrowful parents under the grievous loss, it being a fine son of his own [the father's] name and in its 3rd year." When a child did manage to survive the first years of life, parents were careful to give special thanks to God for sparing them. In a list he prepared of his many blessings, Ebenezer included the "Recovery of my son out of sickness" in September and October 1729 and the "Healing to my son in December of the same year." Abigail Cuming could count no such blessings. [29]

John finally arrived with his captors in Canada and was freed, according to a local 1835 biographer, "by the influence of a French gentleman." Most likely, this unnamed gentleman brokered the ransom. It seems the brotherhood of gentlemen was so powerful that it reached across the battle lines of two nations at war. Even as far from home as he was and without the accoutrements of his house, furnishings, and slaves, John was recognized as part of the brotherhood and was saved. Indeed, the whole point of being a gentleman, of following an international code of behavior, was that it made one instantly recognizable to others of the same status. Whether it was how he spoke, the tattered remnants of his officer's uniform, or the sense he projected of being entitled to approach another gentleman on equal terms, John convinced the French gentleman that he was worthy of his attention. Gentility ensured that no matter where one happened to be, one was among instant friends and protectors. John's only lasting visible scar was the entry wound of a bullet that would stay lodged in his hip for the rest of his life. [30]

Abigail finally had something to be thankful for when John, having secured his release and resecured his identity as a fully autonomous gentleman, made it home to Concord. But what should have been a glorious homecoming was not to be. John returned to a scene very different from the one he had left. No longer did the sound of his daughter's prattle fill the parlor as she bent her head to sew or to sound out the words in one of her father's books. John's little darling, the child whom he had named after his doting mother at a time when few passed on a paternal grandmother's name, was beyond the power of his ability to doctor her to health. His only comfort was that the war that had robbed him of so much was coming to a victorious end. After 1759, the British navy succeeded in emptying the sea of French fleets and thereby managed to cut off French supplies. That and the deterioration of relations between the French and their Indian allies spelled France's defeat. On November 3, 1762, the preliminary articles of the Treaty of Paris were signed.

John might have looked upon Brister, Jem, and any other slaves he owned with new eyes, having experienced the two losses that defined their own enslavement: loss of family and loss of autonomy. But like the judges who heard the Codman trial, John seems to have been unable to empathize across the divide between European and African peoples. In his mind, what he experienced during the period of his enslavement was an unfortunate byproduct of warfare. His captivity was an exceptional occurrence that should not have happened; because he had not been born a slave, it was not his destiny. And so upon returning to his estate, John Cuming the former slave took up the mantle of John Cuming the master once again. By all appearances, the manumission of his slaves did not cross John's mind for another twenty years. His thoughts were solely with his deceased daughter, whom he and Abigail became determined to memorialize for all that she had not yet left a mark on the world beyond the small circle of her family.

There was as of yet no Cuming burial plot where little Helen could be interred. John's father's grave site had never been marked to avoid the expense of having a stone engraved. Feeling it necessary to consider the future needs of Robert's widow and two unmarried daughters, the Cuming family had even forgone reporting his death at the courthouse on account of the fee. The large and elaborately engraved tombstones dotting Concord's two burial grounds were exclusively those of wealthy gentlemen with titles and, on occasion, their wives. But with the financial means to memorialize their only child, John and Abigail decided to break with tradition. They purchased a large stone for their four-year-old daughter and paid one of the colony's foremost stonecutters to engrave it. In the epitaph they chose for Helen's tombstone, John and Abigail attempted to capture their horror that death could rob them of one so young and vibrant, a girl who had yet to flower into womanhood: "Fresh as the morn / the fragrant bud / hangs withered ere it's blown." Scotsman William Park enlarged upon this theme in the imagery he carved to accompany this text. Above the epitaph, the flesh of the death's head has rotted off the bottom part of the face, revealing the skull's rictus underneath, while small rosebuds twine around the face. Helen was remembered by her parents as being still very much alive even as she was already dead. For them, life and death were now inextricably intertwined, and their anguish regarding this most brutal of incongruities was revealed here for all to ponder. [31]

Knowing full well that this would be where they too would await Judgment Day, John and Abigail carefully selected a grave site. Burial Hill provided a fine prospect of the town for those who were considered sufficiently important to be buried on its crest, far above the slaves and later the former slaves who were interred toward the very back of the graveyard on its rear-facing slope, typically in unmarked graves. John's position in Concord was already such that Helen's body could be interred near the top, where the view encompassed the entire town. Her grave faces out toward the church green, where her grandfather Robert's store had been located, and, further, toward where John and Abigail made their home almost three miles away. It was a prospect so well situated for surveying long distances that British officers used the site sixteen years later on April 19, 1775, to take reconnaissance of their troops as they searched the town for hidden military stores. Once it was a lovely site where they had strolled during their courtship; now John and Abigail came here to visit the grave site of their only child and to contemplate their own mortality. [32]

Looking out over the town from this spot, John had to reconcile himself to the fact that he would likely not have any more children. Most Concord couples had a child every two years. If there was a four-year-old in the household, there should have also been a two-year-old and another baby on the way. But the regular pregnancies most Concord women enjoyed had eluded Abigail, whether on account of John's frequent absences or some other reason. With that in mind and a bullet festering in his hip, John must have had little hope he and Abigail would become parents again. He was thus left to imagine other ways to fulfill the gentleman's imperative of being a patriarch. If he could not be a father to his family, he could still be a father to his town and country. The result of experiencing enslavement and the loss of his child was that John would no longer allow himself to be distracted by family pleasures, to loiter at home while the business of empire proceeded without him. He finally committed himself wholly to his father's dream of his ascension. [33]

John's first opportunity to become a patriarch came with the end of the French and Indian War. The defeat of the French opened all of New England for colonization by the British. And so when the colony needed to raise funds to send delegates to the Paris peace conference, officials determined to auction off western lands. In a move that was both patriotic and financially savvy, John organized twenty-six affluent men into a land company. His wealth and newfound status as a lieutenant colonel made it easy to gain their trust. They knew that when it came time in June 1762 to walk into the Royal Exchange Tavern on King Street in Boston, John would appear as the most dignified of gentlemen. The red silk sash and silver-hilted sword he was entitled to wear as a military officer over his scarlet greatcoat said to prospective proprietors that John was an experienced leader. His fashionable attire further made the point that he was also a gentleman committed to decorum and grace. John's expensive wig, laboriously oiled and powdered by his slaves, required him to stand tall and move as regally as he could lest it fall off his carefully shaved head. His silver sword, buckles, and watch chain, also cared for by his slaves, shone. Appearing every inch the pillar of civic-mindedness, enlightened thought, and genteel manners at the auction in Boston, John bid on and won Township Number Five, located one hundred miles to the west of Concord between the Connecticut River and the border of New York in a valley of the Hampshire Hills. Whereas Deerfield had marked the westernmost border of English inhabitation in John's youth, Township Number Five was further west by twenty miles. The work of surveying the area, parceling it into lots, and selling those lots would be arduous and time consuming, and yet John threw himself into this work of expanding an empire he considered very much his own for all that he lived on its periphery. [34]

John's contributions to the work of settling the new township included serving as one of two assessors responsible for visiting the township and inspecting the surveyed lots, sitting on a three-man committee charged with petitioning the General Court for incorporation, and hosting along with Abigail the various meetings of the proprietors at their Concord home. Thus, even as his financial investment in Township Number Five was not as substantial as some of the men in the company who were older than he was, he eventually profited quite handsomely on account of his leadership position. When one of the larger investors had to drop out, most if not all of his lots reverted to John, who began to sell his lots in 1763, ultimately amassing a considerable enough fortune that he was able to speculate in more land. John went on to purchase lots in Marlowe, New Hampshire, and Brandon and Leicester, Vermont. He was poor in off-spring but increasingly rich in the most important colonial currency: land. And the rewards John reaped were more than financial. His efforts on behalf of the land company he assembled for the purchase of Township Number Five were acknowledged on June 23, 1779, when the General Court incorporated the town, ruling that "the said plantation called Number Five be and hereby is erected into a town by the name of Cumington." (The spelling of the name later changed to Cummington.) Here was posterity of a different kind; John would live forever in this very public acknowledgment of his leadership. [35]

John's education, his courageous service as a lieutenant colonel, and now his organization of the purchase of Township Number Five made him a natural choice for a leadership position in local government. In 1763, one year after he headed the purchase of what would become Cummington, John was asked to take on the difficult and prestigious job of moderating Concord's town meetings, gatherings at which the business of the town (concerning property rights, roads, bridges, schools, and the poor) was conducted and town officials elected. These were sometimes quite tense affairs. Resources were finite, and residents of each of the three recognized sections of Concord (North, East, and South) were forever jockeying for position on the board of selectmen. And then there was the fear on the part of people living at the town's edges that town meetings could be packed by those who resided in or near the center of town when the weather was bad. John proved himself particularly adept at managing all of the competing interests. Certainly his position at the top of Concord's social hierarchy garnered him a degree of respect and deference that had the effect of smoothing otherwise ruffled feelings and silencing any simmering resentments. Then, too, John lived on the fringes of Concord himself. Even as other men of means were building new mansion houses along the Bay and Walden roads, John would spend his entire adult life on the estate his father had given him. If the weather was such that he and his fellow outliers could not make a town meeting, the meeting could not proceed. Over the course of the next twenty-five years, John would moderate no fewer than ninety of these meetings. He reaped an even greater civic honor when the Crown made him a justice of the peace, the very honor enjoyed by Charles Chambers, Chambers Russell, and Isaac Royall and the one that secured them the title of Squire. Here was an opportunity to spend time with other members of the elite at the various functions, both social and civic, held during court week every September, when Concord's inns were full of litigants, jurors, magistrates, and barristers. As doctor, town moderator, and now a justice of the peace, John could lay claim to being the foremost leader in Concord of all things political and otherwise. Little happened of which he was not somehow a part. John watched over the residents' health and general welfare from birth to death. When he looked out over the town from his daughter's grave site, he was looking out over his domain.[36]

By 1771, John was asserting himself not merely as a town father but a father to all of Massachusetts. He made a donation that year to the chapel at Harvard, the colony's leading institution. The two brass candelabras he donated were engraved in Latin: "In Sacelli hujusce ornatum et splendorem / phosphoron hoc Munus, benigne contulit / Cummings Armiger, Medicus concordiensis" ("Dr. Cummings, Esq., the Concord doctor, has bestowed this light-bearing gift upon the richness and splendor of this shrine"). A gift to Harvard was both a benevolent and somewhat self-serving gesture on John's part. It was a means of proclaiming to the world that he was an equal to any gentleman in the colony, including Isaac Royall Jr., who had already presented gifts to Harvard of the same sort. As John must have hoped, other gentlemen took notice. In his diary entry for May 14, 1771, a young John Adams, still twenty-six years away from his presidency, noted that John's gift was mentioned at his club, one of many such in England and its colonies in the eighteenth century where men made informal business arrangements, discussed the news of the day, promoted civility, and reinforced shared values of gentility. That the Concord doctor was putting himself into lofty company indeed was duly noted. Adams remarked that James Otis described John Cuming's present as "such as I[saac] Royall [Jr.] Esqr. gave to the Representatives Room."[37]

The reaction at the gentlemen's club to John's gift was not, however, what the donor would have wished for. Adams said of the inscription that "it was much faulted, by the wits of the club — and as it was to be a durable thing for the criticisms of strangers and of posterity, it was thought that it ought to be altered." The "wits" might have been concerned about John's Latin. Phosphoron is not given a normal Latin ending, rather a Greek one. Harvard, however, took the gesture more kindly. In recognition of his benevolence, the school immediately rewarded John with an honorary master of arts degree. John's gift of the candlesticks thus became the means by which he finally obtained a Harvard degree and thereby took his place alongside Concord's other Harvard graduates, even bettering their efforts insofar as his degree was an advanced, if honorary, one. Harvard would again recognize John's benevolence when in 1776 it moved to Concord so that provincial soldiers could be housed in Cambridge. John was accorded library privileges and thereby publicly singled out as someone esteemed by the college for his generosity. [38]

And so, having lost his freedom temporarily and his daughter forever, John fought to achieve the success his father had wished for him. He worked for a professional and a military title. He acquired vast amounts of additional acreage to the north and west of Concord, including lots in a town named after him. And he accepted an impressive amount of civic responsibility as his reward for these accomplishments. It seems Timothy Wesson's wedding gift to John had proven as helpful as Timothy could have wished. Brister and Jem, the only other Cuming slave whose name has survived, made it possible for John to leave behind the work of growing his family's food supply to pursue instead all that John's father had dreamt for him. Their care of his furnishings and wardrobe allowed John to appear as a gentleman on public occasions, whether in his own parlor for land meetings or elsewhere, thereby compelling others to treat him as such.

But for all the rewards John reaped as a slaveholder, he knew he was engaged in a delicate dance. If he leaned too hard on Brister and Jem, he risked becoming another John Codman. He had to be at least somewhat accommodating of his slaves' needs. Well aware that their masters were on edge, slaves across Massachusetts bided their time, waiting for the moment when they could pry the crack in the prison house of slavery made by the Codman slaves into an opening large enough they could all escape through it.

CHAPTER THREE

British Grenadiers

A DECADE AFTER THE CODMAN MURDER, during which time John Cuming began to preside handily over Concord, British officials decided to levy taxes on the colonists in an attempt to pay the substantial debts the government had incurred during the French and Indian War. It was a disastrous move. Colonists once proud to have assisted in the expansion of the British Empire now raged against the government they had fought for so valiantly. By way of protesting the various taxes imposed on them, the incensed colonists boycotted imported goods, harassed stamp distributors, and destroyed the personal property of government officials. By 1768, the situation in Boston had become dangerous and King George sent his troops to occupy the city, which only further infuriated local residents. Political tensions ran high, and within two years the specter of slave insurrection once again swept across Massachusetts.

On March 5, 1770, British soldiers attempted to relieve a cornered comrade who was being taunted with insults and snowballs by a sizable crowd. When the gathered colonists continued to press forward, the British fired at them. John Adams defended the British troops in court on the grounds that former slave Crispus Attucks, the first of five colonists to be killed, was responsible for the carnage. Adams argued that it was the former slave's "mad behavior, in all probability" that forced the soldiers to take what he described as defensive action. His tactic proved effective. In October 1770, Captain Thomas Preston was acquitted of the accusation that he had ordered his men to fire and six of the British soldiers were acquitted on the grounds that they felt threatened by a crowd Adams described as "a motley rabble of saucy boys, negroes and mulattos, Irish teagues, and outlandish jack tarrs." Only two were convicted of manslaughter and branded on their thumbs. The juries were convinced that the threat of advancing "negroes," "mulattos," and other undesirables was sufficient cause to shoot directly into a crowd of people. Pamphlets calling the day's events a "horrid massacre in Boston" and Paul Revere's inflammatory prints of the scene galvanized colonial opposition to British rule but also fanned concerns that area slaves were eager to cause the colonists trouble. One anonymous pamphlet insisted the occupying troops were inciting slaves "to take away their masters' lives and property." Later, when the colonies prepared to declare their independence officially, they considered doing so on the grounds that, among other intolerable actions, George III was intent on inciting slaves to rebel. In his first draft of the Declaration of Independence, Thomas Jefferson wrote that the king "is now exciting" the slaves "to rise in arms among us, and to purchase that liberty of which he has deprived them, by murdering the people upon whom he also obtruded them." This passage, which was eventually struck from the document, pitched the colonists' separation in the same way John Adams had pitched the British soldiers' actions during the Boston Massacre: as an act of self-defense against an impending slave insurrection. [1]

Five years after the Boston Massacre, the Provincial Congress ordered military and food stores to be secreted in Concord in preparation for an all-out confrontation with British troops, at which point fears of a slave rebellion rose to a fevered pitch in the Massachusetts countryside. On March 9, 1775, the *Norwich* (Connecticut) *Packet* reported that "a free negro was apprehended" in Natick, a mere thirteen miles south of Concord on the other side of the neighboring town of Sudbury. He was committed to the Concord jail for being "employed in forming a plot to destroy the white people." It was said "he had enlisted numbers of his own complexion as associates." It appeared slaves were waiting only "until some disturbance should happen that might occasion the militia to turn out, and in their absence it was proposed to murder the defenseless inhabitants." The *Packet* reported that further evidence of the plot had surfaced when "another African, in the vicinity of Natick, was discovered to have been deeply concerned in the above-mentioned infernal scheme." He, too, was committed to the Concord jail. The *New-London Gazette*'s account of these same doings in Natick was only somewhat less hysterical. The *Gazette* wrote that Thomas Nichols, "a Mulatto," was brought before a justice "for being concerned in enticing divers servants to desert the service of their masters" and, worse, "causing the minds of said servants to be inimical towards their masters' persons and property." The article failed to mention that Thomas Nichols had been listed as a "transient person" when his intentions to marry were published in Natick in late 1766. And yet clearly there was more at stake than ridding the town of an impoverished person. Nonwhites were increasingly perceived as dangerous, especially in those instances when there was no white person in charge of them. [2]

With all that was going on in Concord in the spring of 1775, town residents were on high alert. Between one and two in the morning on April 19, when bells tolled the alarm that British regulars were advancing from Boston into the countryside, virtually everyone leapt out of bed. Dressing hurriedly, Concord minister William Emerson rushed from the Manse to meet the mustering provincial troops. A committed Patriot, William had recently exhorted the local militia to set the American colonists "free" from "the encroaching arm of unconstitutional powers," which like so many other colonists he described as "the shackles of slavery." Advancing with Concord's troops to the top of Burial Hill, he eventually saw, as he later reported in his journal, "British troops at the distance of a quarter of a mile, glittering in arms" and "advancing toward us" on the Bay road "with the greatest celerity." It was shortly before 7 A.M. Determined not to give the king cause to accuse them of starting a civil war and unaware that eight locals had been killed by British troops two hours earlier on the Lexington green, the militia turned and headed toward the minister's house with the intention of retreating across the North Bridge, which spanned the Concord River behind the Manse. From a hill on the other side of the bridge, they would be able to keep watch over the town, while their separation from it by the river assured the king's men they would do them no harm. As they passed through Concord's streets, word spread that they had spied the British approaching. [3]

William Emerson's slave man Frank was also out and about that morning. Upon hearing the king's troops were near at hand, he rushed to apprise his mistress. Phoebe Emerson was still on the second floor of the Manse when Frank burst into her bedchamber carrying an axe. "The Red Coats have come!" he cried. Having been warned by her husband earlier that morning to expect their arrival, Phoebe should not have been surprised at the news. But alone in the house, save for her four young children and a few slaves, one of whom stood before her with a lethal weapon in hand, the minister's wife must have been re-minded of the recent plot in Natick "to destroy the white people" as soon as the militia turned out. She fainted.[4]

WHEN WILLIAM HAD BEEN ORDAINED as Concord's new minister al-most ten years earlier, he had inherited a town long embroiled in a fierce reli-gious debate. His predecessor, Daniel Bliss, had been able to capitalize on the spiritual revivals sweeping the colonies, increasing church membership from eighty-three to almost two hundred, but in the process he had caused a schism in the church. There was a vocal group very much opposed to his "extravagant gestures" and raised voice. They squirmed with discomfort every time parish-ioners began to groan audibly and cry out in response to Daniel's exhortations. When Lincoln was incorporated, dissidents within the new town's boundaries eagerly joined the Lincoln church. And while some of the dissidents in Con-cord eventually reconciled with Daniel Bliss, others remained estranged from the Concord church.[5]

After Daniel died at the age of fifty in 1764, William, then twenty-one and fresh out of Harvard, had been called by John Cuming and four other men on the church selection committee to preach in Concord on a trial basis. The son of Malden's minister, William was well poised to inherit a similar post, but cer-tain individuals in town were immediately inclined to dislike him on account of him also being, like the Reverend Bliss, a "new light" or emotional preacher. Dr. Joseph Lee, one of the Concord men still estranged from the church, spent considerable time grilling William, noting in his journal that "we talked over all the matters relating to his coming into town, and how he had spent his time since he left college." William tried to placate Joseph, confessing that he "was very sensible" he had "fooled away" his time and that he "was very much to blame and ought to go to college and study the divinity two years" before he "undertook a pulpit in any place." Assessing the interview later that day, William was pleased, writing in his journal that it had been "a very pleasant, agreeable" one. But Joseph recognized a performance when he saw one. He took offense that William presented himself "as calm as a watch." Others were similarly con-cerned that William would be another Daniel Bliss. When the town vote was taken, William secured only two thirds of the ballots, enough to win the pulpit but also an indication that the road ahead would be a rocky one.[6]

William Emerson might not have struck every Concord resident as the man for them, but he was widely considered good husband material. The ministry was one of the most prestigious positions in colonial society and, should he be awarded a pulpit, William could expect to hold it for life. His "Aunt Cobb," as he called his brother's fiancée's mother, hoped he might form an alliance with Mary Royall, one of Isaac Royall Jr.'s two children. As everyone was well aware, whoever married Mary or her sister Elizabeth stood to receive a very large dowry and someday, on account of Isaac not having any sons, half of the vast Royall estate, now in Medford since its annexation to that town in 1754. That September, when William was at his parents' home in nearby Malden, Aunt Cobb brought Polly, as Mary was called, over from Medford to visit. William returned the call several days later and was, as he noted in his journal, "handsomely entertained." By then, however, William was beginning to set his sights on Phoebe Bliss, the Reverend Bliss's twenty-three-year-old daughter, with whom he became acquainted while boarding with the Bliss family during his candidacy for the Concord pulpit. Phoebe was an accomplished young woman, living up to the promise indicated by the sampler she sewed as a child. Her mother, whose portrait depicted her holding a book at a time when only the most elite women could read and write, had schooled Phoebe well. Although women were not permitted to attend Harvard, Phoebe could hold her own with the graduates of Massachusetts's only college, and William enjoyed conversing with her. On October 1, 1764, before agreeing to preach for two more months, William took Phoebe out for a ride around the town center. He wanted to assess her interest in him before agreeing to stay in town longer. It did not hurt that he also made clear to all who saw them that he was intent on forging links with Concord's past and thereby smoothing the town's transition to a new minister. Ten days after taking Phoebe out, William reported in his journal that he "drank tea at Col. Royall's," but such entries were soon replaced with entries on Phoebe's health. In one of his last diary entries on the Royalls, made that December, William described taking Phoebe to meet his parents after a lengthy supper at the Royalls that kept them from arriving in Malden until eleven o'clock at night. It was clear to William and perhaps he wanted to make it clear to Polly as well that his heart was now firmly in Concord. Six weeks later, the town elected William to be their pastor. He accepted the position and married Phoebe eight months after his ordination.[7]

Formerly a boarder, William became a permanent resident of the Block House, where there was little privacy for the newly married couple. His mother-in-law had nine children, eight of whom had survived infancy. All of them, except her eldest child, still lived at home. Bliss family slaves lived in the Block House as well. Phoebe's father had left them to his wife and daughters jointly. The inventory of his estate referred to two slaves, most likely men, because slave women were rarely counted for tax or inventory purposes. But the family certainly owned slave women. After William married Phoebe, he referred to Bliss family slaves Cate and Phyllis. As if that was not enough people, the Block House was also a boarding house. After Daniel died, his widow needed a way to make money and settled on feeding and lodging people. One of the earliest jobs she took was hosting the celebration of the ordination of her deceased husband's successor, for which she was paid £18. A formidable woman, Mrs. Bliss did not flinch from the vicissitudes of life. No doubt it helped that she was gaining a son-in-law in her husband's stead. [8]

Mrs. Bliss was a relatively young woman when her husband died but she never remarried, remaining a widow for thirty-three years. Just four years after losing her husband, she faced another devastating loss. It was September and she was in her kitchen making pastry during court week while her two slave women did the cooking. William Emerson, who had married into the family only two years before, found himself with the task of breaking the worst kind of news to her. According to William's daughter Mary Moody Emerson, her father "came into the kitchen," walked up to his mother-in-law, and said, "Madam, prepare for heavy tidings." What happened next became part of Emerson family lore, an example of Mrs. Bliss's extraordinary faith and strength. She "took her hands — all flour — out of the pan and knelt right down on the kitchen floor: then she stood up and said 'I am ready.'" William told her that her daughter Hannah's fiancé "had tried to ford the Connecticut at the wrong place and the river was high, and the current had drawn her right out of the chaise and swept her away, and the horse and chaise too." Mary Moody Emerson was an avid reader whom many consider one of her nephew Ralph Waldo Emerson's important influences. She took the line "Madam, prepare for heavy tidings" from a play by C. J. Riethmuller, wanting her listeners to feel sorrowful not for Hannah but for Hannah's mother. Indeed, the heart of the story is not the news that Hannah had been "swept away," but the image of her mother kneeling on the kitchen floor with her hands covered with flour asking for and receiving the strength she needed to survive the horror that awaited her. Apparently, Hannah's fiancé "hardly got to land himself, and was crazy." He ran into Springfield calling out, "Woman drowned! Woman drowned!" But unlike Hannah's fiancé, Mrs. Bliss remained calm. Indeed, she was so strong that her daughter Phoebe found living up to her standards difficult and suffered mysterious illnesses for much of her young adulthood and early marriage. No doubt, her various ills provided a ready excuse for not being as long suffering as her mother. [9]

The Bliss family slave women were silent bystanders in the kitchen on the day Mrs. Bliss heard of Hannah's passing. While Phoebe Emerson and the rest of her family found it extraordinary how much Mrs. Bliss was able to bear, Phyllis and Cate must have had very different feelings regarding what was unfolding before them. Both women bore the standard female slave names that marked them as property. Cate was a popular slave diminutive for Catherine and Phyllis was a name that appeared often in classical pastoral poetry. Cate had recently married Concord farmer Samuel Potter's slave man Boston, named as so many slaves were for a place, but like the Codman slaves she was not permitted to live with her spouse. Phyllis had an intimate relationship with a nearby Concord slave man herself, and at the time of Hannah's drowning had just become aware she was pregnant. That January, when the Bliss-Emerson family noticed her condition, William would perform a marriage ceremony for her and the man he named in his journal only as "Caesar," of whom there were several in Concord, that being the most popular slave name in Massachusetts. If his later decision to squat nearby is any indication, the man Phyllis married was Caesar Robbins. This Caesar was twenty-three years old in 1769 and seems to have belonged to Humphrey Barrett prior to taking his freedom and the last name of Robbins. William charged £6 to perform the ceremony, substantially less than he usually charged on account of the couple being slaves. Although he charged two white couples the same or less, he charged other white couples as much as £45. No doubt Mrs. Bliss paid the bill rather than shoulder the responsibility for illegitimacy. [10]

Like Brister Hoar's mother, Phyllis knew she had to anticipate the loss of her child, perhaps even permanently. Watching her mistress experience a version of that separation herself, Phyllis must have wondered whether Mrs. Bliss would be able to empathize with a slave woman's plight. She never found out. Phyllis died shortly after giving birth to a daughter. By law, Mrs. Bliss owned the now orphaned child and could do with her as she chose. She did not give the infant she named after the baby's mother to Caesar, who was not legally entitled to her despite being her father, nor did she give the baby away to another slaveholder. Instead, she kept little Phyllis for herself.[11]

During this period, William and Phoebe Emerson were still contending with the stress caused by Joseph Lee's outsider status. Joseph had applied for membership in the church a month after William's ordination, hoping to be accepted finally and thereafter reap the civic honors a man of his financial stature was thought to deserve but which had been denied on account of his separation from the church under Phoebe's father. Unhappily for Joseph, members raised objections during the period of probation after hearing that Joseph had acted dishonestly in settling various people's estates. Joseph countered with an anonymous pamphlet accusing William and Phoebe of acting immorally by traveling together to Maine before they were married. In an attempt to give his wife a break not only from her mother but from the scrutiny that came with Joseph's accusations, William sent Phoebe away on long visits to family and friends. Her health, however, continued to decline. On one occasion, William paid a Boston doctor to lance what he described as a "tumor" in her "side," after which John Cuming tended the wound for her. Most likely, Phoebe was bled, thought at the time to be the cure for everything, even depression. What ended up proving most efficacious, however, was the division of the Block House into two parts eight days after the tumor was lanced. William and Phoebe rented half of the house from Mrs. Bliss and separated their belongings into two distinct households. Phoebe finally became pregnant around the date of their second anniversary when she and William were in the process of making further progress toward their complete independence from the Bliss family. William purchased land on the Concord River in April 1770 and the couple set about designing a house for themselves and their expanding family.[12]

The house the Emersons built and which finally gave Phoebe a sense of freedom was close in appearance and layout to the Royalls', the standard of fine living with which William had become so familiar over the years. Like both the Royall and Cuming homes, the Emersons' house had a symmetrical façade with five windows across the second floor and four along the bottom. There were substantial differences, however, between their new home and John's. The Emersons' mansard roof added an additional story to the house where the Cumings had only an attic accessible by a ladder. And whereas the Cumings' home was one room deep, the Emersons' was, like the Royalls', two rooms deep. This amount of space still being rare in Concord, local parishioners called the house a mansion—the Manse. [13]

The inside of the Emerson mansion was just as regal and regimented as the house's symmetrical façade. There were rooms devoted exclusively to genteel and public life and others that were strictly private. This division was further laid over with a far more rigid demarcation than the Cumings had in their home. Whereas Brister and Jem would have slept on the floor in the kitchen when it was too cold to sleep in the barn, the Bliss-Emerson slaves slept year round in the third-story garret, just as the Royall slaves did in Medford. And whereas the Cuming slaves and their servant girls, one of whom would soon run off and marry a British soldier, shared the use of the house's one staircase with the family on those occasions when they had cause to be upstairs, the Emersons had one staircase for themselves and one for their servants and slaves. A grand staircase at the front of the house ran from the central hall to the second floor. This allowed the family to make a ceremonial entrance when company called. A second staircase at the back of the house was meant to keep servants and slaves out of sight when they carried food and bathing materials from the kitchen to the family's bedrooms. It also gave the servants and slaves access to their sleeping quarters on the third floor. Another no less important purpose for front and back staircases was to make clear to the slaves that they were not part of either the family or society.

After the Emerson family moved into this spacious and soon lavishly appointed house, William never again made reference in his journal to Phoebe having health problems. Whatever crises she had weathered in her young adulthood, physical, emotional, or both, Phoebe came through, but only when she was cleared of all charges of immoral conduct and finally established as the head of her own impressive household. She became a very exacting person who demanded others be so as well and she could only be comfortable when she reigned supreme. One of her granddaughters later reported that she was "a real lady" who "didn't like to work." She "sat in her chair and from it ruled the home." Part of what alarmed the exacting mistress of the house on the morning British troops marched into town was that Frank had breached that strict division manifest in the house's design between public and private, enslaved and free, when he burst into Phoebe's bedroom.[14]

William was too busy to care for his now large estate himself. Upon his ordination, he had been immediately thrown into virtually all aspects of local life. A colonial minister was expected to lead not only in religious matters but in civic and social affairs as well. In addition to preaching all day on Sundays and visiting his parishioners, William presided over every local event. He prayed with the troops before they trained, usually four times per year, dining afterward with the officers. He opened each year's September court session with prayer. He visited all of the area schools. William also exchanged with other ministers near and far, bringing to their congregations sermons they had not heard before. Such exchanges were common practice, meant to free ministers from having to write a new sermon each week. Exchanges were also a means of sharing news of the day. In this regard, William served as Concord's representative to the outside world. His diary is a record of trips as far away from Concord as Conway, 80 miles to the west; Portland, Maine, 110 miles to the north; and Gloucester, 45 miles to the east. At a time when white men could easily purchase their own land rather than hire themselves out to work on someone else's farm, one reason so many Massachusetts ministers had slaves was because the work of growing the family's food supply would have otherwise left them little time to write their sermons.

How or where William Emerson procured Frank is unknown. Perhaps, like the Reverend Ebenezer Parkman's father, William's father helped him purchase a slave man out of concern he would otherwise struggle to find time to write his sermons. Either way, Frank freed William to practice his profession in the same way the Bliss-Emerson slave women freed Mrs. Emerson to preside over a fine parlor. Both Frank and the Bliss-Emerson family's female slaves also freed the Emerson children from what would have otherwise been an endless round of chores. The free time they were accorded for literacy and genteel pursuits as opposed to the other young people in the household is made clear in a postscript William added to a letter to Phoebe shortly after leaving town to serve as minister to the Continental troops in 1776. He asked Phoebe to "tell" Billy "to read a chapter in the family [Bible] (when ever his Mamma is able to bear it), every morning, except when there is somebody else can do it better." Hannah was to be told that "she *must* mind what is said to her and everybody will love her" (William's emphasis). And the second to the youngest Emerson, also named Phoebe, should be reminded that "she must learn her book." At the time, Billy Emerson was ten years old, his sister Hannah six years old, and little Phoebe Emerson just three months shy of her fourth birthday. The Emerson parents were initiating their children into the world of English letters and all that it promised. Billy was already sufficiently literate that he could read the Bible, and his father's expectation seems to be that he would read a chapter aloud to the household each morning for both the family's religious edification and to prepare Billy to follow his father into the ministry. But while even three-year-old Phoebe was being taught to read, Phyllis's seven- or eight-year-old orphaned daughter was not. Little Phyllis had essentially been adopted by Cate and Boston. When she was baptized in the summer of 1771, the enslaved couple stood up as her parents and were listed as such in the church records. But Cate's and Boston's ability to parent the child was sharply circumscribed. Boston had to continue to live with his master, and Cate, being illiterate herself, could only school Phyllis in the tasks she would soon need to perform when she took her place alongside her adopted mother as one of the household's laborers, as William clearly expected her to do. In his postscript, William admonished Phyllis only "to be a good girl," which, given her status, meant she must serve his family obediently, not study reading and writing or learn fine sewing. William's daughter Hannah may have been similarly advised to be obedient but not as a flat-out directive to serve. In Hannah's case, it was thought that obedience to her elders, which did not necessarily mean working for them, would win her universal love. Emerson family lore has it that Mrs. Bliss rocked Hannah and Phyllis together. But such an account belies the fact that the two girls were raised radically differently. So too was Ruth Hunt, the Emersons' white indentured servant, who was also directed by William in his letter to Phoebe to be "complying," in addition to "careful" and "active." Ruth was seventeen years old and, in keeping with her place, was presumably only semiliterate. The terms of her indenture, codified in 1772, stipulated that Ruth receive in exchange for her labor, in addition to "good and sufficient meat, drink, apparel, washing and lodging . . . such instruction in reading as shall be suitable for such an apprentice." So whereas Billy and Phoebe Emerson were instructed by their father to work on their literacy, the indentured and the enslaved were told to work and to work obediently. As with Helen Cuming and Brister, the children living in the Emerson home were being raised with vastly different expectations depending upon their status as free, indentured, or enslaved. And it was the labor of the latter and their adult counterparts that allowed Helen Cuming and the Emerson children to focus on literacy and genteel behavior. Billy, for one, eventually ascended to the pulpit of Boston's First Church. He and his wife had the means to raise eight children, one of whom became America's preeminent philosopher: Ralph Waldo Emerson. Little Phyllis would also marry, but her short life, which ended in Walden Woods, would prove far different. [15]

William also sent word in his 1776 letter home to Frank. He asked Phoebe to "tell him to cut up the wood if he has time and take care of the hay in the barn, and the flax on the grass and the corn in the field, that they be kept out of harm's way." The farm chores William referred to in his postscript were the same ones that occupied all of Concord's slaves and nonslaveholding residents in mid-August: chopping wood for fuel, watching over the newly mown and highly flammable hay in the barn so that there would be fodder for the animals come winter, drying and bleaching the harvested flax, which would next be spun into linen fiber for cloth, as well as watching the ripening corn in order to determine the best harvest date. Without Frank to carry out these tasks, William would not have been able to leave his farm that August in order to aid the war effort at Ticonderoga. [16]

Not unlike John Codman, William also expected to be waited on by his slaves as a means of both increasing his bodily comfort and making clear to all his social rank. William wrote to Phoebe from Fort Ticonderoga that social distinctions were made even on or perhaps especially on the war front where it would be all too easy to lose sight of the finer distinctions of genteel society: "This morning I breakfasted just as I would at home, my porringer of chocolate was brought in, in as much order as need be." The chocolate was prepared in "another apartment," he explained to Phoebe, "where the servants keep and dress our provision and bring it in à la mode Pierre." The "order" that prevailed was the social order of distinct hierarchies. Masters and "servants," the latter term a euphemism for "slave" in eighteenth-century New England, had their respective places no matter what political crisis was un-

Figure 6. *Lydia Hosmer,* A Fishing Party *(1812). Concord Museum, Concord, Mass. www.concordmuseum.org. Photograph by David Bohl.*

folding. Officers and ministers lived "in as comfortable [an] apartment of the barracks as any room in our house" in Concord. William would have preferred only that his own slave serve him. He had, he added in another letter home, a "good waiter, but Frank is not yet come, though I expect him every moment." William obviously felt he could count on Frank to travel the two hundred miles from Concord to Ticonderoga without running off, a testament to the continued enforcement of slavery in 1776 New England. Frank would be watched closely on the road and could expect to be continuously questioned as to who he was and to whom he belonged. [17]

Years later, the role of Concord slave men as waiters and personal valets was captured by a young Concord woman in a picture she called *A Fishing Party* and for which she won a prize at the 1812 Middlesex Agricultural Society Cattle Show (Figure 6). At the Bradford Academy, a school for young ladies in Bradford, Massachusetts, Lydia Hosmer made her picture by copying *The Angler's Repast*, a popular print of the day. She changed various clothing details and colors, as well as making her picture look as if it were needlework and not a watercolor painting or engraving, but otherwise she kept the content the same. Three white men and two white women prepare to enjoy a picnic on the banks of a river or lake, sheltered by the branches of several large trees. Their fine apparel and the abundance of food indicate this is a wealthy group of picnickers. But nothing speaks of their wealth as loudly as the fact that one of them is able to keep a liveried servant or slave. Even as the black man in Lydia's picture is placed very much in the background of the picture physically, he makes an important statement, just as Frank would once he finished the harvest, joined William at camp, perhaps donned livery himself, and began to serve William his chocolate in front of the other white gentlemen. A liveried servant made the point that his master used his wealth to buy the leisure time that allowed him to cultivate fine sensibilities, including an appreciation of imported food stuff and, in the case of the Hosmer picture, nature. [18]

But the servile pose of the liveried servant in Lydia Hosmer's picture was no longer a guarantee by 1775. For all that William Emerson conveyed to his wife that he was confidently looking forward to Frank's arrival, he knew to be on guard. Although Frank never raised his axe against his master's family, even on that fateful April nineteenth when he rushed into Phoebe's bedchamber carrying one, another Concord slave recently had. The incident had begun on a wintry Saturday when a local slaveholder's young son decided to amuse himself by acting out the Boston Massacre. He pelted his father's slave with snowballs while the forty-or-so-year-old man performed the endless and arduous task of chopping wood for fuel. The boy's slaveholding father was Samuel Whitney, a leader of the Concord resistance movement who, as his slave Casey well knew, was a member of the Concord Committee of Correspondence, which disseminated news of British actions and rallied local opposition to them, as well as muster master of the Concord militia. After March 1775, Samuel Whitney was also secreting some of the Provincial Army's provisions on his property. As a result, he was in no position to draw attention to himself, particularly to any trouble at his house. With this very much in mind, Casey allowed himself for the first time to retaliate against his victimizer. He threw his axe at the boy. Casey later told George Minot all about it, and George told Henry David Thoreau, who recounted the story in his journal. [19]

Samuel Whitney's father had died in 1749, after which his mother, Abigail, and his eldest sister, also Abigail, made a good living selling cloth, combs, looking glasses, and shoes, among other things, at a shop they owned on Union Street in Boston. When their mother died, Samuel's sister, then approaching forty and still unmarried, inherited the business. Samuel, already a merchant himself in Boston, and another of his sisters each received £400. Samuel used the money to purchase a shop and a large house in Concord less than a year after the British began to occupy Boston. Several years later, when Concord became a hotbed of political resistance, General Thomas Gage, the British commander, who suspected Samuel of involvement in the secreting of military stores, described his house: "Mr. Whitney . . . lives on the right hand near the entrance to the town, at a house plastered white [with] a small yard in front and a railed fence." In later years, the Alcotts, then the Hawthornes, and finally children's author Margaret Lothrop (whose pen name was Margaret Sidney) would own and expand the house into the imposing yet whimsical house Nathaniel Hawthorne dubbed the Wayside. Nathaniel set the novel he was working on when he died in 1864 here. But in asserting in *Septimius Felton* that Samuel Whitney's home at the time of the Revolution was "a small wooden house" and "an ordinary dwelling of a well-to-do New England farmer," the author of *The Scarlet Letter* missed the mark. Like virtually everyone else, Samuel owned and ran a farm for the purposes of feeding his family, but he was the sixth wealthiest man in Concord by virtue of being a prosperous merchant. Like John Cuming's, Samuel's house had two rooms on the ground floor, two rooms on the second floor, and a garret under the steep roof, making it much larger than the average house of his day. There was space for the six children Samuel and his wife brought with them to Concord and the six additional children born to them there. Then, too, Samuel was wealthy enough to own two slave men, one of whom was Casey, a diminutive form of Cassius and thus once again a name that both advertised the slave owner's knowledge of classical antiquity and made a joke about his slaves' lowly position. [20]

At around the same time Samuel moved to Concord, John Cuming was struggling to maintain his stature. His two youngest sisters, Betsy and Amy, or "the two little Miss Cumings" as they were called by friends, were cited in the *Boston Chronicle* on October 5, 1769, for violating the nonimportation agreements, a key means used by the colonists to protest what they regarded as unfair taxation. Thereafter, the sisters were considered enemies of the state and anyone who did not immediately denounce them was similarly regarded. Initially unwilling to disown them, John was regarded with suspicion and stripped of his duties as town moderator. He was replaced in September and October 1774 by Samuel Whitney. [21]

The Cuming sisters were in this very awkward political situation because they had failed to secure husbands at a time when the prospects for single women were exceedingly narrow. Men dominated the public world of business, leaving their wives to preside over the domestic sphere and, in the case of the middle and upper classes, over the domestic sphere only. Robert and Helen Cuming had raised their daughters to be the wives of gentlemen and as such their skills were limited to fine sewing and other genteel arts. They were the first to admit that they had not been bred "to hard labor" and were thus "unfit" to get their "bread in that way." They were, of course, familiar with trade on account of their father having kept a shop, a profession that required little or no manual labor and for which the fashionable were well suited to select appealing wares for importation. But had female shopkeeping of the sort practiced by Abigail Whitney even occurred to Betsy and Amy, their widowed mother had no capital to get them started and John's money was tied up in his land deals. A way finally became open to the two young women when they were taken under the wing of a Boston businesswoman who had begun to import British cloth and other items for sale in her shop when she was herself single and in need of a living. After Elizabeth Murray married Thomas Campbell in 1755, she used her considerable profits to smooth the way for unmarried women struggling, as she once had, to support themselves. By the time Elizabeth determined to help John's sisters, she had already set up her friend Jannette Day with a shop and a "school for young ladies." Taking note of the Cuming sisters' straits and perhaps sensing the good dose of mercantile acumen they had inherited from their father, Elizabeth established them in the millinery trade. With their brother James living in London, where he could negotiate on their behalf with English merchants, and Elizabeth supplying the necessary letters of credit, the sisters were able to import fine cloth and haberdashery, which they sold from a shop in Boston. [22]

The Cuming sisters proved savvy businesswomen, always looking for ways to expand while, like their mentor, assisting other women in need whenever they could. In December 1764, they loaned the relatively small sum of five shillings to a desperate woman willing to mortgage one acre of Concord land with a house and barn as collateral. For whatever reason, it was a loan no one else was willing to make. Betsy and Amy seem to have been motivated as much by good business sense as compassion. Should the woman be unable to repay the debt by the following June, the sisters stood to gain property worth £42. They also expanded their enterprise in the spring of 1768 when Jannette Day married and prepared to leave her school in order to live in London with her new husband. They announced in the papers that they would be opening "a school on the same plan" as hers at their house in Boston. Their advertisement explained they would teach embroidery, accept young ladies as boarders, and continue to sell a variety of imported wares. One embroidery project the young women at their school would undertake was their family's crest or, if their family did not have one, a crest the young ladies selected from the many books published for such a purpose. Whether the contradiction ever occurred to them or not, Betsy and Amy promoted values that were very much at odds with their daily endeavors as businesswomen, namely ladyship, gentility, and the exercise of leisure time born of ancient landedness. [23]

The sisters were effusive in expressing their gratitude to Elizabeth Murray Campbell for investing in "two young inexperienced girls" who were in "no way qualified for business." In one letter, sent to Elizabeth while she was in

London, Betsy Cuming wrote, "My gratitude increases with my days and when I forget the vast debt I owe you, may I be forgotten by them I most wish to be esteemed." She assured Elizabeth it is "the most earnest wish of my heart . . . that I may never do anything you disapprove," and she insisted, "My heart aches when I think how strongly I am attached to you." Betsy and Amy's gratitude was as deep as their knowledge of what would have befallen them without the assistance of Elizabeth, known after her second marriage in 1760 as Mrs. James Smith. Without husbands themselves, their only other option would have been to live with their one remaining brother in Concord. Under John's roof, they would have had to defer daily to Abigail's decisions and preferences, whereas in Boston their business won them independence and, as their letters so clearly indicate, more than a modicum of happiness. And thus a year after the British army began occupying Boston on account of the colonists' increasingly violent protests there, when the pressure to sign and abide by the nonimportation agreements was all the more intense, the sisters chose prosperity over politics. In the fall of 1769, "the two little Miss Cumings" received a shipment in Boston of £300-worth of wrought silk, sewing silk, and haberdashery, all of which they put up for sale in their shop.[24]

For the next several months, the *Boston Gazette* and other papers repeatedly chastised the Cuming sisters for their business activities. The city of Boston and its surrounding towns passed resolutions that, because Betsy and Amy "not only deserted but opposed their country in a struggle for the rights of the Constitution," no one should purchase goods from them or allow others to do so. The Cumings countered that they had never entered into an agreement not to import. They also argued that trade was necessary for their financial survival and that the business they conducted was too small to really matter anyway. Privately, however, they bragged to Elizabeth that they had "more custom than before" on account of friends rallying around them. They even expressed to her their regret that they had not purchased six times more goods than they had. For two unmarried women who had no choice but to look after themselves, business always came first. And when business was good, they rejoiced, no matter what the political cost.[25]

But the political cost was not Betsy and Amy's alone to pay. Their refusal to back down put their brother John in a very awkward position. When eight out of ten Concord men signed a pledge in the spring of 1774 to "break off all trade,

commerce and dealings with all persons . . . who do import," John Cuming decided not to disown his own flesh and blood, although that meant he would be
considered a traitor. Sure enough, John was immediately demoted within the
town ranks. Whereas once his wealth and education secured him a leadership position, the town now turned to those whose political views were in line with the
majority. Samuel Whitney, the town's wealthy new merchant, immediately came
to mind.

In addition to being elected town moderator and serving on the Concord
Committee of Correspondence, Samuel was one of the town's three representatives to the Massachusetts Provincial Congress, which met in Concord in
1774. He served here alongside town patriarchs Colonel James Barrett and Selectman Ephraim Wood, a testimony to how quickly he managed to fill the
space left by John. Then, in February 1775, he was one of eight men elected to
get signatures for another boycott of British goods, this one drawn up by the
Continental Congress. For all intents and purposes, newcomer Samuel Whitney had vaulted over Squire Cuming to take his place among Concord's gentlemen leaders.

Years later, Samuel's slave man Casey remembered that Samuel's response
upon hearing his son could have been killed by Casey's axe was to call Casey "an
ugly nigger." But as horrified as Samuel must have been that his slave was so in-
tractable as to be capable of throwing an axe at a child, his hands, as Casey had
expected, were indeed tied. He could not attract attention to himself on account of the stores he and Casey both knew were hidden on the Whitney property and thus despite telling Casey he would "put him in jail," Samuel was forced
to let the sun go down that Saturday night without taking any punitive action.
He seems to have hoped that the threat would be a sufficient means of eliciting
better behavior. [26]

Taking stock of his owner's inability to act, Casey "ran off" that Sunday, as
Henry David Thoreau later put it, while everyone was at mandatory Sabbath
services. He made his way up the steep embankment directly behind the Whitney house, crossed a swamp and then the Great Field on the other side of the
hill, finally hiding "himself in the river up to his neck till nightfall, just across
the Great Meadows." Concord being a slave town, a place where slaveholders
and nonslaveholders alike helped each other police the town's slave population,
Casey "was pursued by the neighbors" as soon as Samuel sounded the alarm.

Two days after recounting this story in his journal, Henry was moved to remark that "We hear the names of the worthies of Concord, — Squire Cuming and the rest, — but the poor slave Casey seems to have lived a more adventurous life than any of them. Squire Cuming probably never had to run for his life on the plains of Concord." Casey, who did have to flee for his life, managed to outrun his pursuers. Few suspected a man capable of surviving such frigid water, and Casey thus eluded capture by hiding in the tall meadow grasses that lined the river. When darkness fell on Sunday night, the search ended in failure. [27]

Casey told George Minot that later that night he circled back for "something to eat" at the home of "Mrs. Cogswell, who lived," in Henry's day, "where Charles Davis does," or next to what became the Wayside long after it was the Whitneys' home. Emerson Cogswell and his family, comprising his brother, who was apprenticed to him, and two Mrs. Cogswells, Emerson's mother and his young wife, Eunice, had recently moved to Concord, where they had embraced the Patriot cause. Emerson Cogswell purchased the former shop of Robert Cuming from his estate, then being administrated by John, as well as a house next door to the Whitneys, from which one or both of the Mrs. Cogswells may have witnessed the harassment Casey endured. But even if one of the women thought Casey's treatment unfair, the Mrs. Cogswell who harbored him also knew the town could not afford to have Casey attract the attention of authorities. Casey claimed he "cleared far away, then enlisted, and was freed as a soldier after the war." But Casey most likely did not, as he insisted to George, "clear away" that very weekend, for he was still living in Concord in 1781 when he enlisted in the militia. He was indeed free after the war but remained in town until his death in 1822. Perhaps Mrs. Cogswell helped broker his return by somehow assuaging the feelings on both sides. But even if Casey did not manage to run away, he made it plain that the town's Patriot activities had left it vulnerable to the machinations of slaves. No doubt Phoebe Emerson had his actions very much in mind when Frank approached her with axe in hand. [28]

William must have also been recalling the incident with Casey and the axe when he couched his commands to Frank very carefully in his letter to Phoebe. He instructed Frank to cut up the wood, but only "if he has time." In acknowledging that Frank was very busy, William was marking his deference to Frank even as he was giving him orders. William knew better than to leave a highly disgruntled slave with his unprotected family and their food and fuel. He and John Cuming may have been able to pursue professions and prestigious civic responsibilities thanks to their slaves, but the relationship between master and slave was increasingly delicate, with slave masters fearful that if they upset that balance they might well be poisoned or their houses burned down. Their concern only increased as the war progressed.

CHAPTER FOUR

The Last of the Race Departed

ARLY IN THE MORNING OF APRIL 19, 1775, British officers Lieutenant Colonel Francis Smith and marine Major John Pitcairn surveyed upward of seven hundred of their troops marching into Concord. They chose the same vantage point used by William Emerson and the Concord militia earlier that day. Atop Burial Hill, they stood amid the tombstones, Helen Cuming's among them, looking toward the northern of the two bridges that spanned the Concord River (Figure 7). Three companies of light infantry had the task of securing it while four others proceeded across it to search for secreted military stores at James Barrett's farm two miles away on the road to John Cuming's. The British grenadiers stayed in town to search every house and barn, under orders to destroy whatever military provisions they could find. Once these operations were under way, Major Pitcairn, a fifty-two-year-old Scotsman, second in command that day to Colonel Smith, set about finding a place to eat and rest after the seventeen-mile march from Boston.

On earlier occasions during the British occupation, the king's officers had been handsomely entertained in Concord by Duncan Ingraham, a Crown-appointed justice of the peace. Like John Codman, Duncan was a merchant and former sea captain. He had moved out to Concord from Boston in 1773 when he married Mary Merrick, a wealthy Concord widow, promptly purchasing 140 acres of land and building a large mansion house on the road that ran from the center of town to Walden Woods. Like Betsy and Amy Cuming, he continued to sell imported goods in defiance of the Patriot boycotts, on one occasion advertising that he had for sale in Concord "a large assortment of English and West-Indies goods, wholesale and retail, as cheap as any store in Boston." He would take "Good hogshead hoops, lumber, and grain of all sorts . . . as pay-

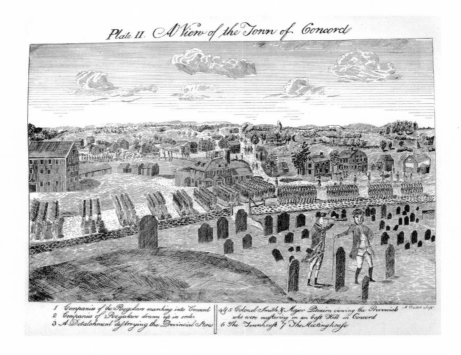

Figure 7. *Amos Doolittle,* A View of the Town of Concord *(1775). Courtesy of the Concord Free Public Library.*

ment for goods." Also like the Cuming sisters, he refused to back down when his Patriot neighbors expressed their disapproval, which they did on several occasions. In one instance, on January 10, 1775, Joseph Lee noted in his journal that "The mob unloaded Capt. Ingraham's boards that were to go to Boston," no doubt the same boards Duncan had advertised he would take as payment for the English goods he continued to sell in the face of the boycotts. On another occasion, twenty to thirty local men surrounded Duncan's mansion while he was entertaining British officers there. The crowd banged on tin pans, creating an unpleasant din in protest of the officers' presence. And on yet another day, when Duncan and his wife were riding through the streets of Concord, someone hung a sheep's head and pluck—the heart, lungs, trachea, and liver—on the back of his chaise. Riding out in a chaise was, like selling imported goods, a brazen defiance of Patriot sentiment. From the French word for chair, a chaise was a two-wheel or sometimes four-wheel carriage that only the very wealthy could afford to import from England. When George Washington ordered a chaise in 1768, the cost was an astounding £315. By the 1770s, anyone still parading around Massachusetts in such an expensive, imported conveyance was most likely a Loyalist and could expect to be attacked. While sheep offal is generally the main ingredient in haggis, a beloved dish in Scotland, it was more commonly regarded in the American colonies as something meant to be discarded, unless one was so poor as to be forced to eat it. For ingesting what he should have discarded—British policy—Duncan was regarded by the Patriots as disgusting and, like the pluck, the refuse of society. Major Pitcairn knew that such a loyal "friend of government" would most certainly issue him a warm welcome and most likely an elegant repast as well. He was still, however, very much on guard when he stepped onto Duncan's property. Just because a gentleman was loyal to the Crown did not mean his slaves were. [1]

This had recently been made abundantly clear to Dr. Charles Russell of Lincoln, who inherited the Chambers-Russell estate when his uncle Chambers Russell died childless in 1766. The first-born son of Chambers Russell's brother James of Charlestown, Charles had already inherited £300 from his great-grandfather Charles Chambers, after whom he was named, which he used to attend Harvard and then to study medicine in London, after which, in 1765, he received a medical degree from Marischal College in Aberdeen, Scotland. Upon returning from Europe, Dr. Russell set up an apothecary shop near the ferry in his hometown of Charlestown where, according to the advertisements he placed in the Boston papers, "Gentlemen Practitioners of Physic in the Country may be supplied with Medicines." No doubt John Cuming, who fit this description perfectly, was one of his customers. [2]

In addition to the Lincoln mansion and land, Charles had inherited six slaves from Chambers Russell, including Brister's sister Zilpah and brother Peter, who were twenty-eight and thirty-eight years old, respectively, when Charles's uncle stipulated in his will that "my negroes shall not be sold; but if any of them through age or other bodily infirmity should become in part or wholly useless; they shall be comfortably supported on my said farm in Lincoln during their natural lives." This did not mean that Chambers Russell intended to free his slaves either at his death or in the future, nor even that he was going beyond what was expected of him in providing for his slaves in their old age. Indeed, his will ensured only that his slaves would remain together on his estate, a stipulation he may have felt necessary for his slaves' continued compliance, if not his nephew's safety. As the Codman murder proved, breaking up families could be a tricky, if not dangerous, business. Charles had also come into possession of the slaves owned by his wife, Elizabeth, Isaac Royall Sr.'s granddaughter by his daughter Penelope Royall Vassall. In some cases, these were the children of slaves who had long been in the possession of the Royall family. Penelope had inherited eight slaves from her father shortly before her marriage to Colonel Henry Vassall. Betsy, as Elizabeth was called, took some of the Royall-Vassall family slaves with her when she married Charles Russell. Her husband, like his uncle Chambers Russell and his great-grandfather Charles Chambers before him, was easily the largest slaveholder in Lincoln or Concord. [3]

One of Charles's slaves, a man he called Luck, had proved to be anything but lucky for Charles when tensions between the Patriots and Loyalists provided Luck with an opportunity to oppose his owner. Early in September 1774, Luck saw one of Betsy's Vassall relatives ride through Lincoln in the Russell chaise, a dangerous flaunting of wealth and loyalty to the Crown. On this particular day, Dr. Russell, who was Lincoln's most prominent Loyalist, was not in his chaise, but he was undoubtedly the intended target of a bullet that suddenly whizzed past. Area residents had already expressed their disapproval of Charles's politics. While he had been the town moderator on many occasions between 1768 and 1773, members of the Committee of Correspondence held the position thereafter, no longer willing to be led in town affairs by a man loyal to the Crown. The message intended for Dr. Russell and Captain Ingraham when their respective chaises were attacked was clear: their Loyalist views made them no longer welcome in the towns over which they would have otherwise presided.

After the firing was reported to him, Charles Russell immediately demanded an investigation. Convinced that the Lincoln committee would be strongly biased in favor of the Patriots, he took his case to the Committee of Correspondence in his attacked relative's hometown of Charlestown, where a good many more Loyalists lived than in Lincoln. Seeking to force the matter, the committee in Charlestown promptly offered to share all expenses with the Lincoln committee. But Lincoln's residents still managed to close ranks. Several people who had been in the vicinity swore they had not heard a gunshot. One man testified he saw the Vassall relative find a musket ball three days later while others searched fruitlessly nearby, proof, he thought, that the relative had planted the evidence.

Luck, who was also in the vicinity at the time of the alleged incident, had to decide whether to side with his master's family or with the Patriots. He could either concur with his master that one of the Vassalls had been shot at and thereby accuse local Patriots of attempted murder or speak out in opposition to Charles's Loyalist views. The latter would provoke his owner's wrath but it would also show Charles that Luck was a political liability and might force Charles to weigh the benefits of continuing to own him. Like Casey, Luck decided to take his chances. He swore the following before John Cuming, who in his capacity as justice of the peace heard the case brought by his medical colleague: "I Luck, a negro servant belonging to Doctor Russell of lawful age, testify that on the 7th instant between daylight and dark I met Doctor Russell's horse and carriage after I had passed a small distance from the place where Mr. Vassall says he thinks a gun was discharged at the carriage." And then he spoke the words that damned the Loyalists, his owner among them: "I heard no gun." Even as the wording of much of his testimony was clearly John Cuming's contrivance (being of "lawful age" was generally a meaningless concept for a slave), Luck made the point that area slaves were willing and able to oppose their owners publicly.[4]

Major Pitcairn was not in a particularly good mood when he stopped to rest at the home of Charles Russell's Loyalist colleague Duncan Ingraham. In the march westward from Boston, he and his men had heard warning bells precede

their advance, making it clear their entry into Concord would not be the sur-
prise they intended. Then, at Lexington, he had had to contend with the local
militia, who had mustered on the town green and were slow to disperse as the
British marched into view. Angered at this brazen show of anti-British sentiment, the major had galloped forward ordering them to "Disperse!" His repeated entreaties had no effect and shots rang out, although who fired first here
or later that day in Concord is still an unsettled question. Eight Lexington men
fell dead while nine others were wounded. The British did not lose any men but
that did not lessen the major's sense that his search-and-destroy mission was spi-
raling out of control.

When he stepped out the back door of Duncan Ingraham's mansion house
after taking some refreshment there, John Pitcairn was still very much on edge.
Spotting a slave man standing in the backyard, his suspicions were immediately
aroused. According to a memoir about Duncan's stepson, written by and for
the Concord Social Circle, a club of the town's most elite men founded in 1782,
the major spied Duncan's slave man Cato "standing by the large pear-tree in the
rear of the house with his hands behind him." The British officer immediately
"commenced on him," according to the memoir, "as he did on the rebels at Lexington Common a few hours previously, by pointing a pistol at his head, and,
in a loud tone of voice, ordering him to give up his arms." The major seemed to
share Phoebe Emerson's concern that area slaves were plotting to take advantage of the political chaos and dispatch their enslavers and any of their friends. [5]

Cato immediately insisted he was unarmed. But he said so in such a way that
indicated he was indeed thinking about ways he might take advantage of the
shifting political landscape. Holding his arms out in front of him, he gave a tart
response: "Dem is all the arms I have, massa." While Cato's retort may not have
been of the same magnitude as the shots the Patriots would soon fire at the North
Bridge, it seems to have come from the same desire to invert what had for so long
been the natural order of things. Cato no longer felt compelled to exhibit the
same obsequiousness toward his owner's guests that he once had. And while the
memoirist colored the account with slave dialect such that Cato's triumph over
the major makes Pitcairn look all the less capable of controlling his troops, let
alone of winning a battle against angry Patriots, it is evident that Cato was anticipating a change in his status and perhaps even plotting how to profit from
what within minutes would prove to be all-out war. The memoirist of Duncan

Ingraham's stepson notes that "At this moment the report of the firing at the North Bridge was heard, and the major precipitately left." The first shot fired in Concord might have otherwise more obviously revealed the degree to which the fear of a slave insurrection was very much in the forefront of the Revolution. As it was, rumors about Frank and his axe shaped the outcome of the day.[6]

Two men from neighboring Acton died instantly at the North Bridge. Four other local militiamen were wounded. On the British side, four officers were wounded, and at least three soldiers were killed and ten wounded. Looking up the hill on the other side of the bridge at the superior number of Patriots and panicking at the sight of their fallen comrades, the remaining British fled, leaving their wounded behind to fend for themselves. One was said to suffer grossly inhumane treatment at the hands of the locals. Having managed to crawl some distance from the bridge, the wounded soldier lay half dead in the road near the Manse when, as William Emerson later explained, someone came along and "very barbarously broke his skull and let out his brains with a small axe . . . of the tomahawk kind." The four British companies returning from their search of the Barrett farm were allowed by the colonists to pass over the bridge unmolested, which gave them ample time to assess the mauled corpse. They were immediately convinced that the victim had been scalped. Years later, Nathaniel Hawthorne would refer to the incident in *Mosses from an Old Manse*, ascribing the deed to someone "in the service of the clergyman" who was chopping wood in the minister's yard that morning. Hawthorne marveled that "this lad should have been so diligently at work, when the whole population of town and county were startled out of their customary business, by the advance of the British troops." But while Nathaniel was unaware of the identity of that person "in the service of the clergyman," many locals were convinced that the perpetrator was William's slave Frank, who had been seen in the vicinity with his axe and who, as Nathaniel only partially understood, had no choice but to be "diligently at work" chopping wood even as everyone else was "startled out of their customary business." Years later, William's descendants tried to clear their slave's name, and local historians began to assert that the culprit was instead Ammi White, a young farmer who had recently moved to Concord and who, it was said, did not scalp the soldier but rather acted mercifully, having been begged by the wounded soldier to put him out of his misery. However, on April 19, escalating fears of a slave insurrection made it seem commonsensical that the minister's slave would be the one intent on carrying out the supposed "plot" reported in the newspapers to murder "the white people." The level of hysteria was such that no one bothered to ask why his first victim would be a regular and not his owner or the owner of one of his fellow slaves. News of the scalping spread instantly and was the first piece of information carried by fleeing British soldiers back to General Gage in Boston. When they encountered an extensive blockade of colonial militia at Menotomy (now Arlington) on the afternoon of the nineteenth, the fear of being scalped by bloodthirsty Americans and their slaves seemed to reinvigorate the fleeing British regulars. The death toll was the heaviest of the day on both sides, with twenty-eight Patriots and forty British soldiers killed.[7]

But British soldiers were not the only ones who ran for their lives that day. Those women and children who were too far from the minister's house to take refuge there hid in the woods, while others simply fled as far away as they could get. Among them was Samuel Whitney's wife, Abigail, who loaded her youngest children in the family chaise and attempted to speed out of harm's way. It was not a good day, however, to flaunt the Whitney family's ability to maintain this most expensive of imported British goods. The tall sides of the chaise may have hidden her and her children's faces from view, but even if onlookers knew who she was and of her husband's central role in the colonial militia's preparations, they were outraged a local resident should choose to flee the scene and in a chaise no less. And insofar as this family was turning tail, it was highly likely they were not true Patriots at all. Outraged at the betrayal of their cause, one Patriot fired at the retreating vehicle, his bullet grazing the head of one of the children inside. Having nearly lost two of their children, one to an axe-throwing slave and the other to a Patriot's ball, the latter on a day when another axe-wielding slave was supposedly wreaking havoc, the Whitneys' commitment to the Patriots began to founder. Not long thereafter, as the political tensions in Boston steadily rose, Samuel determined that it was more prudent to stick with the Crown. Three days after the Battle of Bunker Hill, in June 1775, Joseph Lee noted in his journal that "Mr. Samuel Whitney a very zealous Whig left the town in a fright with all his family." Convinced that the British were well on their way to reasserting control, Samuel returned with his family to Boston where he had to ingratiate himself with British officials. He did not, however, bring Casey with him across enemy lines. He could not afford to take the risk that the slave who had proved himself "an ugly nigger" would reveal his master's treasonous actions at the very moment when he needed to establish his credibility with the British officials still occupying Boston. Instead, he left Casey behind, abandoning him to his freedom. It seems Casey's account of the axe-throwing incident was true after all. He did obtain his freedom as a result of his actions the weekend he threw his axe at Samuel's son, just perhaps not as immediately as he would later insist. His account of how he became free was one intended to stress his own agency, and rightly so.[8]

By the time Samuel Whitney fell from local grace, John Cuming was working his way back into the public's trust. After hesitating to throw himself headlong into Patriot activism on account of his sisters, John began to come around. On April 19, rather than fly from town, he tended to the wounded in the home of Phoebe Emerson's brother, the younger Daniel Bliss, not far from Duncan Ingraham's. Daniel had abandoned his property the month before, after entertaining officers sent by General Gage to gather intelligence on the "quantity of artillery and provisions" secreted in Concord. The Patriots had gotten wind of Daniel's actions and with so much now at stake, rather than serenading the party with tin pans as they did earlier for Duncan, threatened to kill both Daniel and the spies. A few weeks after the British officers escorted him to safety in Boston, Daniel sent for his wife and children. As it did the Cumings, the war pitted siblings against one another. Daniel never returned to Concord, leaving his sister and the rest of the Bliss family behind forever.[9]

Immediately thereafter, having proven his allegiance to the Patriots, John was asked to resume his position as moderator of town meetings. But it was not until British troops evacuated Boston on March 27, 1776, and his sisters and hundreds of other Loyalists left with them for Halifax, Nova Scotia, that John was able to fully resume his leadership position in Concord. It helped, too, that by then Samuel Whitney, the man who had usurped John's position, had fled Concord for Boston and later Maine. The month his sisters departed, John was elected to a year-long term on what had become the Concord Committee of Correspondence, Inspection and Safety. And when the Constitutional Convention met in Boston in September 1779, John and Selectman Ephraim Wood attended as Concord's representatives. John's civic life finally came full circle when the Provincial Congress appointed him to the same position of justice of the peace to which the Crown had appointed him. He suffered the loss of his

sisters, whom he had to worry he would never see again, but with their departure John Cuming regained everything he had lost in the months building up
to the war. He was once again a leader of both town and county. [10]

After April 19, as tensions continued to escalate between the Patriots and
the Crown, other area slaves besides Luck and Casey attempted to play the two
sides against each other for their own advantage. One of those slaves belonged
to the third husband of the Cuming sisters' benefactor, Elizabeth Murray. Ralph
Inman was himself a successful and well-connected merchant. He owned a large
Cambridge estate, fitted out with a three-story mansion and several slaves. After
his only son graduated from Harvard in 1772, Elizabeth was able to throw him
a large party there for over three hundred people, including Thomas Hutchinson, the governor of Massachusetts. But when the war broke out, Ralph was
stuck behind British lines in Boston with other area Loyalists, while Elizabeth
was in Cambridge with the servants and slaves. Rather than join him, Elizabeth
stayed in Cambridge. She explained to her husband that these "poor creatures"
depended on her "for protection" and she did "not choose to disappoint them."
Rather, she was determined to "protect them" to the extent of her "power." But
Elizabeth sorely underestimated the ability of her husband's slaves to look after
themselves. Sensing an opportunity to better his situation in life, Ralph's slave
Job told Continental troops that Elizabeth was a Loyalist and they promptly
took her prisoner on her husband's estate. Elizabeth wrote to Ralph of what she
called "Job's affair" that if she "had not been roused beyond reason to have acted
an uncommon part," the encounter between her and the troops would "have
proved fatal." Elizabeth dodged disaster by allowing the Continental Army to
use her kitchen and several other rooms, as well as pledging not to leave with the
farm's stock. But as Job must have hoped he would, Ralph felt the only safe
course for Elizabeth was to "dispose" of what servants and slaves she could and
bring the rest to town. Elizabeth refused the suggestion until the evening after
the Battle of Bunker Hill, when she was finally forced to abandon the Cambridge farm. Fearing that the colonists would begin to destroy Loyalist property, Ralph's included, and that British troops would attack the headquarters of
the Continental Army in Cambridge, she moved her household further from
the city to her estate in Milton, which was eventually confiscated by the Cambridge Committee of Correspondence. At that point, Job was no longer
counted as part of Ralph's estate. He had proved himself too dangerous for his

owner to feel comfortable continuing to enslave him, thereby contributing to the loss Ralph Inman claimed of £5,000 as a result of the war. [11]

In Concord, yet another slave watched as his owner's political situation grew increasingly tenuous. A week after the battle at the North Bridge, Concord slaveholder Joseph Lee was, as he put it, "seized for a Tory while in bed" by local Patriots angered after seeing him inform British officials of their activities. After questioning Joseph at length, the Patriots decided to confine him to his farm for the next several months so that he could not continue to put them at risk. Ironically, up until this point, Joseph's old rift with the Concord church had been well on the way to mending. In August 1774, the church offered to admit him into full communion if he would apologize for his "many hard speeches, and unjustifiable reflections upon the pastor, church and particular members," a reference to the allegations he published about William and Phoebe's premarital activities and other inflammatory comments he had made. Not only were these gains wiped out, but Joseph literally came under fire when he failed to send someone to serve for him in the army. Joseph wrote in his journal on January 3, 1776, that "a little after sunrise, or between 7 and 8 of the clock in the morning, a company of about 36 or 40 men" returning from the army stopped near his workshop. The men split into two groups and "after some debate and lewd talk . . . the second party shot one gun." Before Joseph knew it, "three or four guns [were] fired loaded with ball." No one was hit but, he explained, "some of the ball struck about my house. Some entered a stick of timber near where I stood, some hit the house, others struck about the cider house." The returning soldiers meant only to frighten Joseph into compliance with their cause, but the firing of weaponry was serious and Joseph could certainly bring charges against them, provided he had witnesses willing to back up his claims. It was therefore of real importance to him that "my son Jonas and a servant . . . [were] near and heard . . . the noise of the guns." One of Joseph's white servants, Lucy Piper, had already "marched off" a month after the battle at the North Bridge, no doubt able to break her contract because no one would have offered to enforce a Loyalist's legal rights. Then, three weeks after the Battle of Bunker Hill, Joseph had sold his slave woman Pegge to one of his acquaintances, a Mr. Turner, in order, as he put it, "to pay various debts." However, he still had his slave man Cato, who was eighteen in 1761 when Joseph inherited him upon the death of his brother John Lee, a merchant and blacksmith in Boston. Joseph's son Jonas often used Cato

to assist him with his own farm work, making it even more likely that it was
Cato standing next to him and his father when the mob opened fire. Joseph
made no further diary entries until six weeks later, when he wrote simply that
"Cato went to the army in the morning." If he valued his and his family's safety,
Joseph needed to make it clear that he was finally willing to send someone to
serve in the army in his stead. As a Hessian officer fighting for the British noted
in 1777, "The negro can take the field instead of his master; and, therefore, no
regiment is seen in which there are not negroes in abundance." That he sent
Cato in particular may indicate that Cato, like Casey and Luck, was threaten-
ing to somehow make Joseph's situation even worse, perhaps by refusing to cor-
roborate the story of the shooting. Cato eventually returned to the Lee estate
after serving out his enlistment but Joseph began to pay him for his services.
Joseph's tenuous, even dangerous political situation had proved an advantage
for Cato, who was no longer a slave. [12]

But even as the Patriots argued vociferously in print and on the battlefield
for freedom from tyranny, many of them, as evidenced by the search party that
acted on behalf of Samuel Whitney when Casey ran away, continued to uphold
the rules of the slave society in which they lived. At least one of the local Loyalists was all too happy to point out the discrepancy. Prior to fleeing town, Daniel
Bliss used the occasion of the death of the Barron family's former slave Jack, whose
estate he was handling, to compose an epitaph for his client that highlighted the
Patriots' hypocrisy. The tombstone toward the back of Burial Hill refers to the former slave as "JOHN JACK," noting that the "native of Africa . . . died / March
1773, aged about 60 years." While Daniel's decision to use two names on the
tombstone may indicate that the former slave went by either name, as was the
case in his land deeds, most likely Daniel was using the full name the deceased
took for himself when he was in a position to finally adopt a last name. His last
name, Jack, was his old slavery name, the switch seemingly a means of creating
continuity between his slave identity and his free one, a move many other area
slaves would repeat and one that allowed the former Jack to take a nonslavery
first name. But for all that he used the new full name John Jack took for himself,
Daniel was less interested in honoring John Jack's new identity than in skewer-
ing his own political opponents. He went on to write in the epitaph of the former slave that "Tho' born in a land of slavery, / He was born free. / Though he
lived in a land of liberty, / He lived a slave." Daniel thus made the case that con-

trary to the complaints of the colonists, William Emerson among them, Britain was the most free nation in the world. He was asking, in effect, the same question Samuel Johnson did when he wondered in 1776, "How is it that we hear the loudest yelps for liberty among the drivers of negroes?" Daniel never seems to have taken an interest in freeing his mother's slave women, Cate and Phyllis, or his brother-in-law's slave man Frank for that matter. He was not an early abolitionist, even though John Jack's epitaph later became a rallying point for them in the 1830s. Daniel Bliss was a Loyalist to the very end, settling in Canada hundreds of miles from his mother, his sister, and his other siblings while his estate was confiscated by the General Court and in 1781 auctioned off. And as a Loyalist, he aimed to show that the Patriots had no business calling for an end to what they had the audacity to claim was their enslavement. [13]

Like Daniel Bliss, the Russells also fled. In the spring of 1775, they felt it expedient to move into a home on King Street in Boston, which they exchanged with another family for their Lincoln estate. After the Battle of Bunker Hill, a turning point for the Whitneys and so many others, the Russells fled the colony altogether. Dr. Russell took his wife, four daughters, and mother-in-law, Isaac Royall Jr.'s sister Penelope, to Isaac Royall's plantation in Antigua. Charles was forced to abandon his Lincoln estate, including the slaves remaining there and the many paintings and books that filled his house. Although the fate of Luck is unknown, it would have been exceedingly difficult if not impossible to carry him across enemy lines into Boston once he had proven himself willing to side with the Patriots. By the time Betsy Russell, then widowed, and her daughters returned to Massachusetts in 1781, her father-in-law James Russell was renting the confiscated Lincoln estate and no slaves were counted in an inventory taken three years later. The former Chambers-Russell slaves were not necessarily absent. Indeed, Peter and Zilpah would spend the rest of their lives near the estate. But having been abandoned, they no longer belonged to anyone but themselves. [14]

Having determined to stay behind when his sisters fled, John Cuming had regained his stature and then some. On July 1, 1776, three months after his sisters departed and while Thomas Jefferson was drafting the Declaration of Independence, John was offered a commission that would have stretched his influence far beyond county limits. Clearly impressed by the honor bestowed upon his friend, William Emerson made sure to report it in his journal. "Colonel Cuming," he wrote, was "appointed by the General Court, Brigadier General of the

3,000 reinforcements cruising for Canada" to engage British troops there. The rank of brigadier general was a step above colonel and only one step below major general, the highest position in the provincial army. John was certainly qualified for the role; he had extensive military experience as an officer and knew the Canadian border well from his service during the French and Indian War. His townsmen had every reason to expect that for the rest of his life they would take pride in claiming General Cuming as one of their own. The day after learning of John's appointment, William Emerson hastened from the Manse to the Cumings' home, intent on congratulating his friend on this greatest of honors and talking over plans for the expedition. He had been invited "to go as Chaplain" himself and, after putting it to a vote, the town had decided to send him. William was shocked to discover, however, that John was not equally excited about his own participation in the upcoming expedition. Although he rarely commented on people's emotions in his journal, William departed from his typically dry entries to note the following: "Waited upon Col. Cuming, who is very low in spirits and exceedingly cast down. His wife utterly against his going." [15]

Abigail well remembered her husband's earlier injury and captivity during the French and Indian War. She had waited anxiously at home in Concord for weeks on end for word of his survival, eventually enduring the death of their only child alone and without knowing if John was also lost to her forever. Bereft of any children, John was the only family Abigail had. So when the opportunity presented itself for her husband to once again go off to battle on the northern frontier, Abigail put her foot down where women seldom if ever did. Phoebe Emerson, in contrast, is not known to have asked her husband to forgo the expedition, even as he left her with a nine-day-old baby and three other very young children besides. Certainly William knew he was asking almost more than his wife could bear. He wrote in his first letter home, "I don't know but you are affronted with me for leaving you so abruptly—but really 'tis too much to take a formal leave." Phoebe may have found her husband's departure difficult, but there was never any question he would go. John, in constrast, was clearly taking his wife's feelings into serious consideration. Abigail had endured much and John had to decide whether he could ask her to endure more. [16]

Four days later, it seemed John was leaning toward accepting the generalship even if it would have meant causing Abigail untold anguish. It was as if his father was by his side urging him on, repeating the stories he had told John in his childhood about the Red and Black Comyns, the great warriors whose names lived on forever in the annals of Scottish history and from whom John was proudly descended. With the weight of the Cuming family's legacy squarely on his shoulders, not to mention his by-now heartfelt commitment to the cause of liberty, John had every reason to want to step into a generalship. When William wrote in his diary after spending the night at the Cuming home on his way to preach in Stow, he used John's new title to describe the visit: "Stopped and lodged at Gen. Cuming's." [17]

But the John who had delayed his military service once before to see his wife through the first months of their baby's life and who must have ever since regretted leaving behind his child to die without him ultimately got the better of the man who was Robert Cuming's son. William reported on the thirteenth that "*Colonel Cuming resigned his Commission!!!!*" Abigail had her way after all, and it was no small victory for her. In a culture built very much on the honor of fulfilling civic and military duties and using the titles with which those duties were rewarded, her husband had decided to forgo what few other men would have been able to resist. William's reaction is striking in comparison to his other daily entries, which are always factual and utterly unemotional, even when recording the deaths of children. In his mind, John had done the unthinkable. As his underlining of the entry and the further addition of four exclamation points indicate, William was aghast. He was still not over John's refusal of the post when he penned a letter to his wife from the road to Fort Ticonderoga the following August. In describing the various regiments, he wrote to Phoebe, "General Brickett's Brigade (which might have been General Cuming's) are encamped by themselves, consisting of about 2 or 3 thousand men." Nor did John easily recover from being what William called "cast down." William's description of John's mental state indicates that his decision left him thoroughly depressed. Colonel Cuming knew exactly what he was giving up, namely his best chance at immortality. [18]

A not-uncaring husband himself, William Emerson delayed his departure for Crown Point until the birth of his daughter Rebecca. He finally left home well behind the troops on August 16, 1776, stopping for his first night at a tavern in Acton, where he penned the letter instructing Phoebe of the chores Frank was to perform in his absence. Thereafter, he stayed when he could at the homes of ministers, where the accommodations were in keeping with that to which he was accustomed. Frank eventually joined his master at Ticonderoga, but not long after his arrival, William contracted camp fever and was discharged. He attempted to return home to his young family. Five days after leaving camp, he had made it only as far as Rutland, Vermont, where he lay sick at the minister's house and wrote what he knew might very well be his last letter to his "Phoebe bird": "I am now on my way homeward, but whether I shall ever reach there is very uncertain." He implored his wife to accept the will of "a kind and gracious Providence" and to "strive for patience" whether God "sees fit to restore me to health or not." William professed himself "willing to leave the matter with him who does all things well." He was only thirty-three years of age when he died in Rutland a month later, suffering the very fate Abigail had so feared for John. [19]

Having forgone the expedition, John was at home in Concord to conduct the sorrowful work of presiding over an inventory of his friend's property. William's many fine furnishings were listed, among them window curtains, two desks, several looking glasses, and a full tea equipage, as well as three wigs, a massive library of 236 books and 194 pamphlets, and even a chaise. These were clearly the belongings of an accomplished gentleman except for the fact that no slaves were listed. Neither Frank nor any other slaves William owned or partially owned were enumerated in the inventory. Emerson family lore has it that William freed his slaves on his deathbed, and there is no surviving evidence that contradicts that account. No military, death, or any other records place Frank back in Concord, let alone on the Emerson estate, after William's passing. But William's decision to free Frank was more likely a practical measure rather than one grounded in William's sense of justice or even benevolence. If William, who was very outspoken from the pulpit on the issue of independence from Britain, had felt slavery was immoral, he would have spoken and acted out against it as well. He never had. Now, with insurrection hysteria gripping Massachusetts, he must have felt it would be too dangerous to have a slave man in his widow's home. To be sure, William had seen fit to leave Frank behind temporarily with Phoebe when he left for Ticonderoga, even after Frank had frightened her so terribly when he rushed into her bedroom with axe in hand on April 19. But William had been very careful to temper his directives to Frank, making it clear in his letter homeward that Frank was to set his own work pace while William was away. In short, William strove to give Frank no cause to follow the example of the Codman slaves. But with his death imminent and knowing very well that his wife was something of a taskmaster, William may have determined that it would have been unwise to send Frank back to a home devoid of a master who could have protected the somewhat tyrannical wife and her young flock. Frank seems to have succeeded in frightening his owner sufficiently that, like Casey and so many other male slaves in the Concord area, he was abandoned to his freedom. Perhaps he struck out from Rutland and attempted to make his way on the northern frontier where there were fewer incorporated towns in a position to expel him through the warning-out process.[20]

Like Frank, Casey, and Joseph Lee's Cato, several other Concord area slaves were also relinquished by their owners during and after the Revolution, many after serving in the army. John and Elizabeth Hoar's slave Brister became a free man sometime after serving in the army for three months in 1777 as a substitute for another Lincoln man. Like John Jack, Brister marked the change in his status by making his slavery name his last name and taking a new first name, in his case Sippio (a variant of Scipio). Sippio Brister was unlikely to have chosen this classical first name for the same reason a slaveholder would have. Most likely he was sufficiently close to another slave man named Scipio that he decided to honor the connection as a familial one. The network of slaves his mother counted on when she presumably surrendered him to Elizabeth Hoar may indeed have provided her son with the kinds of protective bonds slaveholders constantly attempted to sunder.[21]

Whether John Cuming's Brister and Jem made attempts to take advantage of their master's tenuous political position during the Cuming sisters' public travails is unknown. John's diaries and most of his letters have not survived. Brister's military records, however, indicate that if he was not able to make use of John's political troubles then he was able to leverage the difficulty John had later on filling Concord's military ranks. As a member of Concord's Committee of Safety, John was one of the men responsible for making sure the town met its quota of soldiers, an increasingly difficult task as the war wore on and one that resulted in regiments filled with the impoverished and the enslaved or formerly enslaved. John's first step was to contribute money for the hire of soldiers in the campaign to engage General John Burgoyne. His second was to enlist Brister in that same campaign. On September 28, 1777, Brister was accepted into the Continental Army. Like slaveholders generally, John and Abigail must have eventually fed those of their slaves reaching adulthood ample amounts of protein so that they could perform their labor. At five feet seven, Brister was just an inch under the average height for a man born and raised in the North American colonies, and after years of physical labor, he had also become lithe and strong (indeed, well into his late sixties he was able to wield an axe with what would be described as great "celerity"). Brister served for five weeks alongside John in Saratoga, New York, where both were present when General Burgoyne was captured. His name appeared on the roles of "volunteers" as Private Bristol Cuming. Gone, for now, was the diminutive version of his name, Bristo, by which John called him; rather, he is known here by the name originally given him by Chambers Russell in order to link himself to England's great port city. As to the last name of Cuming, either Brister took John's last name as his own or, more likely, it was assigned to him. Whichever was the case, with a last name affixed to his slave name, Brister's public identity was starting to shift. By the following fall, when it had become even more difficult for officials to fill the ranks, John reenlisted Brister, who again served alongside his master, this time for a month. The only difference was that Brister enlisted this time as Private Brister Cummings, using the first name he would prefer for the rest of his life, a small sign perhaps that his status was indeed changing as a result of his service. In 1779, four years into the war, Brister enlisted yet again, this time for a three-year term. Strikingly, he enlisted this time not as Bristol Cuming nor as Brister Cuming, but as Brister Freeman. [22]

Brister's slowly shifting status had finally changed completely and he wanted that change made abundantly clear. In his mid-thirties and after twenty-five years of enslavement to John Cuming, Brister was the free man his new last name proclaimed. This was not, however, because his master had experienced a change of heart and had come to regard slavery as immoral. There was little talk among whites of the immorality of slavery in 1779. Individual slaves had begun to sue for their freedom in 1773, but the first draft of the Massachusetts Constitution, completed in 1778, recognized slavery as legal, and the final draft failed to mention it at all. Historians have often used the rhetoric of exchange to describe how slavery came to an end in Massachusetts, imagining that slaves received their freedom in exchange for their military service. Of course this does not explain how slave women achieved their freedom. Further, it gives undue credit to slaveholders for effecting the demise of slavery in Massachusetts when in fact slaves were doing much to ensure their owners felt compelled to abandon them. Indeed, John must have begun to realize by 1779 what was starting to occur to all of his townsmen: that the conditions that had previously ensured the survival of the institution of slavery were no longer as securely in place as they had been. Concord's slaves had proven they had minds of their own and that they were not afraid to take advantage of any opportunities to endanger their owners and their property, whether physically or politically. And as the number of abandoned slaves living in the region grew, the chances were lessening that the entire town could keep a close eye on enslaved men whose skin color no longer made their status clear. Brister's new name was not meant to proclaim his receipt of a gift or an exchange. Had that been the case he might have kept the name of his supposed benefactor and termed himself Brister Cuming for the rest of his life. Rather, his new name was meant to proclaim a status he had seized as rightfully his own. John Cuming may have believed he gave Brister his freedom in exchange for military service, but for all intents and purposes, Brister took his freedom. He did so by rejecting the arrangement proffered to and accepted by so many area slaves: what amounted to continued enslavement in all but name in return for room and board.

Carefully measuring their ability to live independently should they decide to part ways with their owners, most Concord area slaves were unwilling to take what amounted to a terrible gamble. With no money with which to purchase property, much less to start up a working farm, many slaves, and particularly slave women, decided to accept food and shelter in exchange for their continued labor rather than face certain impoverishment. In short, they remained slaves even if at some point they were no longer legally recognized as such. Cate's husband, Boston, was one of those slaves. The Reverend William Bentley, a former Harvard student who boarded with Boston's owner during the Revolution when the College was moved to Concord, wrote about a visit he made to see Samuel Potter after the war. He reported that "The best good will subsisted" between Samuel and Boston. "The servant was all obedience and the master's will was exactly Boston's pace and Boston's habits and knowledge." He mentioned that Boston was a "servant" to Samuel "above 60 years" and imagined that Boston was more than happy to comply with his owner's every whim, even dying, "as he told him he should, . . . when his Master died," so devoted was he. That Boston had endured living apart from his wife during her lifetime and that he had to be compliant out of absolute necessity were points entirely lost on the

Reverend Bentley. Samuel had made arrangements for Boston in his will, stipulating in 1783 that "my will is that in case . . . my negro man, Boston should stand in need of any support . . . all my heirs assist in his maintenance." Afraid he would otherwise have no place to live in his old age, Boston continued to answer to Samuel's every demand until Samuel died in 1800 at the age of ninety-five. Contrary to the Reverend Bentley's information, Boston outlived his master, dying five years later at the age of eighty-two, presumably at the home of one of Samuel's six children. [23]

The man who came to Joseph Lee's house as an eighteen-year-old slave also never left. After Cato served in the army in 1776 and thereby helped restore Joseph's good standing in Concord, he returned to the Lee mansion house, perhaps free in name but not able to go where he wished. Even after Joseph died in 1797, Cato stayed on, having no better alternatives. Joseph had stipulated in his will his desire that his "faithful servant Cato . . . continue with my beloved wife, while she lives" and that he "be provided with everything suitable and requisite to his comfort." If, on the other hand, Cato outlived his mistress, it was Joseph's wish that "he live with any one or more of my children as he may choose, and when past his labor that he be well provided for at the estate of my sons or their heirs in proportion to the several farms herein willed to them respectively." The catch was that these arrangements were only to be adhered to if "the said Cato will continue to be as diligent in business, and *faithful* to the family as he hath hitherto been" (Joseph's emphasis). Toward the end of his life, Joseph began to pay Cato nominal amounts for his labor, but Cato's board and room were clearly contingent on his continued "faithfulness" and compliance. Cato Lee, as he was formally known after the war, died in 1805 at the age of fifty-four, eight years after his former master's decease and one year before Joseph's widow died. [24]

Cate and Phyllis similarly remained at the Block House, Cate until her death in 1785 and Phyllis until 1795, when she married Duncan Ingraham's Cato. This Cato also continued on with his master, in his case until his master prepared to leave Concord for Medford in order to marry his third wife. Phyllis and Cato were expecting a child and Cato asked Duncan for permission to marry Phyllis so that she and their baby, along with Phyllis's older child, could come with him to Medford, where Duncan would have to support them. According to Duncan's memoirist, Cato's master "consented" to the marriage but only "on condition of" Cato "no longer depending upon him for support."

Rather than be parted from his family, Cato agreed. He and Phyllis were finally free five years after the first federal census, which counted no slaves in the Commonwealth. For Cato Ingraham, Boston Potter, Cato Lee, and many others, little in 1790, when the census was taken, was different from their earlier slavery days. While in some cases their masters now paid them for their labor, other masters did not. The census, which for so long has been regarded as slavery's endpoint in Massachusetts, was, it turns out, a sleight of hand. According to one Massachusetts resident, when the marshal made his enumeration, if someone said he owned a slave, the marshal "would tell him that no other person had given in any." The slaveholder would then change his answer, noting, "If none are given in, I will not be singular." And thus, according to this informant, "the list was completed without any number in the column for slaves." The census thus obscures what Brister Freeman knew to be true: that in joining those who had succeeded in getting themselves abandoned to their freedom and who were determined to make their own way while so many slaves felt compelled to stay put, he was forging radically new ground. [25]

CHAPTER FIVE

Permission to Live in Walden Woods

NOT LONG AFTER THE REVOLUTIONARY WAR ENDED, John Cuming's health began to fade. On March 3, 1788, at the age of sixty, he felt it prudent to resign the position of town meeting moderator "for now and future." His sister Elizabeth had been begging him since 1784 to retire and "enjoy the fruits of your labor," noting in a letter from Halifax that it pained her "much to hear your health declines." John continued, however, to ride out to see patients and make the rounds of the county court. On one such trip, four months after resigning as moderator, John was suddenly taken ill while visiting the home of his friend Ebenezer Bridge in Chelmsford. Their closeness and John's preeminence was such that Ebenezer recounted his illness and the attention it received in detailed journal entries, although despite their years of friendship Ebenezer continued to follow the custom of calling John "the Colonel" in deference to his social rank. He wrote on June 22 that "Col. Cuming — lodged with us — taken suddenly ill." Two days later he wrote that "Dr. Hurd visited him PM and took some blood from him—Doctor Harrington visits him every day." Ebenezer noted, too, that "some of his neighbors of Concord" visited "more or less from day to day since he has been ill," including the Reverend Ezra Ripley. The minister's visit was a sure indication of just how sick John was but also, insofar as Chelmsford was twelve miles from Concord, an indication of John's stature in the community. While the sick were generally watched by women and servants, John's position in the community warranted him the care of no less than three doctors on the Sabbath. When John died four days later, on July 3, his friend mourned his loss while noting with pride that Colonel Cuming was his "good friend, acquaintance and benefactor." [1]

A monument to John and his many accomplishments was erected in the form of an extravagantly carved and unusually large tombstone looking out from Burial Hill over the town John had once led. On it, John is described as a physician, civil servant, magistrate, and Harvard honoree. But those who knew him saw here, too, all John had suffered even as he had soared so high. He had managed to create a durable legacy for himself as Concord's great patriarch but he had not managed to father a second generation. His only child predeceased him by twenty-nine years, her nearby tombstone a stark reminder of his loss. The fact that John was nevertheless able to fulfill each of his many offices is carefully credited in his epitaph to the various aspects of his character. The epitaph begins by noting that John was "naturally active, as to genius and disposition" and that he performed his duties "with spirit and dispatch." In all, twenty characteristics are enumerated (active, useful, compassionate, charitable, particular, animated, warm, earnest, zealous, affectionate, precise, cheerful, affable, prompt, expeditious, punctual, fervent, liberal, pious, and generous). That John should have lived to achieve so much and benefit so many is imagined as strictly a result of traits emanating from within him. In a culture that held so much stock in individual character, the external means by which John was able to achieve all he did go unremarked, namely the substantial advantage he received from his father and the fact that as an owner of slaves, he had been freed from the work of running his farm. [2]

But even as the epitaph finds much in John to praise, the overall tombstone design finally registers some doubts as to whether good works are enough to win an eternity in Heaven. The top of the stone is shaped like a bed board, signifying that on the Day of Judgment John will awake and God will reveal whether or not he had earned salvation. There is a winged angel's head above which are the words "Thro Christ we conquer and reign forever. Here rests in Hope the Body of John Cuming Esqr." The angel's wings have already lifted off the tympanum base, signifying that John's salvation has most likely been achieved. And yet hope for his eternal life in Heaven does battle with despair that he might not have done enough to get there. The angel lifting off in flight is arrested by the skull that sits atop it, behind and around which streams a banner reading "All must submit to the king of terrors." At least John Cuming could be certain his name would live on earth into the distant future for all the reasons enumerated in his epitaph. And indeed for decades after his death, his name was spoken locally with reverence and day-long holidays were declared in his honor. In Concord at least, John Cuming would live beyond the grave. [3]

In the will he penned in 1782, John had taken great care his good works would continue after his death. In addition to leaving his three sisters all of the land that had once been their father's, and a third of his estate to his wife, Abigail, he made several extraordinary bequests, one to the Concord church for £50 to be used to purchase silver communion vessels, one to the town of Concord for £300 to be used for schools and the poor, and one to Harvard, also for £300, "to be appropriated for the Professor of Physic, if any such there be, or shall be." John was a generous man who had clearly thought about how best to use his estate for what he regarded as the common good. Massachusetts had no medical school, and his gift to Harvard, when pooled with other gifts, remedied this situation with the founding of Harvard Medical School. His gift to his hometown would help ensure that its youngest residents had a chance to fulfill the kinds of dreams he had. The money John gave Concord for this purpose was enough to seed a fund that has survived to this day and that the town still continues to draw down annually for its neediest residents. [4]

But it is equally true that John's bequests were meant to solidify his reputation as Concord's town father and even to buy him the kind of futurity that, childless, he lacked. The donation of a silver communion set, for example, was a standard means by which a church member demonstrated not only his or her piousness but also his or her great wealth. The beauty of such a gift for the giver was that immortality was not only garnered within the sight of God but within the sight of the neighbors as well. Comprising an elegant pair of silver flagons with domed covers and scrolled handles, as well as four tall cups, each of the six pieces the church commissioned with John's bequest was engraved with "The gift of John Cuming Esq. to the Church of Concord." John had made an earlier gift in 1774 of two silver tankards, one large silver platter, and three silver goblets to the church in Acton, the town abutting his estate and to which his uncle and aunt had donated the land for the meeting house in 1736. Similar silver communion sets were given by the wealthy to churches all over Massachusetts. One of the givers' hopes was that their position at the head of society would not easily be forgotten by those who read their names each time they took communion. It would forever more be through John's generosity that Concord's residents enacted the last supper, imbibing the blood of Christ from vessels inscribed with his name. [5]

The gift to Harvard to fund a professorship of physic was also a bid for posterity. As John had already experienced, gifts to Harvard were repaid with public declarations of gratitude, the College having thanked him for the brass candlesticks with the honorary master's degree in 1772 and awarding him the library privileges when Harvard moved to Concord while troops were stationed on the Cambridge campus. John well knew that even if a gift was made posthumously, the College would take care to laud him, especially as this would be a gift rivaled by only the most prominent men in the Commonwealth. Despite not being a graduate of Harvard and in exile from Massachusetts, in his 1778 will Isaac Royall Jr. had left to Harvard funds for "the endowing a Professor of Laws in said College, or a Professor of Physic and Anatomy, whichever the . . . overseers and Corporation shall judge to be best for the benefit of said College." He died in England in the fall of 1781, at which point the terms of his will were made public and Harvard endowed a law professorship that exists to this day. John drew up his will in the months that followed Isaac's death, imitating Isaac's gift to Harvard as he had earlier with the candelabras, but focusing on his own professional area of expertise. Isaac Royall Jr. had set a high standard for benevolence and civic-mindedness that John was determined to meet, both on account of his convictions regarding the importance of a good local medical school and his desire to be acknowledged as one of the Commonwealth's great men.[6]

John's generous bequests were indeed made as public as he must have hoped when they were enumerated in his obituary:

> *Characters, respectable and worthy, deserve public notice; especially when through life, and in the final distribution of their worldly substance, they have proved themselves public as well as private benefactors. Upon this ground, Col. Cuming may claim, from many individuals and the public, a grateful tribute to his memory. Charity to the poor, liberality to forward every laudable measure, promote the interest of schools and learning in general, and constant exertions for the good of society, rendered him conspicuous. His generous donations for the benefit of the poor, for the maintenance of schools, for a library in Concord, and to the College in Cambridge, for the support of a professor of physic, are plenary evidence in his favour. Dying without issue, his liberality had scope without exciting complaints.*

As his obituary noted, it was precisely because John died without any children that he was in a position to be so liberal in his bequests. But even so, insofar as his bequests were for the public good rather than for private benefactors, he was thought to deserve "a grateful tribute to his memory." In becoming such a notable man, John had achieved his father's dream.[7]

AFTER A NINE-MONTH ENLISTMENT IN THE ARMY that brought him as far as West Point, Brister Freeman had been discharged on April 20, 1780. He was still a relatively young man and, for the first time in his life, a free man, as the last name he had chosen for himself so loudly proclaimed. But even as he was no longer John Cuming's slave and no longer serving in the army, Brister had not been free to go where he pleased. Although the institution of slavery was waning in Massachusetts, it still existed in each of the thirteen colonies. Had Brister attempted to live where he would have never had to cross paths with John Cuming or any other Concord resident again, he would have run the risk of being captured and sold into slavery. In her novel *Oldtown Folks* (1869), Harriet Beecher Stowe fictionalizes such incidents, which were widely reported to have taken place in Natick, Massachusetts, the town near Concord that Stowe uses as her prototype for Oldtown. She describes how a former slave's children were stolen in the night by kidnappers intent on taking them to New York and selling them into slavery there. The plot is foiled only when outraged white residents intervene on the children's behalf. Should a stranger question or attempt to reverse Brister's free status, only the residents of Concord knew him to vouch for it. Even if Brister had a bill of manumission from John Cuming, officials in any other town could warn him out on the basis that Concord must accept responsibility for him. In the years following Brister's discharge, when more than one hundred former slaves attempted to settle in Salem, hoping to find work in the prosperous Massachusetts port town, local officials, concerned these former slaves would become a drain on Salem's coffers, gave them until December 1790 to leave the town limits. (Three hundred poor whites and their families, in contrast, were given until May, when better weather would make it easier to move.) The paucity of surviving manumission papers in New England speaks to the fact that former slaves were not able to travel far enough away from the site of their former enslavement to need them. Brister may well have wanted to return to Concord to be near his siblings in the only part of the country he knew intimately, but the decision to walk the 170 miles from West Point back to Concord was not really his to make.[8]

The majority of Concord area slaves also seem to have wanted to remain close to loved ones. Either way, like Brister, they were obligated to stay put on account of the warning-out system. John Jack stayed in Concord after being relinquished by Susanna Barron sometime between 1758 and 1761. He lived in Concord a free man until his death in 1773, when he bequeathed his estate to Violet, his former owner's slave woman. (However, his lawyer, Daniel Bliss, fled Massachusetts before settling John Jack's estate, leaving Violet to try to sue for it.) Caesar Robbins, who may have taken his freedom as early as his enlistment in 1776, also stayed in Concord, marrying in succession as many as three local women, the first of whom may have been the Bliss's slave Phyllis. After Phyllis died, Caesar married Catherine Boaz in 1779 and finally, after she died, Rose Bay in 1807. He, too, remained in Concord until his death. In Weston, which borders Lincoln, a slave named Salem after the prosperous coastal town served in the army for both the town of Weston and the town of Lincoln. Like Sippio Brister, he eventually took a name that honored another former slave, living out his days as Salem Middlesex. He, too, returned to the scene of his enslavement. After his wife died in Lincoln in 1781, where both of them were baptized in 1777, Salem married a Weston slave woman named Catherine and had six children there by her. After Salem died in 1799, Catherine moved with one of her sons to nearby Framingham, prompting the town to demand compensation from Weston for their support and eventually insist on her return. She died back in Weston in 1802. The financial complications of this sort that ensued when a former slave attempted to move to another town were not tolerated and served to keep the majority of the former slave population immobile.[9]

Several slaves in Concord disappeared from the local record after their military service but it is hardly likely they were able to settle in other towns. Colonel Charles Prescott's slave man Caesar, for one, never appeared in any official town or state documents after the war. That Caesar lived out his days in Concord is known only because Joseph Lee thought to mention his death in his journal as evidence of the impoverishment of those slaves who, in Joseph's mind, were foolish enough to choose freedom and independent living over continued servitude. Joseph wrote in January 1786, seven years after Charles Prescott's death, "Dies Prescott's negro named Caesar. He had made himself free by leave of his mistress but died miserable enough." As for James Barrett's slave Philip, he last appears in the historical record in 1780, one year after Colonel Barrett's death, when at the age of nineteen Philip served in the army for six months. If he returned to Concord after his discharge, he was facing another eleven years of enslavement, his master's will having stipulated that Philip obtain his freedom only when he reached thirty years of age. But insofar as Philip does not appear in any local records after that, it may be that James's son Peter, who inherited Philip, either relinquished him or sold him out of Massachusetts. As recently as 1772, Peter's brother Stephen had fantasized about the profits to be had from selling Philip. But most of these former slave men lived out their days in Concord either with their former masters, as Cato Lee and Boston Potter did, or alone, like Charles Prescott's Caesar, and so impoverished that they never appeared on tax or probate records, only appearing on the town's poor list if they were lucky enough to garner notice. Not remembered for their exploits, as Brister Freeman would be, Concord slaves Caesar Kettle, Caesar Minot, Sambo Blood, Boston Ball, Colonel James Barrett's Philip, William Emerson's slave Frank, and John Cuming's slave Jem were lost to history. Families and friends did not have the money to record their deaths with the town clerk, nor to supply their graves with headstones. Apparently their former owners were content to see them buried in unmarked paupers' graves. [10]

For those like Caesar Prescott who "made himself free," the first issue facing them was where they were going to live. Town officials and former owners across Massachusetts were quick to point them toward the most out-of-the-way and infertile areas. Beginning in 1792, the town of Plymouth, Massachusetts, allowed four black families to squat on a ninety-four-acre parcel of land, provided that they "clear the same in the term of three years." This was such gravelly and infertile soil, however, that in 1824, when the town attempted to sell the land out from under the squatters, who could not afford to purchase it themselves, no one wanted to buy it. In Gloucester, former slaves squatted at a similarly undesirable location, a rocky portion of the Cape Ann peninsula called Dogtown. In Malden and Woburn, former slaves were allowed to squat on the barren hills overlooking those towns' turnpikes. In Natick, the town's former slaves were permitted to cluster in three places. And while Harriet Beecher Stowe simplified this somewhat in *Oldtown Folks*, writing that "The houses of the colored people formed a little settlement by themselves in the north part of the village," she managed to capture for readers what all New Englanders knew to be true: that former slaves lived in areas that were isolated, usually, as so many examples make clear, by virtue of the soil's poor quality. [11]

This pattern of segregated inhabitation resulted in a term for referring to the burgeoning enclaves of former slaves after the war. "New Guinea" was used to describe the sections of New Haven, Philadelphia, New York, Boston, and Plymouth where former slaves settled. Guinea had long referred to that section of Africa along the western coast where slave ships picked up their cargo. If a former slave had been born in Africa, he or she was generally referred to using this term, as Henry David Thoreau does when he notes in *Walden* of Cato Ingraham, "Some say that he was a Guinea Negro." New Guinea was in the tradition of naming North American regions, cities, and towns after their European counterparts, New England, New London, and New Bedford being well-known examples. But the naming of an area New Guinea was not only a means of noting that former slaves had settled there, it also did the work of keeping the stigma of slavery alive. The status of those who lived in New Guinea, in other words, was made abundantly clear by the name. Readers of the introduction to *The Scarlet Letter* would have known exactly what Nathaniel Hawthorne meant when he describes mid-nineteenth-century Salem as bounded by "Gallows Hill and New Guinea at one end, and a view of the almshouse at the other." In reality, by the mid-nineteenth century Salem's black residents lived on the eastern edge of town near Salem Neck, a particularly noisy section of town that backed up against the railroad tracks, as well as in the area surrounding stagnant Mill Pond in the southwestern part of town. But insofar as Salem was segregated, Nathaniel Hawthorne was right, even if he takes poetic license with the actual location of Salem's black settlements. His placement of New Guinea next to the site where felons were executed captures the fact that former slaves were considered the town's undesirables, forced to settle in the most loathsome of locations. [12]

While the term New Guinea does not seem to have been employed in Concord, at least not in written documents, the town initially had two distinct areas where former slaves were allowed to squat. One of the areas was behind a swamp that backed up to Burial Hill, along the common fence separating the Great Field from the Great Meadows. The area was reached by a lane that branched off the road running from the center of town past the home that formerly belonged to William Emerson and that had come into the possession of the town's new minister, Ezra Ripley, after his marriage to William's widow the year Brister Freeman was discharged from the army. The lane left the road across from the Emerson-Ripley home. It passed through some hills and then forked, one branch leading to the Great Meadows and the other to the Great Field. While the Great Meadows were still carefully managed and diligently harvested for animal fodder, the Great Field had declined dramatically in importance to local residents. As more and more upland had been cleared and plowed into tillage fields, the Great Field continued for a time to be owned and managed by a group of proprietors, but the area no longer constituted the heart of the town's agricultural efforts. The relocation of the fence that once divided the meadows from the Great Field indicated as much. In the decades when the Great Meadows and the Great Field were equally important parts of the town's subsistence economy, the fence had run along the river, keeping livestock sent in to forage after the harvest from swimming or wading away, but allowing animals to roam over the land regardless of whose lots they traversed. After 1740, when most proprietors also had cleared tillage land elsewhere, the official fence was subsequently moved to run between the meadow and the field. It ran along the access path, keeping livestock in the meadows and out of fields that were now more rigorously private than before. Over the three decades that followed, the Great Field shrank in size until finally, on October 26, 1778, the proprietorship of the Great Field was dissolved and the area officially ceased to exist as anything but private land. It was during this period of its waning importance that former slaves were allowed to settle on its edge. [13]

Beginning in 1761, John Jack was allowed to purchase the first of three lots on the edge of the Great Field without any contestation on the part of the town. Then, six years after John Jack's death and a year after the proprietorship of the Great Field was dissolved, Caesar Robbins was permitted by Humphrey Barrett to squat on or near this site on land along the lane and fence, where Caesar built a small house. Humphrey Barrett allowed Caesar to use a nearby woodlot as well, ever after called Caesar's Wood. The nearby spring became known as Peter's Spring and the access path Peter's Path after either Caesar's son or another descendant of former slaves, Peter Hutchinson, who eventually lived here as well. Humphrey Barrett was one of the town's largest landowners, owning a large, contiguous farm that had been in his family since the town's incorporation. (Colonel James Barrett descended from the same original settler, but belonged to a different branch of the family.) In 1771, only John Cuming, Joseph Lee, and three other men had land valued for more than Humphrey's was. But insofar as his land abutted and included lots in the by-then misnamed Great Field, it was Humphrey Barrett who was in a position to help the town manage the settlement of its former slaves on land no one else wanted anymore. Caesar may have been additionally motivated to live here by a desire to be near his daughter Phyllis, if indeed the Bliss-Emerson family slave was his child, but it was solely at Humphrey Barrett's discretion that he was able to do so. [14]

When another former slave, Jack Garrison of New Jersey, married Caesar's daughter Susan in 1812, he was permitted by Humphrey to live in a second room added to Caesar's house and to make use of the Barrett land as well. Humphrey later granted Susan, with whom Jack had seven children, a lifelong tenancy in her half of the house. In 1824, Caesar's son Peter added substantially to the household's size. He married Fatima Oliver of Acton, who already had at least the two children whose births had been recorded with the Acton town clerk: a daughter born in 1804, and a son born in 1805. Fatima also seems to have had a son born sometime around 1800 and named after his father, Peter Hutchinson, also of Acton. There was a problem of some sort with the Robbinses' marriage and Peter proceeded to have his six children by Fatima's sister Almira Oliver, a scandal long remembered by Concord's white residents, who used it as an excuse to shun Peter. Eventually Peter purchased the land on which his family had been squatting, but he lost it soon thereafter on account of debts. His stepson, Peter Hutchinson, purchased the house from the man to whom Peter Robbins had sold it and he and his wife, Nancy, from Danvers, raised the five of their children who survived infancy here. [15]

Another area where slaves were allowed to squat was along the road that ran through Walden Woods east of the pond. Just as the Great Field had once been central to Concord's food chain, this road was once central to the area's transportation routes. And just as the Great Field had declined in importance until its name became what one historian has called anachronistic, so too had what is now called Walden Street or Route 126 declined in importance. Initially only a path when the town was incorporated in 1635, the road past Walden Pond had become a town road in 1671 and the Great County Road, as it was called throughout the eighteenth century, in 1706. The road began in New Hampshire and once it got to Concord ran through the center of town and across the fields on the other side before it hit Walden Woods, where it immediately began to climb up a steep hill, then called Stratton's Hill after the Strattons who once owned the large farm that included it, before curving around Walden Pond to its west side. The road emerged from the woods near the Chambers-Russell estate and continued on toward Boston, which was reached by the neck connecting it to Roxbury. The other way to Boston from Concord ran along the Bay road, now called Lexington Road because it runs through Lexington before reaching Charlestown Neck, where Mark's corpse was gibbeted. On the other side of Charlestown, where John Codman lived until his murder in 1755, travelers could then board a ferry for Boston. The Bay road was also a well-traveled route and as such was lined with shops, taverns, and homes, but for those traveling to and from Boston with conveyances, the Charlestown ferry was not an option, and so the route past Walden Pond was taken. On all but Sundays, local farmers set off on it in the early morning hours to cart their surplus rye, hay, and wood to city markets. The mail stage came through on this road, as did a passenger stagecoach thrice weekly. But at the same time that slavery was coming to a gradual end, the Great County Road was waning in importance. A bridge connecting Charlestown to Boston opened up the road through Lexington to chaises and wagons in 1785. Those who continued to traverse the Walden road now used it to access local destinations, whether Lincoln, their woodlots in Walden Woods, Walden Pond itself, or the distant parcels of their usually scattered farms, reachable by the many bridle, cart, and foot paths that crisscrossed the road. Henry David Thoreau thus recalled the road as it existed in his childhood as "a humble route to neighboring villages" and a route for "the woodman's team."[16]

Considerably less traveled than it had been in its heyday, the edge of the road through Walden Woods became open to squatters in slavery's wake. Former slaves and their families from the Chambers-Russell estate seem to have been the first to arrive. The family of Peter Russell, as Zilpah and Brister's brother came to be called on account of having been inherited by Chambers Russell when Charles Chambers died in 1743, seems to have settled here first. Peter had married a woman named Mary with whom he had a child, Betty Russell, born in December 1755. Peter died shortly thereafter, and his widow married Thomas Cook in April 1759. Mary and Thomas had at least two other children, Hephzibah in 1760 and Beulah in 1762. After Chambers Russell's family fled Massachusetts, the Cook family appears to have squatted in Walden

Woods, not far from where Betty's father and his siblings had been enslaved. By the early 1780s, Mary was dead and Thomas and his stepdaughter Betty, who by then had her own child, were unable to care for themselves. Until the town set up a poor house on the former Stratton farm in the nineteenth century, the poor were boarded with the person who put in the lowest bid for their care. Generally, those in the vicinity of the impoverished person's home won the auction, provided they bid a low enough amount. After the war, Brister seems to have been squatting in Walden Woods himself and from April 8, 1782, through March 1784 was paid by the town of Concord to care for Thomas Cook. On September 25, 1783, the town also paid Brister to care for his niece Betty Russell. [17]

Other former slaves began settling in Walden Woods around this time, although Henry David Thoreau does not mention all of them in *Walden* because they lived much farther from his bean field in the town of Lincoln. A former slave calling himself William Fillis moved onto a small lot on the border of Walden Woods near the Chambers-Russell estate around the time the Russells fled New England. This, too, was less than desirable land, being situated between the road and a steep incline not far behind it. The last name he took, a spelling variant of Phyllis, was presumably a means of honoring a woman in his life who was important to him. Then, around 1779, another former slave managed to purchase land not far from Walden Woods that had until recently been part of the Chambers-Russell estate. Jube Savage, formerly of North Weston, acquired a small lot from Joseph Adams, his wife's former owner. By 1780, Jube was being paid by the town of Lincoln to board Lucy Oliver, a black woman on the poor list and most likely a relative of Fatima and Almira Oliver. These Olivers may have been some of the former slaves of the wealthy Oliver family, which was closely related to the Royalls. The daughter of Isaac Royall Sr.'s second wife married Robert Oliver and later inherited eleven of Isaac's slaves. One seems to have been Robin Vassall's grandmother. The appearance of possible Oliver slaves in the Concord area is an indication former slaves attempted to reforge sundered family ties after the war. The Walden road may have served the region in a diminished capacity, but because of its proximity to a vast estate that once housed numerous slaves and that was closely connected to some of the other finest estates in Massachusetts, it now became a place where former slaves from multiple families were drawn to squat. [18]

Brister was eager, like Jube Savage, to be a landowner, not a squatter. He knew from his enslavement to John Cuming that land was the chief form of wealth in New England and the means by which a person gained a voice in towns like Concord that in essence were land corporations. Land ownership was thus the only way former slaves would be fully able to divest themselves of their former identities as someone else's property and, at least theoretically, gain the right to vote in town meetings. Brister had very little money but he had a friend who shared his ambition. Like Brister, Boston Potter, and Salem Middlesex, Charlestown Edes had been named by his owner, Isaiah Edes of Groton, for a prosperous and cosmopolitan city. Charlestown was, also like Brister, in his thirties. Both men understood what it meant to have served all of one's life as a tool and a symbol for someone else. Charlestown had still been a slave as late as 1781, when he signed over his army wages to his owner. During Charlestown's service in the Fifteenth Massachusetts Regiment, Brister and he met and the two decided to pool their resources. [19]

A large amount of land formerly belonging to the Strattons on the edge of Walden Woods had recently changed hands. John Stratton sold 140 acres to Duncan Ingraham for £2,000 in 1779, the year before Brister was discharged from the army, including 40 acres of woodlot in Walden Woods. In December 1784, Jacob Potter mortgaged to Duncan 80 acres he had purchased of the remaining Stratton farm abutting Duncan's land. The mortgage agreement included 11 acres of woodlot "adjoining Walden Pond" and "one other piece of old field lying up Stratton Hill . . . containing one acre and three rods." Jacob repaid Duncan in September 1792, at which point he had already sold or promised to sell the "old field" to Brister Freeman and Charlestown Edes, despite the fact that the land was mortgaged. The "old field" was small and infertile enough that Brister and Charlestown could afford it, not that they got a break on the price. Brister and Charlestown paid just over £15, whereas Duncan Ingraham had paid an average of just over £14 per acre. The bar for land ownership was being set as high if not higher for them than it was for white residents. [20]

Brister wanted not only the social and civic privileges accompanying land ownership but also to reconstitute his sundered family. The property he and Charlestown had purchased was just fifteen hundred feet from Brister's sister Zilpah, who seems to have begun squatting on the roadside sometime after the Russells fled Massachusetts. Initially, Brister and Zilpah's sister-in-law Mary seems to have also lived nearby with her new husband, Thomas Cook, the two children she had with him, and her first husband's child. Brister was thus able to start his new family alongside his family of origin. He brought with him to Walden a former slave woman seven years his junior, named Fenda, as well as Fenda's daughter Nancy, whom Brister adopted, listing himself as her father when he informed the town clerk of the births of Edward, born to Fenda and him in 1781, and Amos, born three years after that. [21]

Cato and Phyllis Ingraham were the last of the former slaves to settle permanently in Walden Woods. Duncan had refused to support Cato any longer on account of his marriage to Mrs. Bliss's Phyllis. In effect, Cato had not been freed so much as he was abandoned for exerting his will and asking for, in exchange for his labor, the support of not only himself but a wife and two children besides. As Henry puts it in *Walden*, Duncan "built his slave a house, and gave him permission to live in Walden Woods," no doubt concerned that if he did not give him a place to squat, the Concord authorities would seek him out for Cato's support should Cato appear on the poor list. According to Henry's friend Ellery Channing, Cato's home was "directly at the opening of the path from the Walden road to the Goose Pond," and thus a mere 250 feet from Zilpah's. Like her home, Cato's was close to the road. In this regard, Duncan's granting of "permission to live in Walden Woods" was hardly an extravagant gift, much less any kind of real compensation for past labors. The erection of a house by the roadside would disturb a minimum, if any, of Duncan's valuable trees. In short, like Humphrey Barrett, Duncan was allowing a former slave to use land he did not need himself. Indeed, because Duncan was moving to his new wife's home in Medford, he would no longer need to harvest from his Walden lot, which he was planning to sell as soon as he could. Realizing the difficulties Cato faced in squatting on such a small roadside parcel of Walden's sandy plains, Henry quips in his journal of the "permission" granted Cato to live in Walden Woods that Duncan Ingraham was "no doubt . . . thanked" for it. [22]

Cato was forty-four when he moved to Walden in 1795 with his wife, Phyllis, seventeen years his junior. Phyllis's daughter, like Fenda's named Nancy, was six at the time of the move. She may well have been Cato's biological daughter, considering Phyllis's and his proximity to one another during their slavery days. Otherwise Cato essentially adopted her, just as Brister had adopted his wife's daughter. Both Nancys were born into slavery, or at least their popular slave names seem to indicate as much, and it seems both their fathers or adopted fathers were intent on repairing the family ties sundered by slavery, reconnecting and sticking by siblings and wives and becoming fathers to children like Mark's and so many others who were denied their fathers by slaveholders determined to keep enslaved families broken and thus vulnerable to their owners' demands.

The Walden population waxed and waned over the years as more children and then grandchildren were born, residents died, and former slave families in the area, often destitute and suffering the illnesses that accompany poverty, sought shelter there. On one occasion, when the other side of their house was vacated by Charlestown during the final days of what would prove a fatal illness, Brister and Fenda seem to have invited former slave Reuben Burden and his family to live there. Cato and Phyllis Ingraham also shared their home, essentially running a boarding house in the second room of their two-room home. One Concord resident recalled how, in later years, a "friendless negro, a stranger" arrived with smallpox at the home of George Minot's nephew, George Minot Baker, who inherited Jacob and Lavina Baker's farm on the Lincoln edge of Walden Woods. If this stranger was trying to make his way to the Walden enclave, he fell short by only one mile. George Baker and his wife buried the stricken former slave in their Walden woodlot. In all, as many as fifteen former slaves made a life for themselves in Walden Woods, enough that Henry David Thoreau could describe their community as a "small village." [23]

Brister and Charlestown were the only two members of this new community to own the land where they lived. They seem to have incurred the expense of the purchase price and the annual poll tax they would now be assessed on the assumption that Brister would someday receive a bequest from the estate of his former master. John Cuming had penned his will three years before Brister and Charlestown made their purchase, and it was probably not a secret that this most wealthy of Concord's residents, being childless, was leaving several not insubstantial bequests to local residents to whom he felt beholden. He left £20 to the Reverend Ezra Ripley, Phoebe Emerson's second husband and John's longtime minister. He also left half of his clothing to Ezra's stepson Billy. He left the same amount he bequeathed the minister to Eunice Darby, who seems to have been a servant in the Cuming home. The final bequest in his will was "to my two negroes (that was), viz. Bristo and Jem, thirty five pounds sterling each." No other slaveholder in Concord ever left money to his slaves or former slaves.

The most anyone else had ever done was make arrangements for their former slave's care should the former slave remain diligent in his or her labor for the former master's family. But without any children requiring his attention, John had the funds to make substantial parting gifts. [24]

And yet unlike the funds given to the other recipients of John's largess, Brister's and Jem's was not money they would receive directly to do with as they liked. It turns out John's bequest to his two former slave men was not meant to help establish them as free and independent men, let alone to thank them for decades of service. Rather, these bequests were John's means of insuring that his hard-won reputation was never tarnished. Instead of directing that his bequests be paid directly to Brister and Jem, he left the money to the town, stipulating that it was his will "the expending" of his bequests to "Bristo and Jem . . . be under the special direction of the selectmen of Concord." In short, the £35 would cover the cost of providing for his two former slaves should either become so impoverished they had to be put on the town's poor list. The selectmen would stand in for John in his formerly paternal relationship to his slaves so that no one could say he had abdicated his responsibility. Insofar as £35 was roughly the price of a grown male slave in the 1780s, John was essentially asserting that he had paid the town for "Bristo and Jem," even as the town would still have control over them. John's use of the possessive ("my negroes") and the fact of his not using Brister's last name make it clear that in his mind and the town's their status remained largely unchanged. They were still considered property to be managed, and in continuing to manage them John secured his reputation as a benevolent town leader. [25]

Of course Brister's and Charlestown's struggle to make a go of it on an acre of "old field" would prove extremely difficult without any kind of a financial boost of the sort young men starting out as landowners customarily received. Without much or any money, it would prove impossible to buy more or better land, much less stock it with animals and the proper farming equipment.

CHAPTER SIX

Little Gardens and Dwellings

AFTER SHE WAS ABANDONED BY CHARLES RUSSELL, Brister's sister, Zilpah, could have opted for a life similar to the one she led under slavery. Many former slave women, Cate Bliss among them, stayed on with their owners, performing as ostensibly free women the same domestic duties they performed when enslaved. Of course Zilpah's former owner had left the country, but there were still ample numbers of well-to-do white families looking for live-in female help. Former slave women and their unmarried daughters often took such work because it was the surest means of putting a roof over their heads. Elsea Dugan, the daughter of former slaves Thomas and Catherine Dugan, spent her entire life in Concord as a domestic servant, living with and working for Daniel Garfield's family not far from where her family lived on a small, six-acre parcel of land near Old Marlborough Road, the third area of black inhabitation in Concord. Thomas had escaped enslavement in Virginia and after arriving in Concord paid for land there on installment, making his final payment in 1788. He and Catherine had five children, including Elsea. After Catherine died, Thomas had three more children by his second wife, Jennie Parker. Most of the Dugan children eventually left town in search of better prospects. Only Elsea and her half-brother Elisha stayed, but Elisha failed to hold onto his father's land and eventually sank deeper into poverty. Henry David Thoreau describes Elisha and his situation in his poem "The Old Marlborough Road," published in his essay "Walking" (1862). For living on what he trapped, Elisha is described as a "man of wild habits, / Partridges and rabbits." Waxing nostalgic for this kind of backwoods life, Henry imagines Elisha as having "no cares / Only to set snares." And in that he "liv'st all alone," Henry argues, he was able to live "Close to the bone." Elisha, Henry writes, "constantly eatest . . . where life is sweetest." Henry thus glorifies the subsistence life by making literal the expression about living close to the bone. (Elisha is imagined enjoying the sweet taste of bone marrow.) Elisha's poverty makes it all the more shocking that in 1842, Elsea, then thirty-nine, wrote in her will that her entire estate, which eventually totaled over one thousand dollars, should be divided between her employer's two daughters, Louisa and Elizabeth. It seems Elsea was so grateful to the Garfields for her room and board that she felt she owed everything to them, even above and beyond her not inconsiderable labor over the years. She treated Louisa and Elizabeth in her will as if they were her siblings, seeming to want to take her place as one of the Garfield daughters. When the census taker came to the door of the Garfield daughter with whom Elsea was living in 1880, at least part of the reason became clear. Elsea went so far as to get herself listed as white. Her mother, like Thomas, was described as a "mulatto," and Elsea may thus have had a light complexion. Either way, she used the census to disassociate herself from the Dugan family and the lingering associations with her family's slavery past that made them the objects of derision. Ralph Waldo Emerson, for one, did not hesitate to repeat jokes made at the expense of Elsea's half-brother, writing in his journal of an afternoon stroll when he and his companion "fell into the Dugan trail" and caught a "glimpse" of Elisha's "cabin" that it was a "barbarous district." He records how his companion proposed sending the Horticulture Society a note to the effect that they "Took an apple near the White Pond fork of the Dugan trail, an apple of the *Beware-of-this* variety, a true *Touch-me-if-you-dare*." By living with a white family and passing as white herself, Elsea must have hoped she would no longer be associated with Concord's untouchables.[1]

Zilpah took a decidedly different tack than Elsea Dugan. Preferring to take her chances, she sought complete independence at whatever cost. She built or otherwise moved into a small, one-room cabin in Walden Woods. Henry later built himself a cabin out of the remnants of an Irish shanty and described his new home, which was ten feet by fifteen feet, as comparable in size to those of the former Walden inhabitants. The picture of a cabin like his on the original cover of *Walden* (Figure 8) was meant to show readers how little they needed in order to be happy, but after a century in which domestic space had been parsed into distinct rooms for various functions, it was widely felt that only the

Figure 8. *Cover art for original edition of* Walden *(1854). Courtesy of the Concord Free Public Library.*

impoverished should have to cook, eat, work, and sleep in the same room. Zilpah was forced to go one step further than even Henry ever did because she had only the thin strip by the side of the road on which to squat. She used her one room as both her residence and her barn. She housed not only her dogs and cats in her "hut," as one local resident called her home, but her hens as well. By the end of her life, this was so far out of the norm for Concord that the writer of her obituary described her home as a "hovel." [2]

Zilpah's only saleable skills were those she had performed as a slave. One of these was spinning. She took raw cotton imported from the West Indies, wool, and flax and spun them into thread that could then be woven into cloth. In the pre-industrial period, this was an endless task performed at home throughout the year and thus in those households where there were slave women, it was one of the first chores the mistress was happy to hand over. The Royall family was wealthy enough to have a special room they termed the "spinning garret" at the top of their mansion house. They placed "a negro bed cradle and two blankets" there so that slave mothers could watch their sleeping infants while they toiled over their wheels well into the night, much like the miller's daughter in the tale of Rumpelstiltskin, whose pile of straw grows larger every night, a testimony to the never-ending quality of domestic textile production. Like her mother, Zilpah must have spent a good deal of her time at the top or back of the Chambers-Russell mansion house spinning flax into the linen fibers that were then woven into fine table linens and other markers of wealth and gentility. [3]

When slavery ended, at least some former slave women were given one of their master's spinning wheels as a means of providing for themselves. In Windham, Connecticut, slaveholder Mary Jennings knew spinning was her slave woman Ginna's best chance of providing for herself. And thus after freeing Ginna in 1759, she gave her a spinning wheel. Most likely, Zilpah simply took her spinning wheel from her former owner's abandoned estate, where it had been the means by which the Russells made clear their social dominance, in terms of both their mastery of the accoutrements of fine dining, foremost of which were table linens, and their ability to harness the labor of other human beings to that end. Now Zilpah's spinning wheel was the key to her independence. Alone in her little house, she spun flax into linen thread, "making the Walden Woods ring," Henry writes, with her "loud and notable voice." Singing served to make her presence known to passersby and was thereby a means of attracting business. It also, of course, made the long hours spent toiling over her wheel go by more quickly. [4]

Spinning was a risky way to make a living, particularly in such close quarters. Flax is highly flammable, and not a few fires in New England started when a cinder escaped from the hearth and ignited a pile of flax ready to be spun. Nor was spinning an easy task. Zilpah had to place the flax onto a distaff in a fine web and then draw strands of the fibers into one continuous yarn, being careful to draw those strands evenly, while keeping the right tension on the yarn and controlling the speed of twisting, a task particularly difficult with flax because of its lack of elasticity. Zilpah also had to be able to vary her technique depending on whether the yarn was to be used for warping, weaving, knitting, lace making, shoe binding, or embroidery. Over time, the strain on Zilpah's eyes was considerable and she nearly went blind. But for all that Zilpah was remembered by Henry's informants for spinning alone in her Walden house, this was not because it was the means of her independence nor the cause of her physical ailments. Rather, she was remembered as the last of a dying breed. In 1809, a cotton factory opened in Concord with a clothier's shop attached, and spinning wheels were consigned to the past. They did not reappear until the first house museums were opened in Concord and across New England, at which point they were placed by the hearth as if the ladies of the house once did their own spinning and in their parlors no less. In actuality, former slave women had more cause to credit their spinning wheels with their independence than the celebrated mothers of New England's independent farmers and artisans in the age of homespun. [5]

As factory cloth became more readily available and the demand for spinning began to decline, Zilpah needed other means of supplementing her living. Like so many other former slaves, she seems to have taken a cue from the Indians, making and peddling abroad useful domestic objects she made out of freely available natural products. As Henry notes in *Walden*, the former slaves took to a variety of tasks, running what he calls a "basket, stable-broom, mat-making, corn-parching, linen-spinning, and pottery business." And while he does not identify which of the former slaves did which of these jobs, other than that Zilpah "spun linen," Henry provides a clue that seems to indicate Zilpah had ready access to the materials needed to make baskets. He notes that the bricks marking the location of where her house once stood are scattered "amid the oak copse" and that on at least one occasion she "was away." A coppice is a cluster of even-sized tree stems growing up from a common base. It results when the main stems of certain kinds of trees are cut. Coppice growth on oak and ash trees by the road and on barren, unclaimed land was free for the taking and could be harvested for fifteen to thirty years or longer, making an excellent and renewable supply of sticks for baskets, which farmers needed to transport their corn, flax, beans, wool, malt, and rye, and which women needed to store everything from clothes to knives and forks. Like mats, used to cover the floors, and brooms, used for sweeping stables, homes, and stoops, baskets wear out over time, creating a perpetual market for those with the skills who were willing to sell their handmade wares door to door. [6]

Henry does not mention chair seating but no doubt this was also a means of support Zilpah and the other former slaves at Walden used. Chair bottoms were made out of natural materials, required a similar skill set to basket making, and also wore out regularly. Indeed, people remembered in their local towns for making baskets were often remembered for performing the similar work of bottoming chairs. One family in Southbridge, Massachusetts, was said to survive by "swindling flax, chopping wood, weaving baskets and chair-bottoms." Sarah Brown Sprague, a Native American woman in Webster, Massachusetts, sold baskets and bottomed chairs, as did the Nedson family of Southbridge. Simon Gigger and Bets Hendricks, Nipmuck Indians living in Westborough, Massachusetts, were also said to have "often found work in rebottoming the chairs" as well as in making baskets. [7]

Lydia Hosmer's picture *A Fishing Party* (see Figure 6) features several of the items that Henry reports were made by the inhabitants of Walden Woods, if not by Zilpah herself. The picnic repast is spread on a mat seemingly woven of rushes. The fish caught earlier have been stored in a basket on board the boat. A second basket sits next to blue-bordered porcelain plates holding food. And the chair being offered one of the ladies is rush bottomed. Each of these locally made items is depicted by Lydia in great detail and positioned prominently, most notably the chair, which is being carried in such a way that the pattern of the weave on its seat is fully shown. No doubt Lydia was eager to show her not inconsiderable skill in rendering such fine detail. The effect, however, is to collapse time, depicting both bygone slaves in livery and the contemporary contributions of former slaves and their families in the form of baskets, mats, and chair-bottoms. Slavery was over but wealthy whites still relied on former slaves for the material objects on which much of their comfort and pleasure were based.

But while the former slaves were now paid for their labor, they were paid very little. In Williamstown, Massachusetts, one poor family of "whitish mulattoes" was remembered to have lived in a shanty and "eked out a miserable existence by making door mats of corn husks and coarse baskets." Peter Salem, the former slave from Framingham long said to have killed John Pitcairn at the Battle of Bunker Hill two months after the major almost fired on Duncan Ingraham's slave, was described as earning "a precarious livelihood by making and mending baskets, bottoming chairs, and the like." And an 1832 manufacturing census from York, Maine, might as well have been describing the former slaves living in Walden Woods: "The basket makers are indigent persons, living in the back part of the town, on rocky sterile land, who employ themselves in making baskets, as the only means of affording a living." Henry's description of Zilpah's life is similar. He remarks that "She led a hard life, and somewhat inhumane." [8]

The contrast between the magnificent repast enjoyed by the white picnickers in Lydia Hosmer's picture and Zilpah's diet is particularly striking. On the sliver of land where she squatted, Zilpah had enough room for what Henry describes as a "little garden." She did not, however, have enough room to raise the kinds of animal proteins preferred by most Concordians in the form of cows and pigs. She had her hens, which supplied her with eggs and, less frequently, poultry meat. But for the most part, she seems to have lived on what whites considered "the poor man's meat," namely beans and peas, which thrive in sandy soil and can be dried and eaten throughout the year in the form of porridge. Walden Woods, Henry explains, was "bean country," a reputation it seems to have earned on account of the soil quality and the fact that it sheltered the town's most impoverished residents. As Henry well knew, beans are an excellent source of protein. But his predecessors and even his contemporaries regarded them as an inferior substitute for meat. Henry quotes one farmer in *Walden* who said to him, "You cannot live on vegetable food solely, for it furnishes nothing to make bones with." Henry mocks him by noting he is "walking all the while he talks behind his oxen, which, with vegetable-made bones, jerk him and his lumbering plough along in spite of every obstacle." But as one man explained of his childhood in the 1790s, most people made porridge by "boiling" in a cauldron over a fire in the fireplace "a piece of pork, with a handful of beans, till they became soft and smashed." In the mind of Henry's farmer and nearly everyone else, what separated the poor from the rich was how much meat they could add to that daily pot. Indeed, meat was so dear any barrels of it in a person's possession at the time of death were counted as part of the estate's inventory.[9]

Henry includes in *Walden* a story about Zilpah that, when read in light of one of his journal entries, indicates she had little to no precious meat in her simmering pot of beans. The "old frequenter" of Walden Woods Henry mentions in *Walden* who heard Zilpah muttering "Ye are all bones, bones!" over her pot was Henry's friend George Minot, upon whom Henry relied for tales of Concord's yesteryears. Henry notes in his journal that "Minott says he and Harry Hooper used to go to Howard's meadow (Heywood's, by the rr [railroad]) when it was flowed, killing fish by striking the ice above them and stunning them." The two men "gave some to Zilpha as they went by." Few Concord residents consumed local fish in those days. Henry's contemporary, the local historian Edward Jarvis, remembered that the fish were so small they "hardly supplied a meal a year to most families." But he acknowledged that "now and then" there was a "thriftless family" who "depended in great measure on the food the river offered them." George and Mary Minot were hardly thriftless but they were not very well to do, and their genteel poverty was perceived as a form of eccentricity if not laziness by those who were more ambitious. Ralph Waldo's son Edward W. Emerson recalled nostalgically of George that he "kept a cow and raised corn and 'crook-necks' in his little field," supplementing what he grew for himself and his sister Mary with "duck and partridges, horn-pout and pickerel." Most likely Zilpah did not have the bodily strength to strike the ice sufficiently hard to stun the fish below, so she made sure George and his companion heard her lamenting the lack of meat in her pot. Her tactic worked and, on that winter day at least, she received a portion of fish with which to supplement her pot of beans. In the early drafts of *Walden*, rather than noting her caginess, Henry turns this story into evidence that Zilpah was "witch-like." Here and in the final version of *Walden* he has her muttering over her pot like one of the witches in Macbeth, standing over a "boiling cauldron," adding nefarious ingredients to it, and singing incantations in order to produce apparitions. Such depictions of single African American and Native American women were not uncommon. Tuggie Bannocks of Rhode Island, apparently "as much negro as Indian," was also "reputed to be a witch" and was said to have a "full set of double teeth all the way round." It was further said that she could raise from the dead anyone who had ever slept at the old tavern she occupied. But by all appearances, Zilpah did not need to rely on witchcraft to put fish on her table. She relied instead on her not inconsiderable wits. [10]

Zilpah was a conventional Concord resident in only one regard: she was, according to her obituary, "a constant attendant on public worship." She was also, it seems, close to church authorities. When late in her life town officials began to require a last name after years of listing her in the town census as merely "Zilpah," she used the name "White." Insofar as no record of her ever marrying survives and she was always remembered as living alone, it seems likely she chose this name in order to honor or seek protection from John White, who was Concord's deacon from 1784 to 1830. But even Zilpah's Christian devotion may have been a case of her using her wits to acquire food. In 1814, when Zilpah was seventy-six years of age, the wealthier women of Concord formed the Concord Female Charitable Society with the intention of making donations that would help the poor "go regularly to meeting and to school." To that end, they donated to some of the former slaves and their children food and clothes. But while the former slaves at the Great Field were frequent recipients of the society's charity, none of the other Walden former slaves except Zilpah received donations other than when they were on their deathbeds. Zilpah was a regular recipient of tea and sugar, as well as clothing made out of factory spun cloth. Tea and sugar are not required staples but rather popular stimulants the wealthy white ladies of Concord deigned to give only to those men and women they felt were sufficiently proper that they would appreciate having them. Regular church attendance was their benchmark and Zilpah met it. The one direct acknowledgment the society's women may have made to Zilpah's slave past was supplying her with tobacco toward the end of her life. While tobacco was thought to have medicinal qualities for women weakened by poor health, slaves had embraced its use as a leisure activity, fashioning their own pipes out of clay. Zilpah's Christian devotions may have brought her a sense of higher purpose, but they also yielded her comforts on earth she had no other way of procuring than from the Concord Female Charitable Society. [11]

In every way, Zilpah White was a very unusual woman by Concord standards. Unlike so many former slave women, she shunned the de facto slavery of live-in domestic servitude and spun her way to an independent living. Supplementing her meager income from this pre-industrial skill with basket making and other Native American crafts and readily accepting whatever charity she could get, Zilpah was able to live on her own for over forty years, a feat matched by no other Concord woman of her day.

Like Zilpah, Brister Freeman was fiercely ambitious. He was determined to live independently rather than stay on with John Cuming or someone else as a live-in laborer. Former slaves like "Black Cato," as Joseph Lee's former slave Cato Lee was locally known, had all the responsibility of running a farm but, as Brister well knew, none of the privileges of ownership. In one incident recorded by Henry in his journal, a rabid dog showed up on the Lee estate in the middle of the night after wreaking havoc in town during the day. Joseph had stipulated in his will that Cato's room and board depended on his continued diligence and faithfulness and so when Cato "was waked up . . . by a noise among the pigs," he got out of bed, "took a club," and "went out to see what was the matter." Finding the dog in the pigpen, Cato "mauled him till he thought he was dead and then tossed him out." The next morning, concerned both about the estate and fearing recriminations from the dog's owner, Cato had to go out and check on the corpse. Strangely, the dog was no longer there. Later that day, while Cato was out chopping wood, that endless task that occupied both slave men and de facto slave men day in and day out, the dog "reared up at him once more." Having heard in the intervening hours that the dog was rabid, Cato attempted to run away but the dog chased him. After finally bashing the dog with a large stone and not wanting to again make the mistake of leaving the dog behind alive, Cato "cut off his head and threw both head and body into the river." Henry makes Cato into something of a hero for finally dispatching the rabid dog, reporting in his journal that Cato effected what no other Concord resident could. But he fails to consider that Cato never had the option of asking someone else to perform the tasks of tending the pigs, chopping the wood, or generally securing the farm. Cato had to do everything the owner would have otherwise done, in this instance at great risk to his personal safety, but with none of the financial rewards that made Joseph Lee a very wealthy man. [12]

Cato Lee never had a family and would most certainly have been abandoned by his former owner in the same fashion Cato Ingraham was had he insisted on having one. Remaining single and childless or at least separate from one's wife and children was simply one of the things Cato Lee, Cato Ingraham, Boston Potter, and so many other local slaves agreed to in order to secure room and board. In determining to live with Fenda and have a family with her, Brister Freeman jettisoned forever the possibility of working as a live-in laborer, although the last name he adopted in lieu of Cuming makes clear how much he would have hated such a situation anyway. Like Zilpah, he was thus faced with the challenge of raising or otherwise acquiring enough food to feed his wife and their three children.

Brister and Charlestown were particularly concerned with providing their families with what they, like the farmer Henry quotes in *Walden*, regarded as the necessity of animal protein. Every farmer in Concord geared his operation toward raising meat, using his pasture acreage to graze cattle, his meadow acreage to raise winter fodder in the form of hay, and part of his tillage acreage to grow corn with which to fatten hogs. With only one acre, Brister and Charlestown knew they would be unable to fodder cattle and thereby raise beef and so they determined to raise pigs, convincing Jacob Potter to build a corn crib for them as part of their land deal with him. Swine could conceivably be raised on a relatively small amount of land insofar as pigs were allowed until 1817 to forage throughout town during the warmer months under the direction of the town-appointed hog reeve, who made sure the roving animals did not damage local crops. Only in the fall was it necessary to drive the pigs home, pen them, and fodder them on table scraps and corn until they were slaughtered, generally sometime after Thanksgiving when it was cold enough the pork would not spoil before it was barreled. And yet for all their plans, the partners never succeeded in purchasing any pigs. As Nathaniel Hawthorne notes in his *American Notebook*, swine were available fifteen miles from Concord at the Brighton Cattle Market for those "small farmers, mechanics and others who think they can afford to 'keep a pig.'" It may be that Brister and Charlestown, like the farmers Nathaniel gently mocks, were overly ambitious. If they could afford the purchase price, they may not have been able to afford the scraps from their table or have been able to raise enough fodder. Ralph Waldo Emerson describes as "scanty" the corn grown on the marginal land that bordered the Great Field by the descendants of former slaves who lived there, none of whom owned swine either. Of course, as Henry notes in *Walden*, Indian corn "does not require the best" land, but corn is dependent on soil moisture, and the soil in Walden Woods, being sandy, does not retain water well. President Timothy Dwight of Yale certainly did not have Concord's former slaves in mind when he insisted of New England at the turn of the century that even a poor man "has usually a comfortable house, a little land, a cow, swine, poultry, a few sheep, and not infrequently a horse." Whatever "scanty" amounts of corn they were able to grow, Brister and Charlestown could not afford to give it to a pig; rather, they consumed it themselves. Indeed, corn was Concord's most popular crop because it could be ground into meal for "Injun" bread and parched over the fire and added to porridge as a protein supplement. This is what Henry means when he refers to the former slaves' "corn-parching" business. [13]

Living as they did in what was then America's beef country, the former slaves found a means of procuring meat from Concord's burgeoning slaughtering industry. Henry reports in *Walden* hearing from his townsmen that "Cato and Brister pulled wool." By quoting his source directly, Henry conveys several ideas at once. Pulling wool referred to a black man pulling his forelock in deference to passing white folks, a way of tipping an imaginary hat. And yet the former slaves may have only acted deferential as a means of covering their tracks or pulling the wool over local people's eyes, making it difficult to know precisely what they did and thought. But even as Henry is indulging his love of word play here, he also means simply that Cato and Brister pulled wool from sheep carcasses for the local slaughtering industry, which grew in Concord from one slaughterhouse in 1791 to eleven in 1801. Here was where the local farmers brought their cattle and to a lesser extent their swine and sheep to be killed, salted, and barreled for the winter. One of the larger and more successful local slaughterhouses was located within a mile of Walden Woods. Its owner, Peter Wheeler, did a brisk business butchering, packing, and shipping meat to the West Indies, in addition to making soap and candles with meat byproducts. He had to hire agents to purchase animals and drive them to the holding pens behind his house. He needed laborers to kill, butcher, and pack the meat in barrels and to run his smokehouse and soap house. And he needed farmers to transport the barreled meat to Boston and to bring back the copious amounts of salt in which the meat was packed. Both Peter Wheeler and

Brister Freeman had served under the command of Colonel John Buttrick in the march to Saratoga in 1777, Peter as sergeant and Brister as a private. Both men had watched General Burgoyne surrender. Now Peter gave Brister odd jobs at his slaughterhouse, including pulling wool from dead sheep. As one Social Circle member explained of the early nineteenth century, "the principal value of sheep was their wool, — mutton was worth only about two cents a pound." No pelt was allowed to go to waste, even if the animal perished or had to be killed before it could be properly shorn. The pay for pulling wool was low, as pulled wool was inferior to shorn wool obtained from live sheep, but it was labor for which Peter Wheeler would have paid Brister and Cato with meat, albeit the least choice bits.[14]

Henry comments in his journal on the fact that former slaves were often forced to make do with whatever animal parts they could get. His remarks were prompted by seeing Peter Hutchinson return home to the edge of the Great Field one day after several slaughtering jobs. With five children and a wife to feed, Peter worked long hours in the spring shearing sheep and in the late fall slaughtering and quartering pigs. On the day Henry spotted Peter, he was "carrying in the rain a piece of the pork he had slaughtered, with a string through it." While the loin, hams, and shoulders were widely considered the best parts of a pig, Peter received "the head, which is less prized, taking his pay thus in kind." The head and feet yield little meat and only with considerable effort, but, as Henry notes, "these supplies do not come amiss" to a family he describes as "outcast." Animal heads, offal, and even hooves added flavor to the porridge pot, as well as important nutrients. While it seems former slaves and their children were forced to take the least desirable work available, the one benefit from the point of view of the men who did this work was that pay came in the form of meat, even if only what wealthier families considered the least desirable parts of the animal.[15]

With life as tenuous as it was for the former slaves, Brister's wife, Fenda Freeman, sought to earn what money she could for their family. The means she settled upon were long remembered in Concord. All that locals recalled of her in later years was her appearance — according to Henry, Fenda was "large, round, and black" — and that she "told fortunes." Fortune-telling was a popular European folk tradition and women with few resources sought to capitalize on the demand. A widow in Kennebunk, Maine, was one of many single women who made her living telling fortunes. When one of her clients visited Boston in May 1791 to buy a gown and fabric for a new skirt, she recorded in her diary that she was so accustomed to having her fortune told at home that she visited one of the many fortune-tellers there as well. In many instances, former slave women became fortune-tellers, such as Jude, who lived on a tenement farm on Salem Neck in Massachusetts. For Jude and Fenda, telling fortunes was similar to weaving baskets and mats insofar as it required little to no capital to get started in business. And like Zilpah, Fenda seems to have been quite a savvy businesswoman. Henry reports that she told fortunes "pleasantly," seeming to imply that she told her customers what they wanted to hear so she could be sure of repeat business. It is possible, too, that Fenda, who seems to have been born in Africa, if her dark color and African name are any indication, drew on her experiences with the indigenous sub-Saharan African version of fortune-telling. She may have been accustomed to seeing divination practiced and would thus have known various methods of seeing into the future. Indeed, her skills in fortune-telling may have been more than simply a practical means of making money if she retained some of the beliefs of her childhood. It is also possible, given their own backgrounds, that Fenda's fellow former slaves consulted with her about the spirit world in a way similar to their ancestors. [16]

There is evidence in Concord that African beliefs remained an important part of the worldview of the town's former slaves. The fact that they settled so close together may simply be an indication of their enforced segregation from the rest of the town and of their close ties to one another, but perhaps it also indicates a preference for different settlement patterns than those characterizing Anglo-American practices. Concord's European settlers had fanned out across the Concord landscape as soon as they could, but in Walden Woods the former slaves clustered their houses together rather than living as far apart as their squatting arrangements might have otherwise allowed. Out of all of Duncan Ingraham's roadside property in Walden Woods, Cato may have purposefully chosen an acre to build on that was very near to Brister and Zilpah. In Plymouth, Massachusetts, where an enclave of former slaves from four families occupied ninety-four acres, the homes were also built very close to one another. This may have been simply for survival purposes, the idea being that with greater proximity the former slaves would be better able to assist one another. But anthropologists believe clustered building may have also been something the former Plymouth slaves recalled from their African youths. It is clear at any rate that they recalled their African pasts by building their new houses twelve feet by twelve feet rather than the standard Anglo-American bay size of sixteen by sixteen feet. If Zilpah's small house was also twelve feet by twelve feet, which would still have been close to the size of Henry's later cabin, which he compared in size to those of the former inhabitants, she too may have been influenced by African practices. Even the consumption of animal heads and feet may have been less a result of poverty and more of African cooking practices remembered and followed by Concord's former slaves. Without more evidence of the sort an archaeological dig at Walden Woods might provide, it is difficult to determine which decisions were the result of white enforcement and impoverishment and which of cultural preferences. Certainly assimilation was an important tool the former slaves were willing if not desirous to use, as evidenced by the English names they gave their children. But as indicated by Zilpah's decision to live alone in the woods with her family rather than as a live-in servant, the former slaves also seem to have been unwilling to assimilate to the exclusion of all of their other ties, whether to family or Africa or both.[17]

Casey, Samuel Whitney's former slave, left the most evidence of his ties to Africa in the form of comments he made to George Minot and in an artifact he left behind. George told Henry that "Casey used to weep in his latter days when he thought of his wife and two children in Africa from whom he was kidnapped." He "used to say" to George, according to what Henry wrote in his journal, that "he went home to Africa in the night and came back again in the morning." Henry took Casey's comment about going "home to Africa in the night" to mean that Casey "dreamed of home." But Casey was most likely holding on to the West African belief that the soul leaves the body during sleep and travels to wherever it desires. In his mind, he really did go "home to Africa in the night." In later years, former slaves along the Georgia coast made similar statements in interviews. One explained that "My daddy used to tell me all the time about folks who could fly back to Africa. They could take wing and just fly off." Another noted similarly that his "grandmother used to tell me about folks flying back to Africa." The interviewed former slaves were American-born and never had this ability to fly to Africa themselves. Only the African-born claimed to have this power. Casey also kept his African past alive by taking the last name of Feen or Feene (it was spelled variously in his military records), the diminutive form of Josephine, a Catholic name not uncommon among converted groups in West Africa. His white Concord townsmen never honored his desire to adopt what was most likely his wife's name as part of his own, referring to him for the rest of his life as simply Case or Casey and thereby continuing to address him in the same way they had under the regime of slavery. Casey still managed to keep his wife and homeland close to his heart by never remarrying and by flying to Africa each night to reunite with his family. [18]

At some point, perhaps toward the end of his life when his situation became tenuous enough that he was put on the town poor list, Casey turned again to his African past, fashioning a *nkisi* to ward off those people he regarded as a threat. A *nkisi*, often translated as "spirit," is a container or portable shrine into which a spirit of the dead has been metaphorically trapped along with medicine that the spirit is directed to use either for the user or against a designated victim. Along the Guinea Coast, *minkisi* (the plural form of *nkisi*) were typically anthropomorphic sculptures with hollowed-out abdominal cavities for the spirit and the medicine, but they could also be bags or boxes. Mirrors were often added as a means of signifying the power of entrapping the vital spark of the spirit. Typically the *nkisi* also had an element that linked it to its user or the user's victim, such as strips of clothing. Casey seems to have made a *nkisi* out of a small, wooden framed looking glass into which he tucked a piece of paper between the glass and the wooden backboard (Figure 9). The writing on the paper was copied from an eighteenth-century penmanship practice book and seems to comprise a section of Epistle 3 in Alexander Pope's *Moral Essays*, in which Pope writes that "Extremes in Nature equal good produce; / Extremes in man concur to general use" (lines 161 – 62). If he was like the other slaves of his generation, Casey was most likely illiterate or only semiliterate in English, and it is thus possible he stole the practice sheet during his slavery days in an effort to learn to read, feeling the need to hide what he had purloined. Certainly, it was not uncommon for people to use the space between the glass and the backboard as a place to hide documents. In Edgar Allan Poe's "The Purloined Letter" (1844), when the prefect of police searches on numerous occasions without success the apartment of a suspected robber for a stolen letter, the detective from whom he asks assistance says to him, "I presume you looked to the mirrors, between the boards and the plates." The prefect replies indignantly, "Of course." But Casey seems not to have been using the looking glass as a hiding place, nor

Figure 9. *Case Feen's looking glass (circa 1700–1800). The Concord Museum notes that this looking glass is "one of the only documented possessions of an eighteenth-century African-American" (David F. Wood, The Concord Museum, 117). The silver foliating has deteriorated, exposing the hidden piece of paper behind it. Concord Museum, Concord, Mass. www.concordmuseum.org. Photograph by David Bohl.*

the piece of paper as a wedge to tighten the glass, which people also did on occasion. Rather, he seems to have used the looking glass as a means of gaining the power over his life he felt he lacked. George Minot and his sister Mary, who came into possession of the looking glass, thus felt it was sufficiently unusual that it should be given to a local collector of antiquities, along with the words of a prayer Casey would utter when he looked into it. The collector was careful to record the prayer on the back board: "O Lord, I bless thee for another day / and do let the poor Niger / live a little longer." For all that Casey might appear to have adopted some of the Christian ways promulgated in Concord — along, apparently, with white Concord's derogatory attitude toward slaves and former slaves — his prayer that God should let even a "poor nigger" live longer was not imparted solely to the Christian's God. He was also asking the same question of a very different kind of spirit, one he had trapped in the looking glass and empowered with magic. In this regard, Casey was using the looking glass at least partially as a *nkisi*, a means to stop the original owner of the copybook exercise or perhaps just literate whites generally from hurting him in a way that he feared was shortening his life. It seems former slaves turned in times of need to their African pasts for everything from guidance on how to live (by clustering with others), how to make a living (by fortune-telling), and how to go on living (by making requests of the spirit world). This helps explain why Mary Minot was so afraid on that day when she had to carry a watermelon home from Lincoln through Walden Woods. The spirits she imagined there were from an African world that seemed wholly foreign to her own. [19]

Casey was not the only member of the former slave community who perceived himself to be in danger. The one portrait of Brister's character that survives, from Edward Jarvis, includes an account of Brister being "tormented and hooted" repeatedly after it was "said" that he had "stolen a haddock." In those days, a single haddock was large enough to make one or more meals for a large family and, as Edward recalls, "*fresh* fish from the sea" was such a rarity in Concord, it was "eaten with great eagerness" upon the farmers' return from the coast (his emphasis). Once a year, in August, a group of a dozen or more of Concord's farmers went on a fishing trip to the Dorchester section of Boston Harbor in celebration of completing the haying in the Great Meadows. Whether or not Brister did steal such a large fish after the annual trip, it was widely understood in Concord that the fact of his owning such a small amount of land, and infertile land at that, might well have given him cause. A social outcast relegated with his kind to the margins of town, Brister was an easy target for someone looking to recoup the loss of a fish, real or imagined. Brister did not, however, take the abuse lying down. Edward reports that when attacked "he would swear and storm." Perhaps other former slaves though it best to respond to such harassment meekly. Brister's seemingly unusual response resulted in "boys and men" gathering about to witness the show. This only "insulted and violated him to greater passion." Edward was left to conclude that "Brister Freeman was a passionate negro, profane and suspicious." But as much as Edward reveals the lack of respect with which Brister had to contend and that not surprisingly made him "suspicious," he also reveals that Brister was a very proud man. While Casey seems to have called himself a "nigger," Brister was unwilling to accept the view of himself shared by his male townsmen. [20]

Cato Ingraham was also less bold than Brister, staying on with his master for the room and board a full decade after Brister's land purchase, even as that meant compromising his needs. Cato was also much slower to accept the fact that he had been abandoned and not emancipated. Within the first year of coming to Walden, Cato and his family began to feel the pinch of poverty, and Cato traveled to Medford to beg Duncan to come to Concord and bring him and his family supplies. He informed his former owner that he was "out of meal, meat, and wood" and could "stand it no longer." But Duncan refused to give Cato anything, reminding his former slave of their agreement. Cato could marry so long as he no longer "depend[ed] . . . upon him for support." Hungry, cold, and frantic to feed his children, Cato refused to believe his pleas would go ignored: "I don't want to hear any more about that; I tell you I am out of everything." [21]

Cato was out of wood despite having moved to the middle of a two-thousand-acre forest. Walden Woods was divided into privately owned woodlots, and Duncan Ingraham had not given Cato leave to cut the trees on his land beyond the acre on which Cato was squatting. Cutting someone else's wood was stealing, and which wood belonged to whom was always abundantly clear. Henry writes in his journal that he was very much "aware" when walking in Walden Woods that, as he puts it, "I am at a given moment passing from such a one's wood-lot to such another's." Then, too, each woodlot owner knew exactly what was on his lot such that he was easily made aware if he had been robbed of wood. George Minot, Henry writes in his journal, "knows the history of every stump" on his

woodlot and even "how many beech trees and black birches there are." On the occasions when wood was mysteriously missing, it was sometimes possible to tell
who the thief was by reading the trees or stumps for signs of the method of removal. Often as not, the thief never even got that far. Henry notes in his journal
that "some farmers load their wood with gunpowder to punish thieves."[22]

Caesar Robbins fared better than Cato in this regard. He received the tacit
permission or, as his benefactor's memoirist puts it, "the implied consent" of
Humphrey Barrett to take wood from one of the Barretts' lots near Caesar's
house on the edge of the Great Field. The arrangement meant that Humphrey's
woodlot was prudently managed while helping to keep Caesar off the town's
poor list, but it also left Caesar vulnerable to Humphrey's every whim.
Humphrey's Social Circle memoirist tells a story about Humphrey deciding
one day to "get his wood from the lot by Caesar's." He sent two men who
worked for him with teams of horses "to cut only hard wood." As it took long
to grow, most people used hardwood only sparingly, saving it for their building
needs. For fuel, they used faster growing woods and coppice growth. By carefully paying attention to what wood they harvested and how, a family might
never run out of wood. George Minot told Henry that "his and his sister's
wood-lot together contains about ten acres and has, with a very slight exception
at one time, supplied all their fuel for thirty years, and he thinks would constantly continue to do so," even as "they keep one fire all the time, and two some
of the time." But land cleared without thought or overcut could, as Henry notes,
remain bare for fifteen or twenty years. And so upon seeing the men cut more
of the hardwood than he thought prudent, Caesar rushed to the Barrett mansion, "his face covered with perspiration and in great agitation." He proceeded
to tell Humphrey what he had witnessed: "Master Barrett, I have come to let
you know that a parcel of men and teams have broke into our woodlot, and are
making terrible destruction of the very best trees, and unless we do something
immediately I shall be ruined." The memoirist tells the story to highlight
Humphrey's benevolence, concluding the episode with an account of how
Humphrey "had no heart to resist this appeal," particularly one made with such
a great display of deference, if it is true that Caesar called Humphrey "master."
Humphrey sent a note by Caesar to the men telling them "to cut no more wood,
but come directly home with their teams." Of course by then Caesar's careful
management of the woodlot was most likely sorely compromised. Without

such an arrangement, however unsatisfactory for the recipient, Cato Ingraham and other former slaves in his situation, no doubt Brister among them, were left to procure wood in the form of payment for labor or to otherwise scavenge for it, often by the riverside where driftwood collected, or by asking permission to take out stumps or gather wood chips.[23]

Cato Ingraham seems to have wasted a growing season before casting about for ways he could take care of his family himself. But once he put his mind to the task at hand, he devised a creative means of providing his family with much-needed protein while making arrangements for their future. According to what Henry heard, Cato planted a portion of his acre with walnut trees, which after five or so years should have yielded him a good crop of richly flavored and protein-packed nuts. Henry knew a squirrel hunter who harvested walnuts from a local walnut tree that bore "one bushel and three pecks" of shelled nuts in a given season, enough, Henry reports, to supply "him and his family for the winter." Walnut trees are also an excellent long-term investment. They take thirty years to fully mature, but when they do the result is one of the finest woods in the world. Walnut does not shrink and swell as much as other woods, making it extremely valuable to gun and furniture makers, who would have been eager to purchase the finely grained boards that resulted when trees are forced to grow more slowly on the kind of fast-draining, sandy soil that exists in Walden Woods.[24]

Like Zilpah, Cato and his family were also the recipients of the kind of charity that had strings very much attached. Two years after Duncan Ingraham married and moved to Medford, he sold his Walden land to John Richardson, also of Medford, including the land south of Brister's on a sliver of which Cato had been squatting, as well as the eleven acres across the road that would later become part of Ralph Waldo Emerson's woodlot and the spot where Henry would squat forty years later. At the time of the sale, arrangements were made so that Cato could afford to stay on the property. Town officials were concerned Cato and his remaining family might otherwise be evicted by John Richardson and thereafter end up on the town's poor list, a drain on Concord's coffers. The selectmen convinced John to sign a rental agreement whereby Cato, described in the agreement as "a blackman of said Concord," would rent one-half of the tiny house he already occupied and the one acre surrounding it for a mere six cents per year. Selectman Ephraim Wood served as the official witness to the deed. The amount Ephraim induced John to charge was a trifling amount from the property owner's point of view. But John was so wealthy he would not feel the loss of a more profitable arrangement. An enterprising man with cash at his disposal, he would soon own and operate Concord's Middlesex Hotel and eventually as many as twenty hotels in Massachusetts. It seems the rental agreement was a means not of providing John with an income but of keeping Cato from becoming homeless at a point when the town could no longer ask Duncan for assistance. One effect, however, of such a low rental fee was that Cato would be all the more inclined to stay put on Concord's geographic, economic, and social margins. Another effect was that Cato's wife and children would have to leave town after his death if the Emerson-Bliss family was not willing to take Phyllis back. The agreement was binding only for the rest of Cato's "natural life and no longer." It seems Concord was willing to take care of its former slaves but not past the first generation. Cato's signature on the lease is the only mark of his hand that has survived, his testament to the necessity of capitulating to town authorities whose benevolence was hard to distinguish from their attempts to control him. [25]

Similar, although less formal means, were used to house Casey, who had rejected the diminutive form of his name when he enlisted in the army for a three-year term as Case Feen on March 1, 1781. Discharged early on account of being unfit for service, he was back in Concord by January 1782, forced to return, like Brister, to the only town where he could not be warned out, but perhaps eager to put his intimate knowledge of Concord's terrain to use for his own support. The 1790 census places him on property adjacent to George and Mary Minot's father, Ephraim Minot, who was married to one of the daughters of Dr. Abel Prescott, the owner of a large piece of land along Lexington Road, including the land on which his son-in-law lived. Seven years earlier, George had been born in a small house in back of the one where he and his family lived by 1790. When George and his family moved into the larger saltbox house in front of the small house where George was born, Case took up residence behind them. He was back on land that had belonged to the Whitneys until the Battle of Bunker Hill convinced them to abandon both the Patriot cause and Case and flee Concord for Boston. This and Cato Ingraham's arrangement indicate that former slaves were allowed, if not directed, to live on their former owners' property, even if the property had changed hands, as a means of keeping them off the poor list. Case's house and the Minots' new house became connected at one point by a wooden frame until Dr. Abel Prescott moved the frame connecting the two structures and enclosed it at the location where George and Mary spent the rest of their lives. By then, Case's geographical closeness to George had resulted in a degree of friendliness and Case told George about his early years in Africa and his means of escaping enslavement to the Whitneys. This closeness also explains why George and Mary later came into the possession of Case's *nkisi*.[26]

Case ended up on Concord's poor list all the same. Neither pulling wool, spinning, telling fortunes, and bottoming chairs nor making baskets, mats, and brooms could pull the former slaves out of poverty. If Zilpah's life was "inhumane" and Case's destitute, that was because no one paid very much for spinning, baskets, mats, or pulling wool. While Brister's bequest from John Cuming sat in the town coffers, the only reparations he or Concord's other former slaves received for slavery were odd jobs with low pay, the occasional packet of tea and sugar, and permission to live on the town's most marginal land or well in back of its more prosperous houses. In the face of these obstacles, the former slaves drew on each other for strength as well as on their shared African past. The community they built together in Walden Woods managed to survive for four decades, and yet the former slaves living there ultimately failed to plant a next generation. At the end of his chapter in *Walden* on the former inhabitants who preceded him in Walden Woods, Henry David Thoreau wonders about this: "This small village, germ of something more, why did it fail while Concord keeps its ground?"[27]

CHAPTER SEVEN

Concord Keeps Its Ground

THE SLAVES WHO REMAINED WITH THEIR OWNERS after the Revolution began to pass away. Boston Potter's wife, Cate, who stayed on with the Bliss-Emerson family, died in 1785 at the age of fifty. Four years later, Susanna Barron's slave Violet died at the age of eighty. Rose, the slave of John Cuming's Harvard classmate Dr. Timothy Minot, died from burns in 1800 at the age of seventy-four. Boston Potter died in his eighties in 1809, having managed to outlive his master. With their passing, Brister Freeman became increasingly noticeable as a departure from the general rule. Not only was he a former slave living in a household of his own, he owned his house and land. Indeed, for several years after his land purchase in 1785, Brister was the only black man to own land in Concord, for by then John Jack had been dead for twelve years. Thomas Dugan was the third former slave to own land in Concord, making the last payment on his property in 1788, but he had not been enslaved locally and was not upending Concord's rigid social hierarchy in quite the same way. So, until 1823, when Peter Robbins purchased the land on the edge of the Great Field where his father had squatted, Brister was the only one of Concord's former slaves to own the land he lived on. He would soon find that his position made him a target of unwanted attention.

Either Brister had not been able or perhaps he had simply refused to pay his poll tax once he became a landowner and began to be assessed. His debt to the town accumulated over the years until he owed seven pounds and nineteen shillings. At that point, the selectmen decided to use Brister's legacy from John Cuming to pay his back taxes and in the process strip him of legal ownership of his property as well. Land ownership entitled a man to have his say at town meetings, and Concord's selectmen were determined that the town's former slaves would not use this route to become part of the town's civic life. They made their move in late 1790. Under the threat of debtors prison, the selectmen were able to force Brister to sell them the half of the house and land he shared with Charlestown Edes. Brister signed a deed on January 17, 1791, stating that he, "Brister Freeman of Concord," was selling "one half of the house and land that I now live in and upon" in Walden Woods to "Ephraim Woods Esq., Jacob Brown and Asa Brooks, gentlemen and selectmen of Concord and trustees of the legacy given me in the last will of John Cuming Esq late of Concord." The deed stipulated that the selectmen were to pay Brister seven pounds and nineteen shillings, the same amount he owed the town. Presumably, then, the selectmen were not intending to give Brister the money but instead use it to pay off his back taxes. The back taxes, however, proved not to be their primary concern. If that had been the case, they would have taken part of Brister's legacy from John and used it to pay the taxes, leaving Brister his property. Nor were the selectmen interested in actually taking possession of half of the acre of "old field." If that had been the case, they would have seized Brister's property, forced him to vacate it, sold the property, and used the proceeds of the sale to pay the taxes he owed. The fact that they purchased Brister's property with his own money and never asked him to leave indicates that their only goal was to prevent him from legally owning land in town. They did not care that Brister lived out the remaining years of his life in Walden Woods. In fact, they preferred that he have a place to squat so that he did not end up on the town's poor list. Years later, after Henry David Thoreau's refusal in 1846 to pay his own poll tax in protest against what he regarded as the Mexican-American War's extension of slavery, he commented on the town's treatment of Brister when he was surveying a lot in Walden Woods in 1857, trying to show how it appeared in 1797 when Duncan Ingraham owned the land purchased that year by John Richardson. He notes on his drawing that the "Brister Lot" had become "the state's because the owner, Brister, was a foreigner." Having learned about what he seems to have regarded as the selectmen's immoral actions, Henry puts those actions in precise terms: they felt they were entitled to confiscate Brister's land on the grounds that he was not an American citizen, while their actions ensured he would never become one.[1]

The selectmen did not similarly harass Brister's partner Charlestown Edes. Like Thomas Dugan, Charlestown had not been a slave in Concord and in both cases that seems to have made their presence as landowners less of an affront. They were not upsetting what had long been the local status quo in quite the same way. Then, too, Charlestown was in poor health and the selectmen rightly suspected that he would not be long for this world. After five lean years in Walden Woods, Charlestown had developed liver spots on his skin, spongy gums, and nosebleeds. Eventually he lost his teeth, became partly immobilized, and suffered from open, suppurating wounds. Brister and Fenda took him into their side of the house so they could care for him but Charlestown failed to rally. Neither he nor the Freemans could get their hands on the means of what would have been a simple and effective cure. Charlestown had scurvy, which as one physician rightly notes in a book published in 1734, "is solely owing to a total abstinence from fresh vegetable food, and greens." A poor man, Charlestown lacked access to the lemons, limes, and oranges that would have quickly returned him to good health. But his diet must have also lacked tomatoes, strawberries, and carrots, among other fruits and vegetables rich in vitamin C. All of these grew readily in Concord's climate provided one could somehow procure the seeds and the land to grow them. Without land, one had to have the cash or labor to exchange for someone else's produce, know someone compassionate enough to share the fruits of their own garden, or be desperate enough to steal. Brister had planted apple trees on the sloped section of his property, where the trees did very well, surviving long enough to furnish Henry with their fruit during his Walden sojourn. But even if Brister's trees were producing by the time Charlestown began to fail, the amount of vitamin C in apples, let alone cider, which is how most Concordians consumed apples, is not sufficient to cure someone in the advanced stages of scurvy. If Mary Minot feared Walden's ghosts wanted her watermelon, perhaps that was because it was widely known that Walden's former slave residents had suffered vitamin deficiencies that made them particularly eager to procure what fruit they could. Charlestown became one of those ghosts when he was in his thirties. He died of malnutrition at the height of the local vegetable season on August 6, 1791. Brister and Fenda had already lost their son Edward to a fever in the fall of 1788 when he was seven years old. Now they lost their business partner as well.[2]

Brister was well aware that the selectmen had subtly worded the 1791 land deed that legally stripped him of his property in a way that implied he did not actually own his land to begin with. It stated that Brister was selling "half of the house and land that I now live in and upon," not the house and land he owned. He attempted to counter the selectmen on this point, appearing in Middlesex County Court in February 1792 with a deed stating that he and Charlestown had bought the acre of "old field" on Stratton's Hill from Jacob Potter on December 23, 1785. His appearance at the courthouse indicates he was reasserting his right to his land, undoubtedly feeling that the deed he signed for the selectmen should be considered null and void on account of his not having received any money from them. Jacob Potter, however, did not bother to appear in court to sign his deed until 1797, when Duncan Ingraham was in the process of selling his Concord land to John Richardson and needed Jacob to verify the proper bounds. Like so many white Concord residents, Jacob felt compelled to answer only to the richest and most powerful residents. Interestingly, the deed between Duncan and John described the forty-two acres John was purchasing as bounded by "land in the possession of Brister Freeman, a black man." Brister continued to live on and act as if he still possessed his Walden acre, and nearby property owners respected his claim to be there in at least some capacity. Indeed, after a time, Stratton's Hill came to be called Brister's Hill, the name that has stuck to this day. The use of the possessive, however, had nothing to do with legal ownership and everything to do with naming features in the landscape according to the people most closely associated with them. At the Great Field, the woodlot Humphrey Barrett allowed Caesar Robbins to use became known as Caesar's Woods, even though Caesar never owned it. The lack of last names in these and other local instances served to make clear that a former slave was being referenced. Such names were Concord's equivalent of what in other towns was called New Guinea: a way of designating black portions of town. [3]

The house to which Brister clung in the midst of his legal struggles began to grow somewhat crowded. His two surviving children married and had children of their own, although not at anywhere near the rate that characterized more well-to-do families in Concord. In 1791, daughter Nancy married Jacob Freeman of Lincoln and had a son by him that year as well as a daughter seven years later. Brister's son Amos married Love Oliver in 1809, connecting the Freeman family with the Oliver-Robbins family at the Great Fields, and the following year the couple had a son. Neither of the Freeman children was able to establish an independent household and both continued to live with Brister and Fenda. [4]

Cato's children fared even less well. When Duncan refused to supply Cato with food after his initial supply ran out, Cato and his wife were left to watch their baby daughter suffer the ravages of canker or *cancrum oris* (now called noma), a gangrenous disease that eats away the tissue and bone of the victim's face within a matter of days. Many children with canker already have another disease, such as measles or scarlet fever. But malnutrition was and remains the main risk factor in children under the age of five. Cato and Phyllis's daughter succumbed eighteen months after the family arrived in Walden Woods. Her parents had risked everything to be together, giving up the comfort and protection Duncan had provided in what he regarded as a fair exchange for the services he exacted from Cato. Now the baby who had propelled Cato to take his freedom was gone. Nor did the walnut trees Cato planted for the protein of their nuts buy the rest of the family a long future. In the spring of 1805, Phyllis succumbed at the age of thirty-seven to what the doctor described as bilious cholera. There was no local cholera epidemic at that time, making it unlikely she had true cholera as a result of ingesting contaminated food or water. She probably had a virus or bacterial infection that caused acute gastroenteritis, to which malnourished people are particularly susceptible, and which caused her body to shrivel in the same way cholera does. After a short period of severe vomiting and diarrhea, Phyllis died of dehydration. The Concord doctor's diagnosis of cholera was no doubt as much an assessment of Phyllis's living conditions as anything else. Cholera breaks out in places with unsanitary, crowded living conditions. In a letter to one of his daughters describing what he saw of the cholera epidemic in New York in 1832, civic leader John Pintard concludes that the disease was "almost exclusively confined to the lower classes of intemperate dissolute and filthy people huddled together like swine in their polluted habitations." As late as 1866, the *New York Times* was still asserting that "Cholera is . . . the curse of the dirty, the intemperate, and the degraded." The one room the Ingraham family had to live in may have been spotless but insofar as most Concord residents no longer lived in such crowded conditions, the middling and upper sorts, which included the town's record keepers, tended to look with dismay at those who worked, ate, and slept all in the same place.[5]

Cato was unwell himself at the time of his wife's death. He had tuberculosis, then called consumption because its victims seem to waste away or be consumed by the disease. Tuberculosis also causes bloody coughs and fever. It was the leading cause of death in Concord in the first half of the nineteenth century. The Reverend William Emerson's son Billy died consumptive in 1811 at the age of forty-two, leaving his young children, Ralph Waldo Emerson among them, fatherless. Ralph Waldo later lost two of his brothers and his first wife to the disease. Henry David Thoreau died in 1862 at the age of forty-four after several bouts with tuberculosis and prolonged exposure to pencil dust at his father's factory left his lungs severely compromised. Tuberculosis was not understood to be an infectious disease until the 1880s and so family members would often infect one another unknowingly. But not everyone who contracted tuberculosis developed symptoms. Only half of those with a latent infection progressed to the active stage, and those who sickened and died were often those people with a compromised immune system. With such a small amount of land on which to grow food, Cato may have been suffering like Charlestown Edes from malnutrition. Whatever the case, he was not able to withstand his infection. Cato Ingraham died in the summer of 1805, ten years after arriving in Walden Woods. His daughter Nancy died three months later at sixteen years of age, having contracted the infection from her father while caring for him. With her passing, the entire Ingraham family was gone, wiped out over the short span of eight months. Henry knew enough of their story that he was moved to note of Cato's walnut trees that "a younger and whiter speculator got them at last." He was referring to John Richardson, who as the owner of the land Cato rented, came into possession of the valuable trees Cato had planted as an investment in a future that never arrived for him or his family.[6]

Five years after the demise of the Ingraham family, the Freemans also suffered the loss of several family members in rapid succession. First, in July 1810, Brister's three-month-old grandson by his son, Amos, died. That November, Brister's nineteen-year-old grandson by his daughter, Nancy, also died, a victim like Cato of consumption. Then, on February 28, 1811, after living in Walden Woods for more than twenty-six years, Fenda died of what the local doctor called "dropsy." The sudden collapse of her family indicates that Fenda may have been suffering from what is now called nutritional or famine edema, which results from a lack of protein over an extended period of time. She was sixty years old. After Fenda's death, the Freemans' daughter and her husband left town. They had lost both of their children and had no hope of better prospects in Concord. Amos soon followed. After their departure, Brister was left with his daughter-in-law, Love, a grandson born to Love in 1814, and across the road, Zilpah. If, as Henry writes in *Walden*, the road through Walden Woods once "resounded with the laugh and gossip of inhabitants," it was now far more quiet.[7]

The community at the Great Field was larger and flourished much longer, enjoying more and better land on which to raise food. Caesar Robbins's agreement with Humphrey Barrett included thirteen acres of land his son Peter eventually purchased from Humphrey. Caesar's farming operations had been extensive enough that he had been able to build a barn where he and later the two Peters, Robbins and Hutchinson, could store corn, other produce, and perhaps even some livestock. And while Ralph Waldo Emerson called the corn he saw growing there "scanty," the Robbins, Garrison, and Hutchinson families had enough food that they did not seem to feel it necessary, as the Freemans might have, to practice any means of limiting their fertility. The families at the Great Field were the same size or larger than the average white family in Concord of five children. After their marriage in 1779, Caesar and Catherine Robbins had at least three children, including son Peter. Jack and Susan Garrison, who lived in the other side of the Robbinses' two-room house, had eight children over a fourteen-year period beginning in 1813. Beginning in 1831, after Caesar died, son Peter Robbins fathered six children, whom he raised in what had been his father's side of the house. Jack and Susan's son John and his wife, also Susan, had at least three children, beginning in 1840. Peter Hutchinson, who in 1852 purchased the so-called Robbins place, raised five daughters there. In all, between 1779 and Peter Hutchinson's final sale of the Robbins place in 1870 or so, a total of at least twenty children were born on the border of the Great Field.[8]

The experience of Thomas Dugan makes the case that family size was closely linked to land access. By the time this father of eight children died in 1827, he and his family were doing well enough that they owned two lamps and a looking glass. On the other hand, they had only one bed, having invested instead in agricultural equipment, including a hay fork, scythes, sickles, a flail, other equipment for harvesting and processing hay and rye, two steel traps, a gun, and two cider barrels, as well as various cooking implements. They also had a cow and the equipment for collecting its milk. According to Henry, on one hot day, two of the Dugan children invited a passerby to step into their mother's springhouse, a small building built over a spring on the Dugan property as a place to keep food cold. While the portion of Henry's journal where the passerby is identified is torn away, most likely it was George Minot. Henry records George's disgust that a leopard frog was "swimming in the milk, and another sitting on the edge of the pan." But as unappetizing as the sight may have been for George, the fact that the Dugans had the land to pasture a cow must have had a lot to do with Thomas's ability to bring up a large number of children. In contrast, only three children were born in Walden Woods, where Cato Ingraham and Brister Freeman had only one sandy acre apiece. Either the Freemans and the Ingrahams practiced family limitation on account of their small supply of food, or their age and lack of nutrition naturally limited their fertility. Whatever the case, the Walden community failed to produce large families. [9]

But even if the families of former slaves and their descendants at the edge of the Great Field were initially as large as most white Concord families, they were like the Walden former slaves in that they ultimately failed to settle a new generation. Of the twenty children born at the edge of the Great Field, Caesar Robbins's son Peter and Jack Garrison's son John were the only ones who spent their lives in town. One perennial problem that plagued both communities was a high mortality rate compared to Concord's generally. For most people, Concord was a very healthy place to live. While the overall mortality rate in Concord from 1779 to 1853 ranged from thirteen to almost nineteen per thousand residents, the overall mortality rate for the American colonies averaged twenty-one per thousand or 2 percent. At the edge of the Great Field, however, Caesar Robbins and Jack Garrison suffered a 33 percent and 50 percent mortality rate respectively among their children, while Jack's son John and Peter Hutchinson suffered a 100 percent mortality rate among theirs. The difference between whites and blacks in Concord was poverty and isolation. In 1819, one of Jack and Susan Garrison's sons died at five months of rickets. Breast milk is lacking in the vitamin D necessary to grow strong bones and thus after the first few months of life a baby's diet needs to be supplemented. The results are otherwise disastrous. Two years later, in 1821, the Garrisons lost a three-year-old son; five years after that their son Lewis died at eighteen months; and the following fall, they lost a six-month-old son. In the latter two instances, the cause was said to be dysentery. Jack and Susan's son John experienced similar losses. He and his wife, Susan, lost three young children: a two-year-old to scarlet fever in 1842 (the same year Ralph Waldo Emerson's son Waldo died of the disease), a two-year-old in 1843, and a one-month-old in 1845. Peter Robbins lost his daughter Ann Maria at age eleven, but otherwise saw all his daughters live until they were old enough to move away, while Peter and Nancy Hutchinson lost their first child in her infancy and their five other children between the ages of eighteen and thirty-four. [10]

Another ongoing problem in establishing families was a lack of marriage prospects for those descendants of the former slaves who lived to adulthood. In the Garrison family, of the seven children born to Jack and Susan, only son John married and settled in Concord. In the Hutchinson family, only one of Peter and Nancy's six children married. The rest died in Concord single. Neither Elsea nor Elisha Dugan ever married either, while none of Peter Robbins's daughters were able to find husbands locally, and they ended up leaving Concord. One moved to Providence, Rhode Island, in order to work as a dressmaker. Two others ended up in Boston's notorious North End by their late teens. One of the largest black neighborhoods in Boston, the North End was where black laborers and seamen drank gin, smoked, gambled, socialized, and engaged the services of prostitutes in taverns and barrooms. In the Social Circle memoir of Samuel Staples, who held the post of local tax collector, among other positions, and who jailed Henry David Thoreau when he refused to pay his poll tax, his memoirist recalls that after being chosen representative to the state legislature in 1847, Sam reluctantly joined a group of politicians on a tour of the North End slums. Sam was greatly embarrassed when what the memoirist describes as two "black wenches" gave him a warm greeting: "Hullo, Sam! When did you come down here?" The memoirist recounts that Sam "tried to escape," but the two women "insisted" on treating the party to drinks at the tavern where or near which they worked for what they called "old acquaintance' sake." Charlotte and Adaline Robbins, Peter's two eldest daughters, were but fifteen and fourteen at the start of Sam's term and working in a city tavern where their virtue was easily doubted. Their use of Sam's first name is an indication they may have been trolling for clients from the men who passed by. Of course it is just as likely, if not more so, that Sam Staples's memoirist is depicting them in a racist manner. The Concord representative's fellow politicians teased Sam that he must have made several visits to these women before, implying that they provided sexual services. Sam tried to explain that "these wenches" were the "daughters of old Peter Robbins, who raised a large family of girls on the 'Peter's pasture' next 'Caesar's woods,' in Concord" and that they had "drifted," as he put it, into the slums of Boston. But this "didn't quite satisfy his brother members" even though Sam's memoirist would have included the tale only if he was confident of Sam's moral rectitude, just as he was certain that young black women in the North End must be whores. Whether eager to spare others such a fate or on account of wanting to rid the town of other young black women or both, the Female Charitable Society outfitted some of the daughters of former slaves for domestic service out of town, including Jack Garrison's daughter Ellen. [11]

But while the members of the Robbins and Garrison families felt compelled to leave town, they never had to endure the more direct form of abuse that Brister Freeman did. Toward the end of his life, some of his white townsmen, then suffering the woes of a shrinking local economy, decided to make him pay and pay dearly for his attempt to claim a piece of what was fast becoming a smaller Concord pie. What had been a robust American economy began to contract as the Napoleonic Wars between England and France heated up and the United States was pulled into the fray. When the British began to capture and impress American merchantmen and sailors, the American government countered with trade embargoes and blockades. Soon the War of 1812 was in full swing and local export businesses lost their foreign markets. Peter Wheeler felt the full impact of the embargoes on his slaughtering business, and Brister, who "pulled wool" for Peter, found himself an easy target for Peter's anger and frustration. [12]

Peter's early success in the slaughtering business had given him every confidence he would live up to the hopes and dreams of a father who had secured a proud place for himself in Concord lore. Timothy Wheeler had made his fortune as a miller and farmer and was famous locally for managing to protect important provincial stashes on the morning of April 19, 1775. When a British officer entered his barn looking for military stores and regarded with suspicion the many barrels there, Pond Tim, as Captain Wheeler was called on account of his profession, made light of the situation, "I am a miller, Sir. Yonder stands my mill. I get my living by it." He then calmly proceeded to explain the large number of barrels: "In the winter I grind a great deal of grain, and get it ready for market in the spring." The officer had to admit he was not permitted to "injure private property" and thus unknowingly left behind the large store of provincial flour Timothy was secreting for the Patriots. Shortly after the war, when his son Peter married Phoebe Brooks of Lincoln, Timothy was able to build the couple a huge, two-and-a-half-story house next door to his own. While the Cuming mansion, as it was still termed as late as 1800, is two rooms over two, the house Timothy built for his son is, like the Manse, four rooms over four.[13]

After the trade embargoes were enacted and Peter found himself in debt, he was determined to uphold the Wheeler family's good reputation. According to his Social Circle memoirist, Peter put a duct through the side of his house so that court officers could drop their writs directly inside without any of Peter's visitors being the wiser. And he bragged lustily around town when two local lawyers who had found it profitable for a time to buy up promissory notes from Peter's creditors at a discount gave up on account of the notes having grown too large for them to afford. In Peter's mind, better to have once been a successful landowner and businessman than to have never amounted to anything to begin with. Unfortunately, Peter's defiance failed to keep him out of jail. He was imprisoned not far from his house in Concord's new jail until he swore before the magistrate that he would satisfy his creditors by selling all of his property, saving his house and yard. He sold his homestead farm, another local farm he owned, and all of his land in the Great Meadows on April 2, 1810. In all, he parted with three hundred acres, but the proceeds were still not enough to settle all of his debts, which would total over six thousand dollars by 1813. According to his memoirist, Peter comforted himself with the view that "everything was foreordained as to the concerns of men, some being born to grow rich and prosper, while others were to struggle in vain against poverty." By holding to such views, Peter seemed to maintain his "cheerful spirits." But his trials only grew worse in the fall of 1811 when his eldest son and namesake died at sea en route to Boston from Russia. Peter's memoirist kindly names the cause of death "fever," but locals attributed his son's death to "sin," namely syphilis. No matter how much Peter continued to joke and otherwise make light of what by then was a complete reversal of fortune, there was ample evidence he was enraged at having fallen so far from his father's excellent reputation. He directed his ire in at least one instance at a person who he viewed as partially to blame for his troubles: Brister Freeman.[14]

After Fenda's death, Brister had been in need of a new wife to oversee his domestic affairs. Most men remarried quickly and more than once if necessary. Local white man Nathaniel Munroe, for one, married three times, first in 1803, then in 1807, and again in 1826. For those people fortunate enough to see old age — Nathaniel was eighty-four when he died in 1861 — several marriages were not unheard of. Indeed, as the Social Circle memoirist for John Richardson notes of John's mere two marriages, "the usual allowance" in his day was three wives. Brister could have decided it was enough to be looked after by his daughter-in-law Love. She lived in the other half of the small Freeman house and no doubt could have taken on the job of caring for her husband's father. But Brister did exactly what his white townsmen did: he entered into a relationship not long after his wife died with a widow who lived nearby. That he did so is remarkable only insofar as the widow was a white woman. [15]

Rachel Le Grosse was born in Boston to Estes and Rachel How in 1754. By the time she married Francis Le Grosse, a French immigrant from the island of Jersey, she had already been widowed twice. She had a daughter from the first marriage and a son and daughter from her second. When Rachel married Francis in 1804, he was a forty-year-old widower with four children himself. From then until Francis's death five years later, Rachel and her husband lived less than a quarter of a mile from Brister's house. Francis rented a small piece of land with a house and barn on the very edge of Walden Woods, where it came nearest to the town center. Henry David Thoreau marks its location in *Walden*, noting that "Nutting and Le Grosse" lived where he saw a "well and lilac bushes . . . in the now open field." [16]

As Henry takes pains to explain in his book, Walden Woods was not exclusively the home of former slaves. Rather, the former slaves clustered together within a larger enclave of other poor inhabitants who in two cases were outcasts on account of being alcoholics in addition to being impoverished. Barber John Breed also lived closer to town than the Freemans in an equally tiny house. And on the other side of the enclave of former slaves, closer to the Lincoln side, lived John Wyman, a potter who squatted on land owned by Dr. Abel Prescott near the pond, from whose sides the potter dug the clay out of which he fashioned pots and pans for cooking, dishes for the table, jars for preserves or butter, chamber pots, and other items popularly made out of earthenware. Neither barbering nor manufacturing earthenware paid particularly well. John Breed was said to charge as little as six cents for a haircut when he was desperate to buy a drink. In some years, he was so impoverished that his wife's only clothes were those donated to her by more well-to-do Concord women. Earthenware was considered of such small value that pieces of it were rarely reported in estate inventories, whereas china was carefully counted by the piece, and thus, as Henry explains of John Wyman in *Walden*, "often the sheriff came in vain to collect the taxes, and 'attached a chip,' for form's sake . . . there being nothing else that he could lay his hands on." Later, John's son Thomas was somehow able to purchase land in Walden and it was from him that Ralph Waldo Emerson purchased the eleven acres on which Henry began to squat in the summer of 1845. For a short time during his Walden sojourn, Henry was a neighbor of another poor white inhabitant, Irishman Hugh Quoil, who occupied Thomas Wyman's house until his death later that year, after which the house was torn down. Like John Breed, Hugh was found dead in the Walden road of alcoholism. [17]

Rachel knew what it was to be poor before she married Francis Le Grosse. The local justice of the peace refused to marry the couple without the written permission of her town-appointed guardian because Rachel lacked an estate. She did not fare much better once she was married to Francis. The couple was never able to purchase property of their own, renting their Concord land from Peter Wheeler. Nor were they able to make ends meet. When Francis died, he owed his landlord $21.06 for "sundries" he bought on credit at Peter's shop. But rather than pay her deceased husband's outstanding debt, Rachel paid $20 to Brister Freeman for his one acre of land in Walden Woods. [18]

Brister had fought long and hard to purchase and hold onto his land, insisting in court that the land the Concord selectmen had attempted to wrest from him was still legally his. The only indication as to why Brister would sell his land is the timing of the sale. That he sold his land so soon after Fenda's death and to a nearby widow just ten years his junior strongly suggests that Brister and Rachel had a relationship similar to that of a married couple. The only difference was that Brister and Rachel were unable to marry because interracial marriage was illegal in Massachusetts. And without a marriage, Rachel would not be in a position to claim widow's rights when Brister died. A land transfer between the two of them was a means of circumventing this problem by insuring Rachel owned what would have otherwise come into her hands if she was widowed again. Of course there was a risk that Rachel might predecease Brister, leaving him with nothing, but as a man he was more likely to be able to find work and thereby survive somehow. Other interracial couples took the same risk, making land deals meant to procure for the woman the financial security that marriage would have otherwise conferred. In one example in Virginia, David Isaacs, who was white, and Nancy West, who was black, decided in 1796 that Nancy should purchase land legally belonging only to David so that should something happen to him, she could still provide for their eight children. Brister made his sale without anyone disputing his right to sell land to which he no longer held legal title. Perhaps the selectmen were satisfied the land was now in white hands. [19]

Peter Wheeler, however, was not pleased. From his perspective, Brister and Rachel were cheating him out of the $21.06 Rachel owed him at a time when Peter was desperate to get his hands on whatever funds he could. And then there must have been the additionally irksome fact that Peter had not been able to circumnavigate the law, ultimately spending time in prison for his debts, while Brister had managed to wriggle free of it by finding a means other than marriage to pass on what he regarded as his property to a woman who was otherwise legally off limits to him.

Peter's frustrations boiled over in the winter of 1812–13 when he was outside with his hired men and saw his imagined nemesis walking by. Peter's employees were "conferring" with their boss "upon the safest mode" of slaughtering what Peter's Social Circle memoirist describes as a "ferocious bull." Unlike oxen, which are castrated in order to be sufficiently tame to harness and pull together, bulls are allowed to mature with their testicles intact so they can be used for breeding. Their testosterone makes them aggressive and often dangerous. The men had managed to shut the bull in the barn but "were afraid . . . to go in and encounter his fury." Watching the former slave approach, Peter quickly devised a plan for simultaneously dispatching the ornery bull, punishing Brister for his hand in cheating Peter of his money, and regaining some semblance of the social power of which his recent bankruptcy had robbed him. "Giving his men the wink," Peter "inquired very affectionately after Brister's health, and told him if he would go into the slaughter-house and get an axe, he should have a little job to do." [20]

According to Peter's memoirist, Peter hired men of "every shade of character, good, bad, and indifferent." The "bad" men were very bad indeed. One of Peter's agents, Nathan Barnes, is described by Peter's memoirist as a "profane, uncouth, disagreeable fellow" who was called "Peter Wheeler's devil" on account of his ill humor. And then there was the problem of alcohol. In addition to his slaughtering business and farming operation, Peter also kept a store and a barroom in his house where he served rum to the kind of men who did not mind drinking amid the stench of animal feces, blood, entrails, smoke, grease, and meat in various stages of being processed, no doubt his employees among them. Facing not one but a crowd of such men, Brister had no choice but to comply with the request. The sixty-eight-year-old entered the barn and the next thing he knew, Peter and his men had locked him in with a two-thousand-pound beast. [21]

The bull, which had already been worked into a frenzy during an earlier attempt to quarter him, immediately began to charge Brister, who was forced, in the mocking terms of Peter's memoirist, to perform the kinds of moves that "would have established even a French dancing master." For Brister, however, this was no joke. When angry bulls charge, maul, and roll their victims, the results are massive injuries and often death. One nineteenth-century frontiersman describes such an encounter in his journal. He had gone out to feed and water his bull, when the animal "jumped and pinned" him "against the side of the barn." The bull momentarily backed off when hollered at but then gave the man "another boost." The frontiersman recounts how his "clothes were ripped, left side gored, hip raked and several ribs cracked and broken." He barely managed to walk away. Less than a year after recording this encounter, he was attacked and killed by the same bull. Desperate to avoid injury or worse, Brister must have immediately begun to plead with his captors to let him out of the barn. But Peter and his men held the barn doors firmly shut, "watching through the dry knot-holes" as Brister fought for his life. Their only response was to "cheer . . . him on with the most encouraging roars of laughter." Slavery was over but segregated inhabitation and interracial marriage laws helped insure that whites and blacks were socially and thus emotionally as distant as ever. As far as Peter and his men were concerned, they could do with Brister as they liked, even to within an inch of his life. Whether Brister could take the bull by the horns this time was another question. [22]

When he finally found the axe Peter had mentioned, Brister realized he would have to either kill the bull before Peter and his men would release him or die trying. Having worked in the slaughtering business over the years, Brister knew that cattle and swine are easiest to kill if they are first rendered unconscious with a well-placed blow from a blunt object. Once an animal is unconscious, it can be bled to death before it resumes consciousness and, in its distress, hurts people in the vicinity. Typically in Brister's day, a large hammer was used to knock the animal in the head. In this instance, the blunt side of an axe would have to do. Even in the best circumstances, however, additional blows were sometimes needed to knock the animal out if it was not hit properly the first time, and Brister was certainly not in a position to direct the blows of his axe carefully. He could only set about "belaboring his adversary" by "giving him a blow here and there as he had opportunity." Eventually Brister would have had to use the sharp side of his axe either to sever a major artery in the bull's neck, cause a massive brain injury, or cut the animal's spinal cord. Somehow, through one of these means, and no doubt fueled by the adrenaline born of desperation, Brister managed to lay "the bull dead upon the floor."[23]

Writing over forty years later, Peter's memoirist felt compelled to top his accounting of the story with the line that must have punctuated it all the times Peter recounted it himself. He writes that Brister "emerged, no longer the dim, somber negro he was when he entered, but literally white with terror." The transformation was said to be so total that Peter and his men "could hardly persuade themselves to believe it was Brister." That Peter and later his friends could enjoy a joke about turning a black man white with fear indicates how tolerant Concord's white society was of racial harassment in the first half of the nineteenth century. Although famous for never failing to retort when taunted by local boys, Brister "turned his back" on Peter and his men "and departed" without saying a word. Whether he was injured or not was never recorded.[24]

Brister's troubles were far from over. Shortly after the incident with the bull, the home of his sister was burned to the ground by arsonists. As Henry notes in *Walden*, a favorite pastime in Concord of white boys and men was to race to the scene of a fire that, at least in some instances, they had set themselves. He recalls one particular election night in 1841 when the alarm rang and smoke was spotted rising to the south over Walden Woods. Everyone initially assumed the fire must be at "Baker's barn," where Mary Minot's sister Lavina Baker still lived, or at what had become known as "the Codman Place," the former Chambers-Russell estate. After inheriting the property in 1790, the Codman family had sold the estate in 1803, but it retained the name of the patriarch who was murdered by his slaves in 1755 and does so still on account of the family repurchasing the property in 1862 and holding it for over one hundred years after that. That night in 1841, Henry and his white male neighbors ran alongside the fire wagons toward Walden Woods with the intent of passing through to the Lincoln side, but the building on fire turned out to be the former home of barber John Breed, who had died in 1824. Determining that it was no longer of any value, the crowd watched the building burn to the ground. It was rumored that those "who set the fire . . . gave the alarm," but no one was brought up on charges of arson. [25]

In 1813, Brister's sister was seventy-five years old. Although according to Henry she was "away" at the time of the fire, Zilpah had taken the unusual move of shutting all her animals up at home, among them a dog, a cat, and several hens. As would occur in 1841, no one bothered to attempt to put out the conflagration, leaving the animals inside to burn to death and the house to burn to the ground. The fire was blamed, as Henry reports in *Walden*, on "English soldiers, prisoners on parole." The previous August, 267 British prisoners had been taken from the ship *Guerriere* onto the American ship *Constitution* after it famously engaged and disabled the English vessel off the coast of Massachusetts. Several well-to-do naval officers from the *Guerriere* were subsequently paroled in Concord, where they were permitted to take up residence in private houses and inns at their own expense, provided they promised to follow a prescribed code of conduct that limited what they could do, where they could go, and what hours they could be outside. Over the course of the next three months, until they were exchanged in late November for the American crew and officers of two British-captured ships, the *Nautilus* and the *Wasp*, the British officers suffered a rather dull existence under these restrictions. One paroled officer confined to Cheshire, Massachusetts, recorded activities in his diary that rarely varied from day to day. He and his fellow paroled officers walked and rode throughout the town, wrote letters, read, fished, attended church, discussed politics, and played cards and other games, occasionally joined in these pursuits by "the gentlemen of the country." The diarist eventually felt compelled to report that "if it were not for books, we should die of spleen." [26]

But while the officers' boredom might have served to explain actions so uncharacteristic of self-described gentlemen as arson, it seems unlikely that they would have risked being prosecuted by American officials eager to find any excuse to retaliate for what were said to be the horrendous conditions suffered by imprisoned American seamen in Canada. Although Zilpah's home was more hut than house and unoccupied at the time, arson was punishable by death in Massachusetts if the building in question was an occupied house or a barn. Most likely the British officers were blamed for something locals were ashamed to own themselves. It was one thing for the downwardly mobile Peter Wheeler to tell a story in which no permanent harm had come to a former slave man who was ultimately successful in extracting himself from a bad situation. It was another to confess to burning down the home of an old woman and destroying all her domestic animals besides. [27]

It may be that Zilpah was a target of financially straitened whites purely by virtue of being the least likely to be able to retaliate. But the bull incident and the fire occurred in rapid succession, and the former slaves living at the edge of the Great Field were not victims of the same sort of harassment. It may also be, then, that the former slaves living in Walden were being subjected to a specifically targeted reign of terror in the wake of Brister's most recent assertion of his selfhood. Perhaps the locals responsible for the damage to Zilpah's home were following Peter Wheeler's lead, intent on punishing Brister for his continued insistence that he was free to own property and free to live with whomever he chose, even a white woman. Brister may have moved to Walden Woods to be close to and help care for his brother and sister, but that proximity may ultimately have put Zilpah at risk on account of Brister's forward ways. She certainly appears to have been aware that she was in danger. That she had taken the unusual step of shutting her animals in her house is a good indication that she felt it necessary to try to protect her property. Indeed, she may have vacated the premises because she felt it necessary to take shelter.

The following spring, on May 12, 1813, less than a month after his fifty-eighth birthday, Peter Wheeler was killed when he fell from his cart. Nothing about the accident was considered worth remembering by any of the locals. Perhaps a wheel fell off or someone spooked Peter's horse. Whether or not Brister or Zilpah made it their business to get in the way of Peter's cart, they could hardly have mourned the untimely passing of a man who had made it so clear that harassing former slaves was a source of mirth for him. Peter's widow managed to keep the house Peter's father had built the couple, citing dower's rights, even as Peter's creditors received only seventeen cents on the dollar. Daughter Phoebe made a living running an "infant school" there for many years. In 1823, one of her students was little David Henry Thoreau (he changed his name to Henry David later). [28]

In the last months of 1819, Zilpah became sick and the Concord Female Charitable Society, which had already donated regularly to her, loaned her a pair of sheets and night clothes. She died of a fever on April 16, 1820, at the age of eighty-two. A small obituary was printed in the *Middlesex Gazette*, noting that "Zilphah White, a woman of color" was dead. "For a number of years, she had led a life of a hermitess, in a small place, which scarcely would bear the name of a hovel." Her decision to live alone made her an object of curiosity to the very end. But it seems that from Zilpah's perspective, it was better to have died in "a small place" then to have lived in one of Concord's mansion houses leading the life of domestic servitude she was born to on the Chambers-Russell estate. When the Russell family fled Massachusetts, Zilpah had seized a means of living independently in the form of a spinning wheel. And when her house was destroyed, she rebuilt on the same site and resumed her life, living to see a remarkably old age. She may have survived in local memory as a witch, but this seems largely a result of her independence at a time when most women lived with and for their families. [29]

Unlike Zilpah, Brister and his dwindling family were the recipients of the Female Charitable Society's attentions on only two occasions. During the final months of Brister's daughter-in-law's life, the society donated two yards of gingham and a small shirt to the son forty-three-year-old Love gave birth to shortly before her husband left town. But after Love's death in 1820, while the town paid Brister to keep his then six-year-old orphaned grandson, the Concord Female Charitable Society did not give him any additional assistance. Only in late 1821, when Brister was on his deathbed, did the society loan him a pair of sheets and a woolen bed quilt. Other sick and elderly recipients of the society's charity received wine, brandy, crackers, and shirts in addition to bedding, but apparently Brister was not "a constant attendant on public worship," nor otherwise morally redeemable in the society's eyes. His relationship with Rachel Le Grosse had made abundantly clear that he lived by a code of conduct that diverged considerably from the status quo. On January 31, 1822, Brister Freeman passed away. He was in his mid- to late seventies. As the couple had planned, Rachel Le Grosse remained in possession of Brister's property after his death. She sold it to a white farmer from the nearby town of Weston the following year. [30]

Henry David Thoreau asserts in *Walden* that Brister Freeman was buried in Lincoln. In fact, it is Sippio Brister, formerly the Hoars' Brister, who is buried off to the side of the Lincoln cemetery, near only the despised British grenadiers who lost their lives on April 19, 1775. After being separated from his mother and handed over to Elizabeth Hoar, this Brister also survived decades of slavery. He was kept at arm's length by his white townsmen even in death.

Brister Freeman's burial site is neither marked nor known. No epitaph like his master's survives to record for posterity his many character traits. What regrettably little we know of his life story speaks volumes nevertheless. During the years Brister lived in Walden Woods, he demonstrated great fortitude. Not only did he defy those who disrespected and harassed him, he remained resolute about owning his land even when town officials tried to strip him of his property. He insisted to the very end on his right to do with his property as he liked, which for him meant passing it on to the woman he effectively made his wife. In insisting that Concord not treat him as a "foreigner," Brister should be counted among Concord's great revolutionaries. Certainly Henry thought as much, asserting of Brister in *Walden* that he "had some title to be called" Scipio Africanus, the great Roman general who never lost a battle and who is widely considered one of the leading commanders in military history on account of his defeat of Hannibal and his eighty war elephants at Zama in West North Africa. It was a pivotal victory that brought to an end a seventeen-year war between the Roman Republic and Carthage. Indeed, it may be that Henry did not mistake Sippio Brister for Brister Freeman but rather purposefully conflated them in *Walden* in order to associate the heroic traits of Scipio Africanus with Brister Freeman. Henry's is high praise indeed, but had Brister Freeman been asked to think of the great man he most aimed to emulate, he might well have said Mark, whose gibbeted corpse he must have passed in the course of running errands for John Cuming. Mark's exposed remains reminded area slaves that others had made valiant attempts to forge their own independent futures. In attempting to follow suit, Brister and Concord's other former slaves may have failed to plant a next generation in Concord, but Brister took every opportunity to stake his claim to Concord's ground and was able to hold onto his piece of Walden Woods until the very end of his life. That his name survives in Walden Woods at Brister's Hill is a small but sure sign of his tenacity.[31]

After Brister Freeman died, the one remaining Freeman in Concord was his grandson John. As they had with the other children in the family, the Freemans had selected a popular name among Anglo-Americans. But John was not merely a popular local name, it was also the name of the man who had enslaved Brister for a quarter of a century. Having been forced for a time to go by Brister Cuming, perhaps Brister took some satisfaction from turning the tables on John Cuming by becoming grandfather and, after Love's death in 1820, guardian to his enslaver's namesake. But John Freeman never had the chance to make his own mark on Concord. On account of their close living quarters and no doubt the ongoing difficulty of obtaining adequate nutrition, John caught the fever that felled his grandfather. The eight-year-old died eighteen days after Brister. With that, the Freeman family disappeared from Concord.[32]

THE FORMER SLAVES' CELLAR HOLES IN WALDEN WOODS survived for quite a time as the dents that Henry noted in the landscape. The little of Concord's slave history that was still visible by the middle of the nineteenth century was commandeered by local abolitionists, who reshaped the past until it was in line with their own commitment to emancipation. Local officials replaced John Jack's toppled gravestone in the 1830s and a local abolitionist woman carefully tended the gravesite, planting flowers there. By then, it was possible to read John Jack's epitaph not as the indictment of the Patriots' hypocrisy Daniel Bliss intended but as an assertion that Concord was the birthplace of abolitionism. As one local historian put it in 1901, John Jack's epitaph was the "first . . . anti-slavery utterance" ever made in America. It was a bold misreading that has held ever since. Other shifts in rhetoric and emphasis were more subtle but no less powerful. In the 1860s, for example, a carte de visite was made of a very elderly Jack Garrison and distributed throughout the town, not as a somber reminder of Concord's slavery days, but as a testament to the town's willingness to harbor runaways (Figure 10). On the back of one of the photographs, a local woman recalls the story about Jack Garrison that his image elicited for her and no doubt many others. She describes him as "an escaped slave who came to Concord and worked for Mr. Brooks." Here at last he was supposedly safe but only insofar as his townsmen helped to protect him. Or as

Figure 10. *Carte de visite of Jack Garrison (circa 1866). Concord Museum, Concord, Mass. www.concordmuseum.org. Photograph by David Bohl.*

she puts it, "Once when the brother of Mrs. Brooks came from the South to visit, Jack Garrison, fearing it would be found out that he was a slave, left Mr. Brooks and didn't come back till the Southern visitor had gone." That Jack Garrison's slave past was not in Concord was critical to his use as a symbol of the town's commitment to freedom. Of course Jack had escaped from slavery in New Jersey, not as this memoirist implies, the South. By changing the story in this way, the local resident makes the town where he took shelter the antithesis of plantation slavery, even as Jack Garrison was consigned to poverty on the fringes of town. Preferring to hail from the birthplace of liberty, residents allowed Concord's own long and brutal history as a slave town to fade away.[33]

The dwindling numbers of any remaining descendants of local slaves made forgetting the town's slavery past all the easier. Jack's son John had managed to purchase some property locally, but in 1873 John's widow, Elizabeth, felt compelled to sell what was the town's last black-owned piece of property. The year before there had been a "fracas" in the town center, during which, according to the Selectmen's Report, "a dozen men, more or less, attacked in a cowardly and brutal manner two colored persons." Seeing no reason to stay in an increasingly hostile environment, particularly as John's land was burdened by two mortgages, Elizabeth moved to Boston, leaving behind the last few slave descendants, all of whom were elderly and succumbed shortly thereafter.[34]

Two years after Elizabeth left town, Concord celebrated the one hundredth anniversary of the Revolutionary battle at the North Bridge. President Ulysses S. Grant, James Russell Lowell, Mark Twain, Ralph Waldo Emerson, and numerous other luminaries were invited to attend. To mark the occasion, a statue of a white farmer leaving his plow to take up arms against the British was erected next to the North Bridge. With the erasure of the town's slave history and the departure of the long besieged former slave population, the town was able to claim that Concord's farmers tilled their own soil and that in doing so they had garnered the strength to fight for and ultimately secure a new nation's liberty. This became the version of Concord's history that has since been taught to generations of American schoolchildren.

Brister Freeman's Hill

There is no place you or I can go, to think about or not think about, to summon the presences of, or recollect the absences of slaves. . . . There is no suitable memorial, or plaque, or wreath, or wall, or park, or skyscraper lobby. There's no 300-foot tower, there's no small bench by the road.
—Toni Morrison, "A Bench by the Road"

SINCE 2006, VISITORS TO WALDEN WOODS can hike a new path in addition to the well-trodden one that ends at the site of Henry David Thoreau's cabin. Thoreau's Path at Brister's Hill is on part of an eighteen-acre parcel, not far from the pond, that was purchased in 1993 by a nonprofit organization intent on saving the area from development as an office park. The Walden Woods Project eventually decided to use the site to honor Henry's global reach as a "social reformer, naturalist, philosopher, and one of America's most powerful and influential writers." To that end, the organization created a path that wends its way across the hill where Brister Freeman's family lived and marked it with large granite stones carved with the words of Martin Luther King, Mahatma Gandhi, John F. Kennedy, and other freedom fighters and environmental crusaders inspired by Henry's words. Beyond the inclusion of a quotation from *Walden* that refers to him, little is noted of the man for whom the hill is named, other than that Brister Freeman was "a freed slave who lived with his family nearby," a formulation that helps perpetuate the idea that Concord was a place where men were "freed," not enslaved. [1]

The same year that Thoreau's Path was dedicated, the Toni Morrison Society, a group of scholars dedicated to the author's work, launched an initiative aimed at marking the history of slavery near those sites where it would behoove us to recall our nation's slave past and the millions of slaves who lived under its shadow. Heeding Toni Morrison's remarks on this front, the society decided a bench by the road would be a particularly fitting memorial to slavery. A bench is a place to sit, but it is not just any seat. Larger than a chair, a bench — even a small bench — is by definition a long seat meant for more than one person and thus a seat that inspires conversation by its very nature. A small bench by the road is an invitation to stop whatever you are doing, get off the beaten path, and sit down with others to remember and honor our slave ancestors. On July 26, 2008, the society dedicated its first bench. It was placed on Sullivan's Island in South Carolina. Here was where some 40 percent of all the slaves brought from Africa arrived in North America and were quarantined before being sold. [2]

Walden Woods did not play the central role in American slavery that Sullivan's Island did. Indeed, it played no role at all other than to serve as home for a small group of slaves who had managed to take their freedom. But without a bench by the side of the road, the story currently told to visitors of Walden Pond and other famous Concord sites is only a partial story. Concord may have been one of the birthplaces of American liberty, but it was also a slave town. Both are equally true. Concord needs a small bench by the road as a counterpoint to the Minuteman Statue and other local iconography. One particularly appropriate place for such a bench would be alongside Walden Street where it climbs Brister Freeman's Hill, perhaps at the entrance to Thoreau's Path, which is already a popular destination for hikers and tourists. An appropriately marked bench here would be an invitation to recall all that Brister Freeman and Concord's other slaves endured as well as all they were able to achieve. As Toni Morrison said when she finally sat on that first bench by the road: "It's never too late to honor the dead." [3]

DRAMATIS PERSONAE

Barrett and Robbins – Garrison

Lieutenant Humphrey Barrett, farmer, slaveholder (possibly of Caesar Robbins), permits Caesar Robbins to squat on his land at the edge of the Great Field and use his woodlot nearby, gives Susan Robbins Garrison a lifelong tenancy at the edge of the Great Field.

Caesar Robbins, enslaved until the Revolution (possibly by Humphrey Barrett), father of Peter Robbins and Susan Robbins Garrison, possibly the father of Phyllis [Bliss] Ingraham, farmer, squats at the edge of the Great Field with the permission of Humphrey Barrett.

Peter Robbins, son of Caesar Robbins, brother of Susan Robbins Garrison, husband of Fatima Oliver Robbins, father of Almira Oliver's children, farmer, purchases the land where his father squatted at the edge of the Great Field but loses it soon thereafter.

Susan Robbins Garrison, daughter of Caesar Robbins, sister of Peter Robbins, wife of Jack Garrison, mother of John Garrison, receives a lifelong tenancy at the edge of the Great Field from Humphrey Barrett.

Jack Garrison, escaped slave from New Jersey, farmer and day laborer, husband of Susan Robbins Garrison, squats on the edge of the Great Field in the same house as Caesar Robbins with the permission of Humphrey Barrett.

John Garrison, son of Jack and Susan Robbins Garrison, farmer and day laborer, Concord landowner.

Barron and Jack

Mr. Benjamin Barron, farmer and shoemaker, husband of Elizabeth (Betty) Parris Barron, father of Susanna Barron, owner of John Jack and Violet Barnes.

Elizabeth (Betty) Parris Barron, daughter of the Reverend Samuel Parris of Salem Village, in her girlhood one of the instigators of the Salem witchcraft hysteria, wife of Benjamin Barron, along with her daughter Susanna inherits John Jack and Violet Barnes upon Benjamin Barron's death.

Susanna Barron, daughter of Benjamin and Elizabeth (Betty) Parris Barron, owner with her mother of John Jack and Violet Barnes, relinquishes John Jack after her father's death.

John Jack, slave of the Barron family until Susanna Barron relinquishes him, first former slave landowner in Concord, owns and farms land at the edge of the Great Field, leaves his estate to Violet Barnes.

Violet Barnes, slave of the Barron family, goes by Violet Barnes when she sues for John Jack's estate after lawyer Daniel Bliss Esq. flees the country before settling it.

Bliss – Emerson

Reverend Daniel Bliss, minister of Concord, husband of Phoebe Walker Bliss, father of Phoebe Bliss Emerson Ripley and Daniel Bliss Esq., owner of Cate and Phyllis [Bliss], among others.

Phoebe Walker Bliss, wife of the Reverend Daniel Bliss, boarding house proprietor after her husband's death, along with her daughters inherits Cate and Phyllis [Bliss] from her husband, co-owner of Phyllis [Bliss] Ingraham along with her daughters.

Daniel Bliss Esq., son of Daniel and Phoebe Walker Bliss, Concord lawyer, author of John Jack's epitaph, flees Massachusetts for Canada during the Revolution.

Phoebe Bliss Emerson Ripley, daughter of Daniel and Phoebe Walker Bliss, wife of the Reverend William Emerson, inherits Cate and Phyllis [Bliss] along with her mother and sisters, co-owner of Phyllis [Bliss] Ingraham along with her mother and sisters, marries the Reverend Ezra Ripley after William Emerson's death.

Reverend William Emerson, minister of Concord after Daniel Bliss, husband of Phoebe Bliss Emerson Ripley, grandfather of Ralph Waldo Emerson, part owner of Cate and Phyllis [Bliss] after his marriage, owner of Frank [Emerson] until relinquishing him during the Revolution.

Cate [Bliss], slave of the Reverend Daniel Bliss until inherited by Phoebe Walker Bliss and her daughters, wife of Boston [Potter], adoptive mother of Phyllis [Bliss] Ingraham.

Phyllis [Bliss], slave of the Reverend Daniel Bliss until inherited by Phoebe Walker Bliss and her daughters, mother of Phyllis [Bliss] Ingraham.

Frank [Emerson], slave of William Emerson until relinquished by him during the Revolution.

Chambers – Russell

Squire Charles Chambers, Charlestown merchant, justice of the peace, first owner of the Chambers-Russell-Codman estate (in what is now Lincoln), owner of Caesar, Jack, Chloris, and Lincoln [Chambers], among others.

Squire Chambers Russell, grandson and heir of Charles Chambers, second owner of the Chambers-Russell-Codman estate, justice of the peace, owner of Lincoln [Chambers], Zilpah [Russell], and their children Bilhah, Peter, Ishmael, and most likely Zilpah White and Brister Freeman, appears to give Brister Freeman to Timothy Wesson.

Dr. Charles Russell, namesake of Charles Chambers, nephew and heir of Chambers Russell, third owner of the Chambers-Russell-Codman estate, inherits six slaves from his uncle, probably including Bilhah, Peter, Ishmael, and Zilpah White, becomes the owner of certain Vassall slaves upon his marriage to Colonel Henry and Penelope Royall Vassall's daughter Elizabeth Vassall Russell, also the owner of slave man Luck.

Lincoln [Chambers], slave of Charles Chambers and then Chambers Russell, husband of Zilpah [Russell], father of Bilhah, Peter, Ishmael, and most likely Zilpah White and Brister Freeman as well.

Zilpah [Russell], slave of Daniel Russell and then Chambers Russell, mother of Bilhah, Peter, Ishmael, and most likely Zilpah White and Brister Freeman as well.

Zilpah White, most likely the daughter of Lincoln [Chambers] and Zilpah [Russell] and thus seemingly the sister of Brister Freeman, probably enslaved by Chambers Russell and then Charles Russell until the Revolution, spinner, squatter in Walden Woods.

Codman

Captain John Codman, former ward of Charles Chambers, grandfather of John Codman III (fifth owner of the Chambers-Russell-Codman estate), sea captain, Charlestown merchant, owner of Mark, Phoebe, Phyllis, Tom, and Scipio [Codman], murdered by his slaves.

Mark [Codman], slave of John Codman, hanged and gibbeted for the murder of John Codman.

Phoebe [Codman], slave of John Codman, sold to the West Indies for the murder of John Codman.

Phyllis [Codman], slave of John Codman, burned at the stake for the murder of John Codman.

Cuming

Robert Cuming, Scottish immigrant to Concord, father of John, Amy, and Elizabeth Cuming, shopkeeper, land speculator, probable slaveholder.

Colonel John Cuming, son of Robert Cuming, husband of Abigail Wesson Cuming, father of Helen Cuming, doctor, farmer, land speculator, justice of the peace, owner of Brister Freeman, Jem, and probably others, relinquishes Brister and Jem during the Revolution and later leaves each of them £35 in his will.

Amy and Elizabeth Cuming, daughters of Robert Cuming, sisters of John Cuming, Boston merchants, flee to Canada during the Revolution .

Abigail Wesson Cuming, wife of John Cuming.

Mr. Timothy Wesson, father of Abigail Wesson Cuming, Lincoln selectman, seems to give Brister Freeman to John Cuming as a wedding present.

Helen Cuming, daughter of John and Abigail Cuming.

Dugan

Thomas Dugan, escaped slave from Virginia, farmer, third former slave to own land in Concord after John Jack and Brister Freeman, farms land near the Old Marlborough Road.

Elisha Dugan, son of Thomas Dugan and his second wife, backwoodsman in Concord.

Elsea Dugan, daughter of Thomas Dugan and his first wife, domestic servant in Concord.

Freeman

Brister Freeman, most likely the son of Lincoln [Chambers] and Zilpah [Russell], probably enslaved by Chambers Russell and later Timothy Wesson before becoming the slave of John Cuming, relinquished by John Cuming during the Revolution, husband of Fenda Freeman, father of Nancy, Edward, and Amos Freeman, farmer and day laborer, Walden Woods landowner.

Fenda Freeman, wife of Brister Freeman, fortune-teller.

Love Oliver Freeman, probably a relative of Almira Oliver and Fatima Oliver Robbins, wife of Brister Freeman's son, Amos, mother of John Freeman.

John Freeman, grandson of Brister Freeman, son of Amos and Love Oliver Freeman, the last descendant of local slaves to reside in Walden Woods.

Hoar

John Hoar, husband of Elizabeth Hoar, owner of Sippio Brister.

Elizabeth Hoar, wife of John Hoar, may have acquired her husband's slave Sippio Brister by taking him from his mother at Cambridge .

Sippio Brister, slave of John and Elizabeth Hoar until after the Revolution, changes his name from Brister [Hoar] to Sippio Brister, confused or conflated with Brister Freeman by Henry David Thoreau.

Ingraham

Captain Duncan Ingraham, Boston sea captain and merchant who moves to Concord in 1773, justice of the peace, owner of Cato Ingraham until Cato marries in 1795.

Cato Ingraham, slave of Duncan Ingraham until his marriage to Phyllis [Bliss] Ingraham in 1795, father or adoptive father of Nancy Ingraham, father of Phyllis [Bliss] Ingraham's second child (name unknown), day laborer, squatter and then renter in Walden Woods.

Phyllis [Bliss] Ingraham, daughter of Phyllis [Bliss] and Caesar (perhaps Caesar Robbins), slave of Phoebe Walker Bliss and her daughters until her marriage to Cato Ingraham in 1795, mother of Nancy Ingraham and a second child (name unknown), inhabitant of Walden Woods.

Lee

Dr. Joseph Lee, farmer and sometime doctor, church dissident, owner of Cato Lee among others, relinquishes him during or after the Revolution.

Cato Lee, slave of Joseph Lee, relinquished by him during or after the Revolution, paid laborer on the Lee farm after the Revolution.

Royall – Vassall – Russell

Squire Isaac Royall, Sr., father of Isaac Royall, Jr., and Penelope Royall Vassall, plantation owner in Antigua, justice of the peace, owner of over thirty slaves, moves to Charlestown and establishes an estate there.

Squire Isaac Royall, Jr., son of Isaac Royall, Sr., brother of Penelope Royall Vassall, inherits his father's plantation in Antigua as well as his father's Charlestown (later Medford) estate and eighteen of his father's slaves, justice of the peace, abandons his slaves to their freedom when he flees Massachusetts for England during the Revolution.

Penelope Royall Vassall, daughter of Isaac Royall, Sr., sister of Isaac Royall, Jr., wife of Colonel Henry Vassall of Cambridge, mother of Elizabeth Vassall Russell, inherits eight slaves from her father, among them Robin [Vassall], gives some of the Vassall slaves to her son-in-law, Dr. Charles Russell, loses the Vassall estate in Cambridge during the Revolution.

Robin [Vassall], inherited by Penelope Royall Vassall upon her father's death, becomes property of Penelope's husband Henry Vassall of Cambridge, sold to Dr. William Clarke after he tries to run away, purported accomplice of Mark, Phyllis, and Phoebe [Codman] in the murder of Captain John Codman.

Whitney and Feen

Mr. Samuel Whitney, Concord merchant, owner of Case Feen and one other male slave, probable owner of other slaves as well, abandons Case to his freedom when the Whitney family flees Concord for Boston during the Revolution.

Case Feen, formerly Casey, slave of Samuel Whitney until abandoned by him during the Revolution, takes the last name of Feen when he enlists in the Concord militia, squats on Lexington Road thereafter.

The following abbreviations appear in the notes.

CFPL	Concord Free Public Library, Concord, Mass.
J	Henry D. Thoreau. *The Journal of Henry D. Thoreau.* Edited by Bradford Torrey and Francis H. Allen. 14 vols. In 2. 1906. Repr., New York: Dover, 1962.
JP	Henry D. Thoreau. *Journal.* Edited by John C. Broderick et al. 8 vols. to date. Princeton, N.J.: Princeton University Press, 1981–.
MHS	Massachusetts Historical Society, Boston, Mass.
MP	Middlesex County, Massachusetts, Probate Record Number
MRD	Middlesex Registry of Deeds, Boston, Mass.
MSS	*Massachusetts Soldiers and Sailors of the Revolutionary War*
NEHGS	New England Historic Genealogical Society, Boston, Mass.

Introduction

[1] Thoreau describes the Minot house as "small, square, one-storied and unpainted house" in a journal entry made on November 25, 1857 (J 10: 207). George Minot is described in the Social Circle's memoir of Ralph Waldo Emerson by Ralph Waldo's son Edward W. Emerson, who writes of Minot that he "had never been in the railroad cars, nor but once to Boston, when with the Concord company he marched there in 1812." Edward W. Emerson also notes of George Minot that he was "a man somewhat of the Rip van Winkle type, then more common in Concord than now" (Social Circle, vol. 2, 137). Thoreau writes in his journal on March 23, 1854, that "Minott confesses to me today that he has

not been to Boston since the last war of 1815" (JP 8: 47). That Mary Minot and Elizabeth Potter lived together is clear in Thoreau's journal entry for February 27, 1861: "Miss Minott and Miss Potter have both died within a fortnight past, and the cottage on the hillside seems strangely deserted" (J 14: 321). On Mary Minot's customers, including her sister and Ralph Waldo Emerson, as well as on her business relationship with Miss Potter, see Mary Minott Record Book, CFPL. (Minot is spelled variously in Concord.) Edward Jarvis describes Mary Minot as "a tailoress of the second-class, for working men and boys" (quoted in Thoreau, *Walden*, 24 n134). In *The Personality of Thoreau*, Franklin W. Sanborn writes that Thoreau's "garments were usually cut by the village tailor, and made up by Miss Mary Minot, sister of Emerson's neighbor, George Minot, farmer and sportsman" (24–25). For a selection of Thoreau's journal descriptions of his clothing, see Thoreau, *Walden*, 25, n136. On the Baker Farm, see Brain. This farm is now the home of the Walden Woods Project.

[2] Thoreau notes in his journal of watermelons that "The first are ripe from August seventh to twenty-eighth (though the last is late), and they continue to ripen until they freeze; are in their prime in September" (September 2, 1859; Thoreau, *Wild Fruits*, 107). Thoreau tells the story of the watermelon being dropped in the middle of the Walden Road in the same entry: "I remember hearing of a lady who had been to visit her friends in Lincoln, and when she was ready to return on foot, they made her the rather onerous present of a watermelon" (Thoreau, *Wild Fruits*, 109). Bradley P. Dean, the editor of *Wild Fruits*, the recently recovered volume of Thoreau's journals in which the watermelon story appears, notes that the saying about not being able to carry a watermelon under one arm was attributed by Thoreau to Mary Minot "on another MS page." And thus he concludes of the "lady" who dropped a watermelon that "Likely this lady was Mary Minot, who spoke of the difficulty of carrying watermelons" (Thoreau, *Wild Fruits*, 324). On the history of the major roads that ran through Concord, see Frederic Wood, 119–23.

[3] Thoreau writes in his journal that "You can walk in the woods in no direction but you hear the sound of an axe" (JP 5: 459). On the annual fishing trip to the Dorchester section of Boston Harbor, see Jarvis, *Traditions*, 60–61. Regarding this fishing trip, Thoreau writes in his journal on August 5, 1854, that "Formerly they [farmers] used to think they had nothing to do when haying was done & might go a-fishing for 3 weeks" (J 6: 424). Thoreau, *Walden*, 246.

[4] In his *Autobiography of Seventy Years* (1903), George Hoar recalls hearing the story of the Indian doctor from Walden Woods resident Tommy Wyman: "When I was a small boy a party of us went down to Walden Woods. . . . There was an old fellow named Tommy Wyman, who lived in a hut near the pond, who did not like the idea of having the huckleberry-fields near him invaded by the boys. He told us it was not safe for us to go there. He said there was an Indian doctor in the woods who caught small boys and cut out their livers to make medicine. We were terribly frightened, and all went home in a hurry." Running away in fear, George and his friends "met old John Thoreau, with his son Henry, and I re-

member his amusement when I told him the story. He said, 'If I meet him, I will run this key down his throat,' producing a key from his pocket" (quoted in Thoreau, *Walden*, 253 n57). Thoreau, *Walden*, 247. Thoreau, *Wild Fruits*, 324. Thoreau, *Walden*, 246.

[5] Ralph Waldo Emerson, "Concord Hymn."

[6] A 1990 survey of college teachers conducted by the Modern Language Association found that *Walden* was the book mentioned most frequently as being particularly important to teach in nineteenth-century American literature courses (Schneider, 1).

[7] Thoreau, *Walden*, 11. For a reading of the Walden Pond State Reservation as sacred geography, see Ackerman. On paying homage at Walden to Thoreau, see Buell, 311–38.

[8] Thoreau, *Walden*, 88, 313–14.

[9] Thoreau, *Walden*, 324–25.

[10] On the puns in *Walden*, see Michael West. Thoreau, *Walden*, 62, 3.

[11] Thoreau, *Walden*, 247–48.

[12] For the author's first book, see Lemire, "*Miscegenation.*" The few scholars who addressed slavery in New England prior to the recent explosion in New England slavery studies, include Greene, Litwack, McManus, and Zilversmit. More recent studies include Chan, "The Slaves of Colonial New England" and *Slavery in the Age of Reason*, Sweet, and Melish. Melish shows how after the Revolution New England cultivated a version of its history that purposefully contrasted with the South's such that "the North" became commensurate with the idea of free, white labor, while "the South" and "the South" only became commensurate with slavery (3). The history of Northern slavery was thereby obscured and remained obscured for well over one hundred years. Some of the more recent books about Concord include Petrulionis and Maynard. Maynard's book, *Walden Pond: A History*, begins in 1821 with Thoreau's first visit to Walden Pond and thereby manages to largely ignore the history of Walden Woods as a black enclave.

[13] The following thirteen slaves were counted in the 1771 tax assessment, which only includes male slaves between the ages of fourteen and forty five: 1) slave of Phinihas Blood; 2) slave of Deacon Simon Hunt; 3) Brister, slave of Colonel John Cuming; 4) Jem, also slave of Colonel John Cuming; 5) slave of Lieutenant Humphrey Barrett (perhaps Caesar Robbins); 6) slave of Squire John Beatton; 7) Boston, slave of Samuel Potter; 8) Caesar, slave of Captain George Minot; 9) slave of Timothy Hoar; 10) Casey, slave of Mr. Samuel Whitney; 11) another male slave of Mr. Samuel Whitney; 12) Cato, slave of Dr. Joseph Lee; and 13) Caesar, slave of Colonel Charles Prescott (see Pruitt). The Reverend William Emerson's slaves were not taxed and included 14) Frank; 15) Cate; and 16) Phyllis (orphaned daughter of Phyllis [Bliss]). In addition, the names of the following slaves appear in other Concord records, indicating they were also in town in 1771: 17) Amy, who died in town in 1828 at age 100 (*Concord, Massachusetts*, 345); 18) Catherine, who died in town in 1785 at age 50 (*Concord, Massachusetts*, 418); 19) Catherine,

who died in 1786 at age 45 (*Concord, Massachusetts*, 419); 20) Fenda, if Brister Freeman's wife was locally enslaved prior to their living together in Walden Woods (*Concord, Massachusetts*, 331); 21) Jane, who died in 1790 at the age of 24 (*Concord, Massachusetts*, 420); 22) Jane, who married Nero in 1757 (*Concord, Massachusetts*, 191); 23) Rose [Minot], who died in 1800 at the age of 74 (*Concord, Massachusetts*, 423); 24) Violet Barnes, who died in 1789 at the age of 80 (*Concord, Massachusetts*, 419); 25) Mrs. Martha Stone's "negro servant," who died in 1801 at the age of 42 (*Concord, Massachusetts*, 423); 26) Philip [Barrett], who was too young to be assessed in 1771 (see Chapter 2, note 25); 27) Nero, who married Jane in 1757 (*Concord, Massachusetts*, 191); 28) Nancy, who was sold at the age of two in 1740 to Sarah Melvin (the bill of sale is reprinted in Elliot and Jones, 7 – 8); 29) Titus , who was sold to Jonas Heywood in 1755 (the bill of sale is reprinted in Elliot and Jones, 10 – 11); and perhaps 30) Reuben Bootin, who was married to Cate Jube in Concord in 1787 (*Concord, Massachusetts*, 255); and 31) Cate Jube (*Concord, Massachusetts*, 255). Captain Duncan Ingraham arrived in town either shortly before or after his 1772 marriage and brought with him 32) Cato (see Chapter 4). One of if not the last former slave to pass away in Concord was former slave woman Amy, who died in 1828. While she should have been "past her labor," as the expression went, former slave woman Rose was still working for and living with the Timothy Minot family when she died in 1800.

[14] On the soil in Walden Woods, see Peragallo. Thoreau, *Walden*, 255.

[15] William Ellery Channing, who often walked with Thoreau, writes the following in the first biography of his companion: "Three spacious tracts, uncultivated, where the patches of scrub-oak, wild apples, barberries, and other plants grew, which Mr. Thoreau admired, were Walden woods, the Estabrook country, and the old Marlboro' road" (quoted in Blanding, 3). Blanding argues that Channing was referring to Thoreau's journal entry for June 10, 1853, in which, as Blanding points out, Thoreau also mentions a fourth: the Great Fields (JP 6: 192). Of the four wild tracts he identifies in Concord, Thoreau settled in Walden Woods, where Ralph Waldo Emerson allowed him to squat on his eleven-acre woodlot there.

Chapter 1. Squire Cuming

[1] The story of how the Hoars came to acquire their slave boy Brister was first written down in a letter by Mary Blake of Wellesley Hills to Susan W. Loring, who lived in the former Hoar house with her husband, Robert Loring, in the 1930s. Blake implies that her account was passed down by the Hoars' nieces and nephews to their children (Lincoln Public Library, Stories — Remembrances. 2003.053). A popular story in Lincoln, the Hoars' story was most recently told in the June 2000 edition of the *Lincoln Minute Man Dispatch*.

[2] On slave mothers and infanticide, see Sweet, 155 – 56.

[3] On the Bristol, England, slave trade, see Morgan, and Richardson (1986 and 1987).

Munro notes of Bristol, Rhode Island, that "In choosing Bristol for its name, the settlers cherished a hope that, as in the case of its English namesake, it would become the great city upon the west" (14–15). On the slave trade in Rhode Island, see Coughtry.

[4] On social classes in colonial and revolutionary New England, see Main. On the titles Esquire (or Squire) and Mr., see Main, 215–20. On the role of a squire in Concord, see Gross "Squire Dickinson and Squire Hoar." In *The Minutemen and Their World*, Gross rightly points to a correlation between slave ownership and wealth: "In 1771 eleven taxpayers were assessed for ownership of a 'servant for life,' age fourteen to forty-five: nine were in the top 20 percent of wealth-holders the previous year and two in the next highest quintile. They owned a total of thirteen slaves" (230 n52). But being wealthy did not necessarily mean a person owned a slave. There were thirty-three men in Concord in 1771 with an "annual worth of the whole of real estate" of over £10. Only seven of these men owned slaves (just over 21 percent). There were also four slaveholders who were worth less than £10. Melish looks instead for a correlation between slave owner-ship, professional status, and wealth. She cites data from Main, pointing out that in Connecticut "By 1774 half of all ministers, half of all lawyers and public officials and a third of all doctors owned slaves; about two-thirds of persons leaving estates valued at more than 2,000 pounds and over forty percent leaving estates valued at 1,000 pounds to 1,999 pounds owned slaves" (17). The data in Concord is even more striking. Virtu-ally all of the ministers in the seventeenth century and most of the eighteenth century (until the end of the Revolution) owned slaves, and virtually all of the doctors, includ-ing Alexander Cuming, Joseph Lee, Timothy Minot, and John Cuming, also owned slaves. All three of the lawyers in town prior to the Revolution owned or were from slave-holding families (Hoar, Bulkeley, and Bliss). This correlation between having a profession and owning a slave makes sense insofar as a man needed a slave or hired labor if he was to leave his field and follow a profession. But not all Concord slaveholders were ministers, doctors, or lawyers. The Concord data show that slaveholding most closely corrolates to the possession of a title, an honorific based on multiple factors, in-cluding wealth, education, leadership, profession, ambition, and family background. Indeed, of the fifteen known slaveholders in town in 1772 (Phinihas Blood, Deacon Simon Hunt, Colonel John Cuming, Lieutenant Humphrey Barrett, Squire John Beat-ton, Samuel Potter, Captain George Minott, Timothy Hoar, Mr. Samuel Whitney, Dr. Joseph Lee, Colonel Charles Prescott, the Reverend William Emerson, Captain Dun-can Ingraham, Colonel James Barrett, and Dr. Timothy Minot), ten had a professional, military or civic title. One was called by the honorific Mr. Until the Revolution, Mr. was accorded men with leadership positions who did not have another title. No doubt Phinihas Blood (who became a selectman and moderator in Carlisle after it split off from Concord), Samuel Potter, and Timothy Hoar were given the honorific Mr. at least on occasion. Further evidence of the correlation between title and slaveholding is the fact that there was no one in Concord or Lincoln who had the title of Squire but did not own slaves. It seems an ambitious man with sufficient education and wealth to pur-sue a title typically used slave labor and the prestige of owning slaves to ensure his rise.

On Chambers Russell, see Margaret Mutchler Martin, 40–64. On Timothy Wesson, see MacLean, 180.

[5] The Reverend Ebenezer Parkman's diary is a detailed account of the difficulty of finding hired help. His father finally purchased a slave man for him so that he would have a reliable labor source, but the slave died shortly after Ebenezer brought him home. Ebenezer continued to struggle in his seasonal attempts to find hired help. On the various forms of slavery and servitude in Massachusetts, see Towner. Insofar as Timothy Wesson's daughter married John Cuming, who owned Brister Freeman prior to his emancipation, I am assuming Timothy's and John's Bristers were the same person. That Timothy baptized his Brister one month before John's marriage to Abigail Wesson further indicates that Timothy gave John the not uncommon wedding present of a slave child.

[6] Brister's hair is called "wool" in the "Memoir of Peter Wheeler" (Social Circle, vol. 1, 141). Another young slave in New England, eight-year-old Venture Smith, was employed at the kinds of tasks a young child could accomplish : "The first of the time of living at my master's own place, I was pretty much employed in the house at carding wool and other household business." But when he turned nine "I then began to have hard tasks imposed on me. Some of these were to pound four bushels of ears of corn every night in a barrel for the poultry, or be rigorously punished. At other seasons of the year I had to card wool until a very late hour" (12). There is no concrete evidence that Benjamin Barron acquired his slave John Jack from Anne Cuming. Jack was a popular enough slave name that the two Jacks might not have been one and the same. The dates, however, indicate that this could be the same man. Anne rented her Jack to a farmer in 1736, at which point the Barrons' Jack would have been twenty-three. The Barron land parcels worth more than the Barrons' slave man were a seven-and-a-half acre parcel, a six-acre parcel, a sixteen-acre parcel, and a property described as "half the dwelling house and land that was Benjamin [illegible]." (MP 1283).

[7] The baptism of Timothy Wesson's slave boy Brister is recorded in the Church Records of Lincoln Church (Lincoln First Parish Collection, Lincoln Public Library). Considering that Brister Freeman died at the reported age of seventy-eight on January 31, 1822, he would have been approximately nine years old when he was baptized, if these are indeed the same Bristers. On the use of Christianity to police slaves, including quotations from Cotton Mather, see Greene, 257–89.

[8] On Isaac Royall, see Chan, *Slavery in the Age of Reason*. The Royall estate was annexed to Medford and is now open to the public. In her dissertation, "The Slaves of Colonial New England," Chan includes her transcription of Isaac Royall Sr.'s account book. His purchase of "a mahogany desk for Isaac" was made in January 1738 (436); he purchased a horse for £20 that same month.

[9] On John Cuming's desk, see David F. Wood, 16–18. The only wooden parts of John Cuming's desk that are not mahogany are the four pine drawer bottoms. Even the lopers, the pieces of wood that extend from the side of the desk to support the lid when

folded down, are solid mahogany. The Concord Museum thus rightly concludes of this piece that "the maker was truly flaunting the use of spectacular wood" (David F. Wood, 18). The desk resides now at the Concord Museum, which dates the desk to the 1750s, noting that dense, dark mahogany was used in the Boston area in the 1750s and that Boston-area craftsmen changed their designs for such desks by the 1760s. Later still, Boston case furniture was made of lighter, redder mahogany. It is the timing of the desk's manufacture that suggests it came into John's possession at the time of his wedding. On the link between the polished properties of mahogany and the polished manners of gentlemen, see Anderson.

[10] On the triangle trade, see Coughtry.

[11] Goodwin cites Lawrence Stone's study of English merchants from a 340-year period, noting that only 6 percent were able to buy their way into the landed elite (56). Helen's father, Sir Alexander Cuming, was the baronet of Coulter in the county of Aberdeenshire. Dobson shows a Robert Cumming arriving in Boston in 1717.

[12] Robert Cuming's purchase of land in Littleton is recorded in MRD 20-243 and 20-244. His first purchase of land in Concord is recorded in MRD 20-709. On the 1721–22 outbreak of smallpox in Boston, see Duffy, 51–52. Robert's purchase of a shop in Concord is recorded in MRD 57-186. Isabella and Alexander are not listed in Concord's vital records, indicating that they were born prior to their parents' arrival in town.

[13] On why the meadows in Concord made this particular area attractive to European settlers, see Donahue. For more on Concord's settlement by Europeans, see Wheeler, and Shattuck. For the history of Native Americans in Concord, see Blancke and Robinson.

[14] On the radial road system in Concord, see Lenney, 164–67.

[15] On land corporations in New England, see John Frederick Martin. On how the First and Second Divisions were carried out, see Donahue. On the size of the woodland now known as the Walden ecosystem, see Schofield, 155. On the number of parcels owned by the average farmer, see Donahue, 107.

[16] On rewarding proprietors with land, see John Frederick Martin. On Peter Bulkeley's position and the size of his Concord estate, see Wheeler, 5–8.

[17] On Charles Chambers and his purchase of the Bulkeley grant, see Margaret Mutchler Martin, 16–31. For a history of the Chambers estate in Concord from Charles Chambers's arrival to its more recent incarnation as the Codman estate, see Margaret Mutchler Martin. On the new world of imported goods and the importance for the upper classes of knowing how to use them, see Hunter, and Bushman.

[18] On Charles Chambers's slaves, see Margaret Mutchler Martin, 26–27.

[19] The legal agreement with Jack is cited in Margaret Mutchler Martin, 26–27.

[20] Robert Cuming's Concord purchases include MRD 27-133, 24-221, 24-126, 24-316, 22-627, 22-703, 23-317, 23-358, 23-445, 23-45, 27-384, 25-287, 25-187, 15-188, 25-214, 25-215, 25-679, 26-1. He also purchased investment properties in the following towns: Groton: 23-306, 25-147, 25-714, 25-715; Haverhill: 25-187; Dunstable: 23-314, 27-201; Littleton, 22-628, 45-574; Lancaster: 24-127, 25-286, 25-680, 26-169; Sudbury: 25-713; and Worcester: 27-384. Only four of the Cuming children are listed in Concord's vital records: Robert (born on February 22, 1723/24, died in infancy); James (born July 18, 1726); John (born March 1, 1728); and Amy (born September 19, 1733). See *Concord, Massachusetts: Births, Marriages, and Deaths, 1635–1850*, 109, 117, 119, and 135. Amy appears in various records as Ame. Here and throughout the book, I have modernized the spelling of names. Phebe thus becomes Phoebe and so on. I am assuming Amy is older than Elizabeth because she is listed first in a deed of land signed over to the sisters by their mother in 1760. Alexander Cuming and his wife, Anne, appear in various local documents. In 1736, for example, Anne Cuming deeded two acres of land for a new meeting house when the "southern" part of Concord broke away and formed the town of Acton in 1735. The deed describes Anne as "wife of Mr. Alexander Cuming Surgeon now abroad and attorney of said Alexander Cuming." Shattuck asserts that "Alexander Cuming came to Concord about 1726" (239). Whether Alexander was Robert's brother or related to him in some other way seems likely but has not been substantiated. Elizabeth Cuming made her remarks about "hard labor" in a letter to Elizabeth Murray, quoted in Cleary, 97. Robert's case regarding his servant girl is recorded in Middlesex Court of Common Pleas, folio 11-B-V.

[21] Robert Cuming was referred to as Mr. Robert Cuming only in 1782 when his son John inventoried the remaining portion of his father's estate. The rules of deference relaxed considerably after the Revolution, and "Mr." came to be used indiscriminately. On Robert Cuming's dealings with those indebted to him, see records at the Middlesex County Inferior Court of Common Pleas. The families Robert Cuming brought to court included the Strattons, the Wheelers, the Nuttings, and the Bloods.

[22] On John Beatton, see Wheeler, 88–90. Robert Cuming made a land gift to his daughter Isabella and her husband in MRD 45-727.

[23] Alexander was listed in a land deed as a mariner (MRD, 47-191). I have assumed that he was lost at sea insofar as he never returned to Concord to settle on his land or sell it to John, who treated it as his own legally. A letter from sister Elizabeth Cuming to Elizabeth Smith [Murray], dated November 20, 1769, refers to her brother James as being in London: "I hope you will see my brother James in London" (James M. Robbins Papers, MHS). The extant copy of James's will in the Concord Special Collections is undated but clearly refers to James's family and property in the Isle of Man (Concord Antiquarian Society Collection, 1422–1957, Cuming/Cumming Papers, box 1, folder 62, CFPL). The fact of its turning up in Concord is evidence that James, like Alexander, also pre-deceased John. John made bequests to his surviving sisters in his will, but mentions no surviving brothers.

[24] On the Comyn clan, see Young. Wheeler notes that Robert Cuming used the Comyn shield, but I have not been able to track her source (102). On Isaac Royall's use of three wheat sheaves as his family crest, see Chan, *Slavery in the Age of Reason*, 120–21. Royall was not related to the Comyns, but used this crest as a means of accruing the patina of ancient landedness.

[25] Quoted in Morison, 375. On the social aspects of class rankings at Harvard, see Morison, Dexter, and Shipton (1954).

[26] For a list of John's classmates in ranked order, see Shipton, vol. 12, 102. Benjamin Prescott's Harvard biography appears in Shipton vol. 12, 200.

[27] For biographical sketches of Timothy Minot Sr., see Shipton vol. 12, 194–95, and Shattuck, 244–45.

[28] On Robert Cuming's land purchases, many of which were clustered along the Concord / Acton border, see note 20. His land gift to John and Alexander is made in MRD, 47-191. As with Isabella two years before, there was a nominal price the brothers had to pay in order to make the gift legal, and as it had been for their sister that sum was £5. Robert essentially gave his sons the land, as made clear in the deed, in which he cites "the love and good will I bear toward Alexander Cuming Mariner and John Cuming of said Concord." On the size of an average farm in Concord, see Gross, "Culture and Cultivation," who notes that "the average size of a farm was no bigger in 1800 than it had been before: around sixty acres" (521). In his will, the Reverend Daniel Bliss, who died in 1764, explains that he is not giving his eldest son any land because he had "already given him his proportion in his education" (MP 1944). On Chambers Russell, see Margaret Mutchler Martin, 40–64.

[29] Lincoln and Zilpah's marriage and the subsequent baptism of their children is recorded in Wyman, 1059–60. Zilpah White's obituary (reprinted in *The Concord Saunterer*, 14.1 [Spring 1979], 27) lists her age at the time of her death as seventy-two, town records as eighty-two (*Concord, Massachusetts*, 338). I have assumed the town clerk was more accurate and that Zilpah White was born at around the time Zilpah and Lincoln were still having children. In Genesis, Bilhah and Zilpah are the slaves of Leah and Rachel, respectively, said by some ancient commentators to be sisters, Bilhah the older sister and Zilpah the younger. That Zilpah and Lincoln's eldest daughter was named Bilhah and their younger Zilpah would have been in keeping both with Genesis and with the New England custom of naming a child after her parent. I have also assumed that Brister was part of this same family based on his role after the Revolution in caring for certain individuals related to the Chambers-Russell slave Peter as well as Brister's subsequent decision to settle in Walden Woods.

[30] Quoted in MacLean, 82–83. On Lincoln's separation from Concord, see MacLean, 79–150. For an account of Daniel Bliss's role in the split, see Gross, *The Minutemen and Their World*, 18–21, and Shattuck, 173–74 n2.

[31] See MacLean for a list of Lincoln's twenty largest estates (154). MacLean notes that Timothy Wesson was sometimes listed as a "Gentleman" in town documents (224). There is no concrete evidence that Chambers Russell gave Brister to Timothy Wesson. But insofar as Timothy had a slave boy named Brister and insofar as Brister Freeman decided to live in Walden Woods, it appears Brister Freeman may very well have been born on the Chambers-Russell estate prior to becoming the property of Timothy and later John Cuming.

[32] On John Cuming's stint teaching school, see Wheeler, 102.

[33] Concord Antiquarian Society Collection, Cuming/Cumming Papers, box 1, folder 62, CFPL, and Winnifred Sturdy Collection of Papers and Records, box 2, folder 15, CFPL. On the genteel art of letter writing, see Bushman, 90–92, and Goodwin, 190–92.

[34] On the study of medicine at the University of Edinburgh, see Morrell.

[35] Concord Antiquarian Society Collection, Cuming/Cumming Papers, box 1, folder 62, CFPL, and Winnifred Sturdy Collection of Papers and Records, box 2, folder 15, CFPL.

[36] The house and grounds of the Cuming mansion house are described in detail in an 1810 newspaper announcement that the property was for sale (Concord Antiquarian Society Collection, Cuming/Cumming Papers, box 1, folder 62, CFPL). The road that once ran in front of the house has since been rerouted to run behind it. In addition to John Cuming's desk, the Concord Museum owns a tea table, a looking glass, and two engravings that belonged to him.

[37] Robert Cuming wrote his will in 1749. On January 17, 1753, John, Amy, and Elizabeth signed a statement that "we the children of Robert Cuming deceased are fully satisfied with the will and testament which he has left in favor of our honored mother" (MP 5439). It was presented for probate by his wife on January 7, 1754. By all appearances, then, Robert died shortly before John Cuming wed Abigail Wesson on February 8, 1753.

[38] The description of Brister comes from "Memoir of Peter Wheeler," Social Circle, vol. 1, 139.

Chapter 2. The Codman Place

[1] Parkman, 291. For an account of John Codman within the context of his relationship to Concord residents, see Margaret Mutchler Martin, 32–39. A transcript of the Codman trial is reprinted in Goodell. John Cuming's slave man Jem is mentioned only in John's will (MP 5420). When he acquired Jem is unknown.

[2] Goodell, 7, 12. The bill of sale for Nancy is reprinted in Elliot and Jones, 7–8. The bill of sale for Henry Spring's Cato is reprinted in Trumbull, 7. In 1765, Lincoln farmer Joshua Brooks sold his slave woman's nineteen-month-old son Peter to another Lincoln farmer. See MacLean, 216–17.

[3] For an account of Robin Vassall's robbery and escape plan, see Batchelder, 65 – 67.

[4] See Wyman, 1059, on Mark being warned out of Boston. It appears that Mark was born either in Africa or the West Indies. During the trial, he was asked if he knew if cashew nuts were used to poison his master. He responded that he had "not seen a cushoe [sic] nut since I have been in this country" (Goodell, 19).

[5] Abba and her family attempted to forge new family ties but these were eventually sundered as well. Robin's sister Cuba, named for a place as was one of the slave-naming customs, married one of the Vassall slaves, a man named Tony. In later years, when Henry Vassall began to suffer the financial effects of spoiling his only child, the future wife of Chambers Russell's heir, he would clear some of his debts by selling Cuba and her children, but not Tony, to his nephew John Vassall. Shortly afterward, in the spring of 1769, when Cuba gave birth to a son, Darby, her new owner, a member of Christ Church in Cambridge, gave the child to George Reed of South Woburn, an occasional attendant of that church. So acute was Cuba's family's pain that, according to Darby, when Henry Vassall "was dying and asked his servants to pray for him, they answered that he might pray for himself" (Batchelder, 35). On Henry Vassall, his wife, Penelope Royall Vassall, and their slaves, including Cuba and Tony, see Batchelder. For a list of the Royall slaves and their division at Isaac's death, see Chan, *Slavery in the Age of Reason*, 146 – 48.

[6] For a transcription of Belinda's statement, see Chan, "The Slaves of Colonial New England," 446 – 47.

[7] For Mark's reported statement, see Goodell, 17.

[8] On Samuel Parris, see Margaret Mutchler Martin, 18 – 19. On Betty Parris's connection to Benjamin Barron, see Nelson, 23 – 24. On John Jack, see Tolman, and Benjamin Barron's will and probate papers (MP 1283). A receipt signed by Anne Cummings dated December 22, 1736, notes that she received £20 from Edward Flint for one year's service of her "negro man named Jack" (Winnifred Sturdy Collection of Papers and Records, box 2, folder 15, CFPL).

[9] MRD, 69-341 and 69-342. Historians refer to a third plot of land that John Jack bought in the Great Field but I was not able to locate a deed for it.

[10] Mark and Phyllis attempted to implicate each other throughout the trial and in this way revealed their purported involvement in the fire. Goodell, 7.

[11] Goodell, 9, 6.

[12] For a genealogy of the Codman family, see Wyman, 224 – 26.

[13] Jefferson, 288. Venture Smith, 14 – 15.

[14] Reprinted in Waters, 786.

[15] Parkman, 33 and 37.

[16] Goodell, 12.

[17] At the trial, Mark insisted he had procured the lead from a man named Essex Powers, who belonged to Thomas Powers, a blacksmith. Essex seems to have been working for the potter John Harris. Mark argued that he intended only to settle a dispute with Tom, his master's slave, as to whether the lead would melt in the fire or not. Essex, listed perhaps erroneously as a "negro woman" in Thomas Powers's estate inventory, was never charged for the murder of John Codman.

[18] Goodell, 10, 11.

[19] Goodell, 14.

[20] The report on the Antigua plot is quoted in Chan, *Slavery in the Age of Reason*, 54.

[21] Parkman, 295. Broadside quoted in Sweet, 148.

[22] A broadside printed in Boston on March 17, 1758, advertised the pay scale for each rank (MHS Proceedings, 2nd Series, vol. 6 [1891], 25). On September 27, 1755, a list was made "of the men's names that are going in this expedition to Crown Point in the Regiment whereof Josiah Browne Esq. is Colonel which Company is under the Command of John Cuming Esq. Lieutenant Colonel of said Regiment." In addition to the forty-three men at his command, John had a captain, lieutenant, and ensign under him. Transcription of portions of Ebenezer Bridge's diary by Henry S. Perham for George Tolman, Concord Antiquarian Society Collection, Correspondence and Records, box 1, folder 47, CFPL. William Emerson, 17–18.

[23] Dr. Caleb Rea of Danvers is quoted in Goodell, 30.

[24] On the relative importance of stitchery over literacy, see Ulrich, 148.

[25] The inventory made of John Cuming's estate at the time of his death counted almost one hundred books (MP 5420). The deed for "a negro boy named Philop, seven years of age" is in the Allen French – Ruth Wheeler Collection of Papers and Documents Relating Primarily to Concord, Massachusetts, 1668 – 1852, series II, folder 5, CFPL. Cambridge vital records show a Francis Jr. and Phoebe Moore in Cambridge who had a son, also Francis, on March 30, 1782. Judging by his military records, Colonel Barrett's Philip should have been twelve in 1772. But if he intentionally overstated his age when he enlisted in 1780, it is plausible that this pretend deed refers to him.

[26] Brister's mark appears on the following land deeds: MRD 124-399 and MRD 195 – 224.

[27] On John Cuming's capture by Indians, see Shattuck, 253.

[28] John Cuming's friend Ebenezer Bridge reported in his journal on August 26, 1756,

that "My brother John Bridge arrived here on his way from Lake George, he being one that was taken by the French and stripped by the Indians, when Fort Wm. Henry was taken from us" (Waters, 786).

[29] William Emerson, 29, 30. Parkman, 21, 35.

[30] Shattuck, 253.

[31] On the changing iconography of death symbolism on gravestones, see Harris, 114.

[32] Concerning burial of slaves and former slaves, Abiel Heywood's memoirist wrote in 1853 that in Concord deceased blacks were "consigned by themselves to a far corner of the graveyard" ("Memoir of Abiel Heywood," Social Circle, vol. 2, 232).

[33] Between 1750 and 1770, the mean number of children in Concord in a first marriage was 7.66 (Harris, 99). The story of how John Cuming was struck by a ball that lodged in his hip, where it remained for the rest of his life, was passed down in Concord for generations, a testament both to the town's pride in the military valor of its citizens but perhaps also a coded means of explaining his lack of any further progeny after Helen's death. In Laurence Sterne's novel *The Life and Opinions of Tristram Shandy, Gentleman*, published in nine volumes between 1759 and 1767, the character Uncle Toby has been injured in the groin, also in battle. Much of the novel is about the impact on his sexual potency. The wealthy woman who pursues Uncle Toby is eager to ascertain if he will be able to perform "the marriage function." Rather than answer, Uncle Toby beats a hasty retreat.

[34] On Township Number Five or Cummington, see Foster and Streeter.

[35] Quoted in Foster and Streeter, 26.

[36] On the percentage of Concord residents who lived near the meeting house, see Gross, *The Minutemen and Their World*, 7. On town meetings, see Gross, *The Minutemen and Their World*, 8 and 10.

[37] Tuesday, May 14, 1771, John Adams Diary, Adams Family Papers: An Electronic Archive, MHS. This is the only surviving source for the inscription. Harvard University has been unable to locate the actual brass candelabras. My thanks to Frank Farrell for the translation. The benefits of high-profile philanthropy are made clear in a letter dated January 30, 1764, from colonist Margaret Mascarene to her husband, reminding him how he might induce a certain colleague to help rebuild Harvard after the devastating fire there in 1764: "if he gives any thing worth while, he will have the public thanks of the college, and his name will be enrolled among the worthy benefactors to this luminary, and will live when the building themselves are crumbled into dust" (quoted in Goodwin, 85–86). On the link between civility and clubs, see Hunter, 142–43.

[38] John Cuming's honorary degree is in the Concord Antiquarian Society Collection,

vault A70, CAS unit 1, oversize box 1, folder 9, CFPL. It is reprinted in Foster and Streeter, 157. On Harvard's recognition of John Cuming when the College moved to Concord, see Teele, 64.

Chapter 3. British Grenadiers

[1] Adams quoted in Dershowitz, 57, and Sweet, 189. The anonymous pamphlet, "A Short Narrative of the Horrid Massacre in Boston," is transcribed online at www.law.umkc.edu / faculty / projects / ftrials / bostonmassacre / anonyaccount.html. Jefferson, 22.

[2] Thomas Nichols is listed as transient in Baldwin, 169.

[3] William Emerson, 65 – 66, 71.

[4] The account of Phoebe Emerson fainting when Frank came into her room with an axe in hand is told by her granddaughter (William Emerson, 73). On other women in the countryside who feared they would be murdered by area slaves, see Quintal, 34.

[5] Description of Daniel Bliss's mannerisms quoted in Gross, *The Minutemen and Their World*, 20.

[6] Joseph Lee quoted in Gross, *The Minutemen and Their World*, 21. William Emerson, 18.

[7] William Emerson, 13.

[8] Mrs. Bliss's payment is recorded in William Emerson, 20.

[9] Mary Moody Emerson's account of Mrs. Bliss receiving the news of her daughter's drowning is quoted in William Emerson, 50 – 51.

[10] William Emerson recorded the marriages of Boston to Cate and of Caesar to Phyllis in his journal. See William Emerson, 38, 50.

[11] Based on her daughter's birth date (extrapolated from her age at the time of her death), it would appear that Phyllis died sometime between March 1768 and March 1769. See *Concord, Massachusetts*, 327.

[12] William Emerson, 33.

[13] Ruth Wheeler argues in *North Bridge Neighbors* that William and Phoebe Emerson's house was a remodeling of an existing house. "It seems probable that the central hall and the two north rooms were added, the roof raised to make four chambers upstairs, and a second chimney built to provide four more fireplaces" (quoted in Brooks, 4). But as Paul Brooks notes, "Recent research . . . has revealed no trace of a former building incorporated into the present one" (4).

[14] Quoted in William Emerson, 120.

[15] William Emerson, 103. Phyllis's baptism is recorded in First Parish in Concord Records, 1695 – 1994, vault A30, unit A1, CFPL. Indenture of Ruth Hunt to William Emerson and his wife, November 12, 1772, Concord Town Archives (1772 folder), C. pam 3. item 69, CFPL.

[16] William Emerson, 103.

[17] William Emerson, 111, 113.

[18] For an account of the Hosmer picture *A Fishing Party*, see David F. Wood, 131 – 33.

[19] Thoreau's journal, February 18, 1858; J 10: 284 – 85.

[20] On Abigail Whitney and her store, see Cleary, 60. On the Whitney family's genealogy, see Pierce, 86 – 87. Gage is quoted in Ronsheim, 8 fn9. Hawthorne, *The Elixer of Life Manuscripts*, 4. Samuel Whitney was taxed for two slaves in 1775. Henry David Thoreau's journal account places Casey in the Whitney home and otherwise makes it clear that Casey was one of those slaves. Diminutive forms of classical names were popular as slave names. James Fenimore Cooper's slave character Agamemnon in *The Pioneers* was called Aggy for short. Casey was a diminutive form of Cassius, for Gaius Cassius Longinus, the Roman senator behind the conspiracy against Julius Caesar.

[21] The reference to Elizabeth and Amy as "the two little Miss Cumings" is quoted in Cleary, 134. The story of the Cuming sisters being accused in the newspapers of violating the importation agreements is told in Cleary, 133 – 34.

[22] No death record survives for John's mother, Helen Cuming, but she disappears from the historical record after a land gift she made to Elizabeth and Amy of the Rutland acreage (MRD 57-186). Amy Cuming quoted in Cleary, 97. On Elizabeth Murray, see Cleary. In a letter dated November 20, 1769, Betsy Cuming wrote to Elizabeth Murray, "I hope you will see my brother James in London. I know it will be of some service to us to have things properly represented" (James M. Robbins Papers, MHS).

[23] MRD 65-507. The Cuming sisters' April 1768 advertisement is quoted in Cleary, 98. On the popularity of selecting and embroidering a family crest, see Ring, vol. 1, 60 – 75.

[24] Letter from Elizabeth Cuming to Mrs. Elizabeth [Murray] Smith, November 20, 1769, James M. Robbins Papers, MHS. Elizabeth Cuming reported the worth of the shipment she and her sister received in a letter to Elizabeth [Murray] Smith, November 20, 1769, James M. Robbins Papers, MHS.

[25] The Boston resolution that Amy and Elizabeth Cuming "not only deserted but opposed their Country in a struggle for the Rights of the Constitution," appears in the Boston Town Records of March 12, 1770 (quoted in Cleary, 135).

[26] Thoreau's Journal, February 18, 1858; J 10: 284.

[27] Thoreau's Journal, February 18, 1858; J 10: 284. February 20, 1858; J 10, 285.

[28] Thoreau's Journal, February 18, 1858; J 10: 284. A thirty-seven-year-old "Case" Whitney (original quotation marks) was engaged for the town of Lancaster on March 5, 1781 (MSS, vol. 17, 157), but appears in no muster rolls. A forty-year-old Case Feen (also spelled Feene) was engaged for Concord on March 1, 1781, and appears in muster rolls taken in July, August, and September 1781 and one taken in January 1782 (MSS, vol. 5, 589). Case Feen was described as black and his birthplace listed as Guinea. It is probable that these are the same person and that the engagement for Lancaster did not turn into an enlistment. This would mean that Casey or Case did manage to clear away for a time. Either way, Henry David Thoreau and census records place Casey back in Concord and it thus seems likely that the Casey who used to belong to Samuel Whitney thereafter called himself Case Feen.

Chapter 4. *The Last of the Race Departed*

[1] MRD 80-253. Duncan Ingraham's advertisement appears in the *Boston News-Letter*, February 15, 1773. Joseph Lee quoted in William Lee, 156. The stories of Duncan Ingraham being harassed by Loyalists are told in "Memoir of Duncan Ingraham," Social Circle, vol. 1, 127 – 30. George Washington's chaise is described in Wiencek, 90 – 91.

[2] Quoted in Margaret Mutchler Martin, 100. On Dr. Charles Russell, see Margaret Mutchler Martin, 99 – 124.

[3] MP 19591. The inventory of Chambers Russell's estate included six slaves: Caesar, Mingo, Titus, Osmund, and Peter. Strangely, no value was placed on them. MacLean assumes they were "evidently rather old or infirm" (218), but it is highly unlikely that all of Chambers Russell's slaves were past their labor. There were most likely female slaves as well who simply were not listed in colonial inventories or for tax purposes. Chambers Russell's wishes regarding his slaves were reported in the obituary published in the Boston newspapers (quoted in Margaret Mutchler Martin, 60). For a list of Royall slaves inherited by Penelope Royall, see Chan, *Slavery in the Age of Reason*, 146. On Henry Vassall, his family, and their slaves, see Batchelder. In 1763 the Vassalls still had at least seven slaves at their Cambridge home. Six years later, only five adult male slaves were listed in the inventory taken at the time of Henry Vassall's death, a year after his daughter's marriage, evidence perhaps that she took some with her, which would have been customary.

[4] Luck's statement on the shooting, made to John Cuming, is in *Letters and Affidavits to the Charlestown Committee of Correspondence*, September 20, 1774, MHS.

[5] The story of Major Pitcairn stopping at Duncan Ingraham's house is told in the "Memoir of Tilly Merrick," Social Circle, vol. 2, 58 – 59. Melish explains in her book on New England slavery that she "deliberately avoided where possible (though it was not always possible) the hundreds of antiquarian histories of New England towns, cities, and countries, most written in the 1880s and 1890s." She writes that "although they offer a rich va-

riety of anecdotal information about the institution of slavery in New England and also about individual slaves and free persons of color," she is "deeply suspicious of their rather uniformly 'fond' reconstruction of the relations between slaves and slaveholders." She explains that she only "resorted" to these sources when she could not otherwise find detailed information "on an important event or practice" (9). I share Melish's view that local histories and memoirs are often strongly revisionist. But I believe these sources are still valuable so long as the historian attempts to separate what can be corroborated from what is based solely on nostalgia or some other emotion. On the Concord Social Circle, see Gross, "The Biography of a Town." I have assumed that the slave referred to in the story is Duncan Ingraham's slave Cato because he was counted as having only one slave in the Boston 1771 tax assessment (see Pruitt).

6 "Memoir of Tilly Merrick," Social Circle, vol. 2, 58 – 62, 58.

7 William Emerson's statements on the matter were recalled by the Revered William Gordon of Roxbury, in a "Letter to a Gentleman in England," dated May 17, 1775, and intended for the public. It was printed in two Massachusetts Almanacs in 1776 and is quoted at length in McLaughlin, 41. Hawthorne, *Mosses from an Old Manse*, 10. On the role of Ammi White, see Gross, *The Minutemen and Their World*, 127. On the role the scalping played in exacerbating the violence on April 19, 1775, see Bradford, 51 – 52, 78 – 79.

8 On the incident with Mrs. Whitney and her chaise on the morning of April 19, 1775, see Pierce, 86. Joseph Lee quoted in William Lee, 161. Thoreau's journal, February 20, 1858; J 10:284 – 85.

9 On Daniel Bliss's political views and his removal from Concord, see Tolman, 10 – 13.

10 Decisions to stay in the countryside or retreat behind British lines made strong statements about a person's politics. It was reported of one man, for example, that because he "withdrew himself from Cambridge and retire[d] to Boston on the day of the late unhappy commencement of hostilities" in the spring of 1775, he "increased the public suspicions against him." On the flip side, when another man decided not to go to Boston, a Crown supporter concluded "if Mr. Bass had been truly loyal, I can't see how it was possible for him to stay at Newburyport, a place so much in favor of the other part" (quoted in Batchelder, 46).

11 For a description of the graduation party, see Cleary, 161 – 62. The story of "Job's affair" is told in a letter from Elizabeth [Murray] Inman to Ralph Inman quoted in Cleary, 175 – 76.

12 Joseph Lee quoted in William Lee, 160. The church's offer is quoted in Gross, *The Minutemen and Their World*, 61. Joseph Lee quoted in William Lee, 162 – 63, 160, 161, 163. On September 11, 1775, Joseph wrote in his journal that "Jonas with Cato & team to work on his [Jonas'] farm" (William Lee, 162). Cato stayed on Jonas Lee's farm in Ashby, Massachusetts, until September 23. The Hessian officer is quoted in Nash, 10.

In Concord, thirteen blacks in all served for the town during the Revolution: Caesar Minot (43 days in 1775 and 3 months in 1776); Charleston Hodon (1775); Cato Lee (1776); Caesar Quaco (1777); Samuel (Sambo) Blood (3-year term in 1777); Brister Cuming Freeman (1 month and 11 days in 1777, 1 month in 1778, and 9 months in 1779 at the age of 31); Caesar Kettle (1778 at the age of 32); Francis Benson (1778); Philip Barrett (1780 at the age of 19); Boston [Potter?] Bill or Ball (1779 at the age of 30); Case [Whitney] Feen or Feene (3-year term in 1781 at the age of 40); Charles Adams (3-year term in 1781 at the age of age 18); and Richard Hobby (3-year term in 1781 at the age of 18). See MSS under individual names.

[13] Samuel Johnson, "Taxation no Tyranny: An Answer to the Resolutions and Address of the American Congress" (quoted in Sweet, 189). An 1830s replica of John Jack's tombstone still sits on the back side of Burial Hill, not far from John Cuming's grave.

[14] For an account of the Russells' final years in America and their subsequent flight, see Margaret Mutchler Martin, 111–15. The man with whom the Russells exchanged houses was Henderson Inches, whose daughter was baptized in Lincoln on October 1, 1775. The 1784 inventory of the Lincoln estate included "a clock, a glass globe, a broken looking glass, two and a half dozen broken china plates and platters, six tea dishes, and a china bowl . . . eight large maps, three large pictures, eleven of a middling size, sixteen of small size, six large glass pictures, nineteen smaller ones, and another twenty-three pictures . . . eighty-six bound books" and a myriad of other objects (Margaret Mutchler Martin, 129–30).

[15] William Emerson, 99, 100, 101, 100.

[16] William Emerson, 102.

[17] William Emerson, 100.

[18] William Emerson, 100, 109.

[19] William Emerson, 115.

[20] Two inventories were made of William Emerson's estate, one of which was signed by John. MP 6980.

[21] On Brister Hoar's enlistment and substitution for Mr. Joshua Child Jr., see MacLean, 294.

[22] Brister's "celerity" is described in "Memoir of Peter Wheeler," Social Circle, vol. 1, 140–41. MSS, vol. 4, 207, 208, 214; vol. 6, 32. John called his slave men "Bristo and Jem" in his will. MP 5420.

[23] Quoted in Pierson, 26. Samuel Potter, MP 17816.

[24] MSS, vol. 11, 627. Joseph Lee, MP 13934. Joseph Lee's Diaries, entries for May, September, and November 1794, NEHGS.

[25] Joseph Lee recorded the death of "Cate Bliss" in a March 1785 diary entry (Joseph Lee's Diaries, NEGHS). "Memoir of Duncan Ingraham," Social Circle, vol. 1, 128–29. Among the earlier historians of New England slavery, Greene and Zilversmit assumed slavery was over in Massachusetts by the 1790 census. Historians of Concord have made similar assumptions. Gross writes that "By 1790 there were no slaves in Concord or anywhere in Massachusetts" (*The Minutemen and Their World*, 185). More recently, historians have revisited this assumption. Sweet notes that "even the census of 1790 may have obscured slaves still held there." He cites a letter to historian Jeremy Belknap explaining how the marshal of Massachusetts convinced slaveholders not to claim a slave for the purposes of the 1790 census (248 – 49).

Chapter 5. Permission to Live in Walden Woods

[1] Selectmen Minutes, March 3, 1788, Microfilmed Concord Town Records, 1777-1790, box 1, roll 3, CFPL. Letter from Elizabeth Cuming to John Cuming, Halifax, July 15, 1784, Concord Antiquarian Society Collection, Cuming/Cumming Papers, box 1, folder 62, CFPL. Transcription of portions of Ebenezer Bridge's diary by Henry S. Perham for George Tolman, Concord Antiquarian Society Collection, Correspondence and Records, box 1, folder 47, CFPL.

[2] The inscription on John Cuming's tombstone reads as follows: "Naturally active, as to genius and disposition, he early appeared on the stage of life, where he conducted with spirit and dispatch, and acquired honour in different stations. As a Physician, he was beloved, useful and celebrated. His compassion for the distressed hastened him to their relief and husband[.] [W]as as charitable as healing to the poor and as a Magistrate he magnified his office, nor held the Sword of justice in vain. Constitutionally particular, animated and warm in his disposition and temper, earnestness and zeal, affection and precision were his characteristics — hence from his youth, in conversation, he was cheerful and affable, in civil business, prompt and expeditious[,] in private and public worship, punctual and fervent[,] in charity, liberal, in piety devout. His learning, dignity and donations procured him an honorary degree at Harvard College[.] [T]o that society, for the support of a Professor of Physic and to the Church and Town of Concord, for public charitable and religious purposes, he made generous donations, in his last will."

[3] On this kind of iconography, see Benes, *Masks of Orthodoxy*.

[4] MP 5420.

[5] On John Cuming's gift to the Concord church, see Teele, 234, and Benes, *Two Towns*, 135. John had no way of knowing that his gift would be upstaged by Duncan Ingraham's wife, Mary, who donated similarly engraved silver to the church of Concord in 1790, four years before she died at the age of sixty-four, whereas John's set was not finished until 1792. See Teele, 234. On John's gift to Acton, see Phalen, 249. Anne Cuming was acting as her husband's attorney when on February 5, 1736/7, she made a gift of two acres of land to the township of Acton as "a spot for a meeting house" (MRD 37-383).

[6] Royall will quoted in *Rules and Statutes of the Professorships*, 34.

[7] *Independent Chronicle*, July 24, 1788.

[8] Stowe, 297–307. A local history of Natick also mentions that "several attempts were made to kidnap" Caesar Thompson and his wife "and sell them into slavery in the southern states, but without success" ("Black Slaves in the Revolutionary War"). On Salem's slavery and postslavery period, see *African American Heritage Sites in Salem*.

[9] Peter Salem is sometimes said to appear in one public record as Salem Middlesex, but these are not the same two men. Peter Salem died at the Framingham poor house in 1783 and Salem Middlesex died in Weston in 1799. If Caesar Robbins was not the Caesar whom William Emerson married to Phyllis [Bliss], then Caesar Robbins married only twice.

[10] Joseph Lee Diaries, January 1786, NEHGS. Colonel Charles Prescott died in 1779 at the age of sixty-eight. His wife, Lucy, died on April 23, 1799, at the age of eighty-two.

[11] On the black enclave at Plymouth called Parting Ways and comprising four families, see Deetz. On the black enclaves in Natick, see "Black Slaves in the Revolutionary War." Stowe, 47.

[12] Deetz explains that New Guinea was "a fairly common term used over much of Anglo-America for separate black settlements" (139). Gorea was also the name of a part of the African coast where slave traders stopped and Bristol, Rhode Island, thus named the district in which its former slaves settled "Gorea" (Munro, 18). On Nathaniel Hawthorne's use of New Guinea in *The Scarlet Letter*, see Sokolow.

[13] For a history of the Great Meadows, see Donahue, and Gupta.

[14] I am assuming Caesar Robbins began to squat next to the Great Field at or about the time of his marriage to Catherine Boaz in 1779.

[15] On Caesar Robbins's use of Barrett land, see "Memoir of Humphrey Barrett," Social Circle, vol. 1, 64. Local histories, including Jarvis, generally refer to two separate houses for the Robbinses and Garrisons but the deed recording the sale of Barrett land to Caesar Robbins's son Peter indicates that the two families shared one house. The 1823 deed describes five acres with a dwelling house and a barn situated on "the river meadow." The deed stipulates that Susan Garrison has "the right to occupy herself and family the easterly half of the house, and the easterly half of the cellar during her natural life" (MRD 248-376). Jack and Susan Garrison lived here with the four of their seven children who lived past their first birthdays, but eventually purchased a different piece of property not far away. The birth of Fatima Oliver's first two children is recorded in *Vital Records of Acton*, 85. Peter Robbins's children were recorded as illegitimate by the town clerk. See *Concord, Massachusetts*, 317. Jarvis writes of Jack Garrison in *Houses and People in Concord* that "He was

a respectable man and his wife had the same character. People were accustomed to visit them. Their children were like themselves in public estimation." Then he adds in a foot-note, "Except Peter Robbins" (188–89). Jarvis's remarks about the Garrisons are mis-leading, however, insofar as the Garrisons were visited by local women bestowing charity upon them. They were not locally regarded as the equals of white residents. See Lemire, Review. Both Peter Robbins and Peter Hutchinson seem to have wanted to show alle-giance to the Barrett family for protecting them. Both named one of their daughters after Ann Maria Barrett, born to Joseph Barrett, Esq. and his wife, Sophia, in 1827. Ann Maria Robbins was born in 1831 and Ann Maria Hutchinson was born in 1833. Peter Robbins was not able to hold onto his land for more than seven years and sold it to Daniel Shat-tuck. Peter Hutchinson purchased "the Robbins Place" from Shattuck in 1852.

[16] On the transformation of the Great Field from the cornerstone of Concord agricul-ture to "a barely breathing anachronism," see Donahue, 119–20. For a history of Con-cord's changing road network, see Frederic J. Wood, 52, 119–23. On farmers and their use of the Boston markets, see Gross, "Culture and Cultivation," 525. On the stage-coach schedule, see Jarvis, *Traditions*, 6. According to Lenney, when Herbert W. Glea-son mapped the paths of mid-nineteenth-century Concord, he included twenty miles of paths used by Henry David Thoreau, most of which were in Walden and Estabrook Woods (171). Lenney notes that "As currently mapped, the mesh-size of the Walden path-net is generally about one and a half to six acres, which agrees with its longtime use as woodlots by the Emersons and other Concord families, who would need to get around to cut trees and collect firewood" (171). Thoreau, *Walden*, 246.

[17] That Peter Russell's daughter Betty and her half siblings were not listed as "negro" in Concord's birth records (*Concord, Massachusetts*, 207, 254, 259) may be because they were born free, "negro" being less a means of stipulating a racial identity than a person's legal status. John Cuming, for example, referred to Brister as "my negro" rather than his slave. On the history of caring for the poor in Concord, see Heath. After Brister cared for Thomas Cook for a time, Nathaniel Nutting did so until Thomas died on February 5, 1785. Nathaniel may, like Brister, have lived near Walden Woods. Henry David Thoreau places a Stephen Nutting next to Le Grosse in Walden Woods (Thoreau, *Walden*, 253).

[18] The location of William Fillis's property is shown in Glass and Little. On Jube Savage and Lucy Oliver, see MacLean, 305.

[19] *MSS*, vol. 5, 207–8. Charlestown Edes's note signing his military wages to "my master Isiah Edes" is at the Groton town clerk's office. Laura Wilkes notes that Charlestown Edes was at Bunker Hill "shouldering his pick with the well-known 'Spirit of '76.' He entered the army at the very beginning of the trouble and was afterwards in Colonel Bigelow's company of the Fifteenth Massachusetts. He was not discharged until December 3, 1780" (27). Presumably Charlestown was not warned out of Concord because he came to town already a landowner. Brister's and Charlestown's periods of service in the army do not ap-pear to overlap but records of enlistment are incomplete in many cases.

[20] The Stratton family house was located at the current intersection of Walden Street and Brister's Hill Road. John Stratton's land sale to Duncan Ingraham in 1779 is recorded in MRD 80–253. Jacob Potter's mortgage to Ingraham is recorded in MRD 88-350. Jacob's land sale to Brister Freeman and Charlestown Edes is recorded in MRD 124-397.

[21] The absence of any land deeds that refer to a Zilpah White, along with Edward Jarvis's and Henry David Thoreau's description of the hut's location as on the edge of the road from Concord to Lincoln, indicate that she was squatting, living on the roadside by permission of the selectmen. As Donahue notes, "By the middle of the eighteenth century . . . [t]he only legal commons left were along the highways" (174). Jarvis in *Houses and People in Concord*, provides the most detailed description of the house's location: "Just at the bottom of the hill, on the south side and west of the junction of the Watertown road and the land leading to what is now the picnic grounds, was a hut where an old colored woman, Zilpah White, lived" (98). *Concord, Massachusetts*, 271.

[22] "Memoir of Duncan Ingraham," Social Circle, vol. 1, 129. Thoreau, *Walden*, 247. William Ellery Channing quoted in Thoreau, *Walden*, 248 n13. Thoreau made his remark that Duncan Ingraham was "no doubt... thanked" in an undated entry in his journal during the Walden period (1845–47; J 1: 420).

[23] Reuben Burden appears next to Brister Freeman in the 1790 census. Three people are listed as members of the Burden household and seven as members of the Freeman family. Thoreau Society president Walter Harding argues that Cato Ingraham "and his wife apparently kept a guest room for transients" but he never noted his sources (Thoreau, *Walden*, 247 n 6). For the story of the stranger with smallpox, see "Memoir of Dr. Josiah Bartlett," Social Circle, vol. 2, 179.

[24] MP 5420.

[25] MP 5420. Greene notes that "In 1770 Dr. Joseph Warren, famous Revolutionary hero, paid £30 for a Negro boy" and that "George Wyllys, Secretary of the State of Connecticut, paid £30 in 1777 for a Negro woman." He reports that "The average price of a slave during the eighteenth century was probably between £40 and £50 sterling" (45).

Chapter 6. Little Gardens and Dwellings

[1] Thomas Dugan's land purchase on installments is recorded in MRD 115-481. (The Concord Historical Commission is mistaken in its assertion that 212 Williams Road was the Dugans' house at one point [see Forbes]. The family's property and tax records indicate that they would never have been able to afford such a large home. They did, however, live nearby.) The deed stipulates that Thomas had already paid Captain John Minot six dollars during Captain Minot's lifetime and that upon the captain's death, having paid the executor of his estate nine more dollars, he was now in possession of six acres near Nut Meadows Brook (now called Jennie Dugan's Brook). Thoreau and Emer-

son, *Nature and Walking*, 83. MP 14017. Emerson's journal, October 28, 1848, quoted in Edward Waldo Emerson, 117.

[2] Jarvis, *Houses and People in Concord*, 98. *Middlesex Gazette*, April 22, 1820.

[3] Chan, "The Slaves of Colonial New England," 411.

[4] On Mary Jennings and Ginna, see Greene, 110. Thoreau, *Walden*, 247.

[5] On the steps involved in spinning flax, see Ulrich, 86–95. On Concord's cotton factory, see Hammond. On Concord's first house museums, see Patricia West, 39–91.

[6] Thoreau, *Walden*, 255, 247. On basket making in New England, see Wolverton, "'A Precarious Living,'" and Ulrich, 42–74. On coppice growth in Concord, see Foster, 76–78.

[7] Quoted in Wolverton, "'A Precarious Living,'" 342. Quoted in Wolverton, "Bottomed Out," 180. On New England chair bottoming, see "Bottomed Out."

[8] Quoted in Wolverton, "'A Precarious Living,'" 344, 343, 342. Thoreau, *Walden*, 247.

[9] Thoreau, *Walden*, 246. On Walden Woods as "bean country," see Gross, "The Biography of a Town." Thoreau, *Walden*, 9. Sheldon, 26.

[10] Thoreau, *Walden*, 247. Thoreau's journal, November 5, 1857, J 10:163. Jarvis, *Traditions and Reminiscences of Concord*, 61. For a comparison of Jarvis and Thoreau, see Gross, "The Most Estimable Place in All the World." "Memoir of Ralph Waldo Emerson," Social Circle, vol. 2, 137. On Tuggie Bannocks, see Ulrich, 355, 360.

[11] *Middlesex Gazette*, April 22, 1820. Concord Female Charitable Society Records, 1814–1943, CFPL. Donations of tobacco given to Zilpah appear in the January 1818 report and in the July 1818 report. On the presence of smoking pipes at the slave quarters on the Royall estate, see Chan, *Slavery in the Age of Reason*, 183.

[12] Thoreau's journal, November 28, 1853; J 11: 524–25.

[13] MRD 124-397. In 1817, the town voted "that the Swine shall not go at large the ensuing year," after which the title of hog reeve became purely an honorary one typically bestowed on newly married men. Ralph Waldo Emerson and Nathaniel Hawthorne each served their terms. Hawthorne is quoted on the web site of the Brighton Allston Historical Society (www.bahistory.org/ historycattle.html). For the poem "Peter's Field" with its description of corn, see Ralph Waldo Emerson, vol. 9, 363–64. Thoreau, *Walden*, 61. Dwight, vol. 2, 269. Thoreau, *Walden*, 255.

[14] Thoreau, *Walden*, 255. "Memoir of Peter Wheeler," Social Circle, vol. 1, 138–42. On the price of mutton, see "Memoir of George Minot Barrett," Social Circle, vol. 3, 98–99.

[15] Thoreau's journal, December 12, 1856, J 15: 179–80. A local farmer like George Minot Barrett could have as many as 350 sheep, the wool of which was sold to manufacturers in Lowell. On one occasion, George volunteered to sheer sheep for one of his uncles alongside Peter Hutchinson. The two competed to see who could sheer the most sheep in a day. George's Social Circle memoirist calls it "an exciting contest." The men sheared all day long. "For hours they sheared, neck and neck." But, according to the memoirist, "Peter lost heart, and when the struggle was over, could show but sixty sheep to Mr. Barrett's sixty-two — a third more, at least, than was counted a great day's work in that art." It is hard to imagine that Peter Hutchinson could afford to beat "Mr. Barrett," insofar as George was a prosperous sheep farmer who, like his uncle, may have hired Hutchinson on occasion to help with his own shearing. That George was "Mr. Barrett" and Peter Hutchinson merely "Peter" in the recounting of the contest is enough to indicate the social hierarchies that Peter Hutchinson had to negotiate. In a contest of strength and skill, the man with the greatest social and economic capital must win. That the two men finished within two sheep of one another seems to indicate that Peter may have held back out of future economic necessity ("Memoir of George Minot Barrett," Social Circle, vol. 3, 100).

[16] Thoreau, *Walden*, 248. On fortune-telling client Eliza Wildes, see Benes, "Fortunetellers, Wise-Men, and Magical Healers," 127–28. Thoreau, *Walden*, 248. On fortune-tellers in New England, see Benes, "Fortunetellers, Wise-Men, and Magical Healers." In addition to describing Zilpah in early drafts of *Walden* as "witch-like" and Fenda as a fortune-teller (Thoreau, *Walden*, 248), Henry may have meant to describe Jennie Dugan as a witch as well. He tells in his journal sometime around October 31, 1850, of Jennie Dugan's boys showing someone the interior of her springhouse, where the visitor spotted a frog in her milk pan. A frog in milk was a witch's means of pulling other people's cream into her house (J 3:125). All three women were slaves or, in Jennie's case, the descendant of slaves, and it seems they were generally regarded with suspicion by locals.

[17] See Deetz for the archaeological work done on the former slave enclave in Plymouth. Deetz notes that at Parting Ways in Plymouth, most of the animal bone found during excavation of the black enclave there were of cow's feet: "Such parts were of little value to Anglo-Americans, although they could be cooked to yield nourishment." But he concludes that "we must not overlook the possibility that these bones might reflect in part a different cuisine" (153).

[18] Thoreau's journal, February 18, 1858; J 16: 285. On flying home to Africa, see Gomez, 117–18. On Casey's name Feen and Feene, see *MSS*, vol. 5, 589.

[19] On *minkisi*, see MacGaffey, and Thompson, 117–31. Poe, 197. Cummings Davis, the collector of Concord antiquities whose collection formed the basis of the Concord Museum, noted the provenance of the looking glass on its back: "Mary Minott died in / Feb 181861 [*sic*] / C. E. Davis / Concord 1860 / George Minott died in 1861."

Casey's prayer quoted in David F. Wood, 116. The Concord Museum has not opened the mirror to examine the paper tucked behind the glass. I have inferred that one of Pope's epistles is written there based on the words that are visible.

[20] The story of Brister stealing a haddock is in Jarvis, *Traditions and Reminiscences of Concord*, 105. On the rarity of seafish in Concord, see Jarvis, *Traditions and Reminiscences of Concord*, 60–61.

[21] "Memoir of Duncan Ingraham," Social Circle, vol. 1, 9.

[22] Thoreau quoted in Foster, 95, 105.

[23] "Memoir of Humphrey Barrett," Social Circle, vol. 1, 64. Thoreau quoted in Foster, 95. In another journal entry, Thoreau insists of wood that "the pleasure of picking it up by the riverside" is far superior to purchasing it (quoted in Foster, 105).

[24] Quoted in Thoreau, *Faith in a Seed*, 143.

[25] "Memoir of John Richardson," Social Circle, vol. 1, 159–63. MRD 474-125.

[26] Case Feen's military service is recorded in *MSS*, vol. 5, 589.

[27] Case was cared for by Caesar Robbins in 1815, by Jack Garrison in 1816, and by Caesar Robbins again in 1817 and 1819. See Records of the Overseers of the Poor, 1810–20, box 3, roll 13, CFPL. Thoreau, *Walden*, 255.

Chapter 7. Concord Keeps Its Ground

[1] Brister Freeman's back taxes owed were extrapolated from various town records on microfilm at CFPL. MRD 124-399. Thoreau quoted in Moss, 7.

[2] Physician quoted in Brown, 82. In his "Record of Concord Deaths," Jarvis listed "Charlestown, a Negro" as dying of scurvy in 1791 at thirty-two years of age (Edward Jarvis Papers, 1796–1886, CFPL). But in his 1780 military records, Charlestown was listed as thirty, making him thirty-six when he died (*MSS* vol. 5, 207–8). I assume the Freemans took Charlestown into their side of the house because he was not counted in the 1790 census but was still alive and living in Concord, where he died. Reuben Burden is listed in the 1790 census next to the Freemans. On September 2, 1859, Henry notes in his journal of watermelons that "The farmer is obliged to hide his melon patch far away in the midst of his corn or potatoes" (J 12: 312).

[3] MRD 124-399. MRD 124-333.

[4] *Concord, Massachusetts*, 358, 364, 291.

[5] For the death dates of Cato Ingraham's daughter and wife, see *Concord, Massachusetts*, 422, 327. The causes of death are given in Jarvis, "Record of Concord Deaths" (Edward Jarvis Papers, 1796–1886, CFPL). Pintard is quoted in "Plague: How Cholera Helped

Shape New York," the *New York Times*, Tuesday, April 15, 2008, F4. 1866 *New York Times* article quoted in Sontag, 143.

[6] The deaths of Cato and Nancy Ingraham are recorded in *Concord, Massachusetts*, 327. Causes of death are given in Jarvis, "Record of Concord Deaths" (Edward Jarvis Papers, 1796–1886, CFPL). On consumption in Concord, see Manoli-Skocay. Thoreau, *Walden*, 247.

[7] The deaths of Brister Freeman's two grandchildren and his wife are recorded in *Concord, Massachusetts*, 425 and 331. Causes of death are given by Jarvis, "Record of Concord Deaths" (Edward Jarvis Papers, 1796–1886, CFPL). Thoreau, *Walden*, 246.

[8] See entries by name in *Concord, Massachusetts*.

[9] MP 6495. Thoreau's journal entry made October 31, 1850; J 2:77. The spring was known as Jennie Dugan's Spring. It and Jennie Dugan's Brook, formerly called Nut Meadow Brook, are the only Concord sites known by a black person's first and last names.

[10] Concord's early mortality rates are given in Harris, 109. Jarvis, "Record of Concord Deaths" (Edward Jarvis Papers, 1796–1886, CFPL).

[11] "Memoir of Samuel Staples," Social Circle, vol. 4, 138. On blacks in the North End, see Horton and Horton, 2–3, 5, 34, 35.

[12] Thoreau, *Walden*, 255.

[13] Timothy Wheeler quoted in Shattuck, 107–8.

[14] "Memoir of Peter Wheeler," Social Circle, vol. 1, 138–42, 138.

[15] "Memoir of Nathaniel Munroe," Social Circle, vol. 2, 114. "Memoir of John Richardson," Social Circle, vol. 1, 163.

[16] Thoreau, *Walden*, 253.

[17] On John Wyman's pottery in Concord, see Watkins, 44. Jarvis on Breed quoted in Thoreau, *Walden*, 249, n 27. The Concord Female Charitable Society recorded donations to John Breed's wife in their reports for June 1816 and January 1817 (Concord Female Charitable Society Records, 1814–1943, CFPL). Thoreau, *Walden*, 253.

[18] The town clerk wrote of the marriage of Rachel Harrington to Francis Legross [sic] that it was "by the written approbation of her guardian, Jonathan Maynard, Esq." (*Concord, Massachusetts*, 360). For a list of money owned Peter Wheeler see his Estate Papers, CFPL. MRD 195-224.

[19] Brister Freeman might have sold his land out of financial necessity but this does not seem to have been the case. In 1811, he either had secured a career for himself or was at least feeling hopeful that his lot was about to change. He indicates in the land deed (MRD 195-224) that he was no longer a mere laborer, a term then used to describe a person gen-

erally known to lead a precarious existence on account of being landless and which he used to describe himself in 1785 when he originally purchased the land. Rather, he describes himself as a barber. The fact that Brister was remembered nevertheless as a laborer or "handy Negro" by Henry David Thoreau and his informants indicates that if Brister barbered, he did not barber for long. In his annotated version of *Walden*, Walter Harding notes that in addition to working as a barber, Brister also worked as a nurse (250). I have not been able to find any documentation that corroborates Harding's assertion, although the barbering and medical professions were then still somewhat related and Brister might have known some medical procedures if he had ever assisted his former master, John Cuming. On David Isaacs and Nancy West, see Rothman, 74–75.

[20] "Memoir of Peter Wheeler," Social Circle, vol. 1, 140–41.

[21] "Memoir of Peter Wheeler," Social Circle, vol. 1, 139.

[22] "Memoir of Peter Wheeler," Social Circle, vol. 1, 141. Record of "Laroy" for December 30, 1885 (www.llewellyn.com/archive/fate/58/).

[23] On slaughtering methods in U.S. history, see Skaggs. Death by loss of blood also lengthens the amount of time the meat remains fresh. "Memoir of Peter Wheeler," Social Circle, vol. 1, 141.

[24] "Memoir of Peter Wheeler," Social Circle, vol. 1, 141.

[25] Thoreau, *Walden*, 250.

[26] Thoreau, *Walden*, 247. Paroled officer quoted in Dietz, 185–87. On prisoners of war during the War of 1812, see Dietz.

[27] On January 1, 1814, the *Boston Patriot* printed an advertisement for a book called "Barbarities of the Enemy" that details the conditions suffered by American prisoners.

[28] Jarvis, "Record of Concord Deaths" (Edward Jarvis Papers, 1796–1886, CFPL). Sanborn, 39.

[29] Concord Female Charitable Society Records, 1814–1943, CFPL. Zilpah White's obituary is reprinted in *The Concord Saunterer* 14, no. 1 (Spring 1979): 27. The obituary lists her age as seventy-two whereas town records list it as eighty-two (*Concord, Massachusetts*, 338).

[30] Concord Female Charitable Society Records, 1814–1943, CFPL. On Love Freeman's death, see *Concord, Massachusetts*, 338. On the payments Brister Freeman received for the care of his grandson, see Records of the Overseers of the Poor, 1810-1820, box 3, roll 13, CFPL. On Brister Freeman's death, see *Concord, Massachusetts*, 340. Rachel Le Grosse's sale of her Walden lot is recorded in MRD 251-92.

[31] Thoreau, *Walden*, 248.

[32] Jarvis, "Record of Concord Deaths" (Edward Jarvis Papers, 1796–1886, CFPL). Nancy, who remained a Freeman on account of that also being her husband's last name, was thirty-one when her second child died (*Concord, Massachusetts*, 424). Whether she lived to have others is unknown. An Amos Freeman died a pauper of dysentery at the age of sixty-six in September 1850 in Monmouth County, New Jersey. But while he shared a birth year with Brister's son, Amos Freeman was such a popular name it is difficult to know if this is the same man.

[33] For local interpretations of John Jack's epitaph, see Tolman, 20. The story on the back of one of Jack Garrison's carte de visite is reprinted in Trumbull, 59.

[34] Peter Hutchinson and Elsea Dugan both died in 1882. Elisha Dugan followed in 1896. See the Concord genealogy boxes at CFPL. Selectmen's Report, 1871–1882, CFPL.

Epilogue. Brister Freeman's Hill

[1] It might have been interesting to include the words of Malcolm X on one of the granite stones in light of the fact that Malcolm X was introduced to Thoreau's ideas while in prison at Charlestown, after which, when he was moved to the Concord prison, erected on the former Cuming estate, he became committed to Islam and racial justice. Of course the extent of the role Thoreau's ideas played in Malcolm X's own work would need to be explored first. Whatever the case, Malcolm X's transformation while living on land formerly owned by John Cuming and farmed by Brister Freeman is another important event in history yet to be marked or even remarked upon in Concord.

[2] See Felicia R. Lee.

[3] Quoted in Felicia R. Lee.

BIBLIOGRAPHY

Ackerman, Joy. "A Politics of Place: Reading the Signs at Walden Pond." *Reconstruction: Studies in Contemporary Culture 5* (Summer 2005), http://reconstruction.eserver.org/053/ackerman.shtml.

African American Heritage Sites in Salem. Rev. ed. Salem, Mass.: Salem Maritime National Historic Site, 2003.

Anderson, Jennifer L. "Nature's Currency: The Atlantic Mahogany Trade and the Commodification of Nature in the Eighteenth Century." *Early American Studies* (Spring 2004): 47–80.

Baldwin, Thomas Williams, compiler. *Vital Records of Natick, Massachusetts, to the Year 1850.* n.p.: Stanhope Press, 1910.

Batchelder, Samuel Francis. *Notes on Colonel Henry Vassall (1721–1769), His Wife Penelope Royall, His House at Cambridge, and His Slaves Tony and Darby.* Cambridge, Mass.: 1917. Rpt., Whitefish, Mont.: Kessinger Publishing's Rare Reprints, 2006.

Benes, Peter. "Fortunetellers, Wise-Men, and Magical Healers in New England, 1644–1850." In *Wonders of the Invisible World: 1600–1900*, ed. Peter Benes, 127–42. Dublin Seminar for New England Folklife. Annual Proceedings, 1992. Boston: Boston University Press, 1995.

------. *Masks of Orthodoxy: Folk Gravestone Carving in Plymouth County, Massachusetts, 1689–1805.* Amherst: University of Massachusetts Press, 1977.

Benes, Peter, ed. *Two Towns: Concord and Wethersfield, a Comparative Exhibition of Regional Culture, 1635–1850.* Concord, Mass.: Concord Antiquarian Museum, 1982.

"Black Slaves in the Revolutionary War." Natick, Mass.: Natick Historical Society, n.d.

Blancke, Shirley, and Barbara Robinson. *From Musketaquid to Concord: The Native and European Experience*. Concord, Mass.: Concord Antiquarian Museum, 1985.

Blanding, Thomas. "Historic Walden Woods." *Concord Saunterer* 20 (Dec. 1988): 3–74.

Bradford, Charles H. *The Battle Road: Expedition to Lexington and Concord*. Boston: Rotary Club of Boston, 1975. Rpt., Eastern National, 1986.

Brain, J. Walter. "Jacob Baker's Farm." *Concord Journal*, July 7, 1994. Rpt. in *Thoreau Society Bulletin* 211 (Spring–Summer 1995): 13–14.

Brooks, Paul. *The Old Manse and the People Who Lived There*. Concord, Mass.: Trustees of Reservations, 1983.

Brown, Stephen. *Scurvy: How a Surgeon, a Mariner, and a Gentleman Solved the Greatest Mystery in the Age of Sail*. New York: Thomas Dunne Books, St. Martin's Press, 2004.

Buell, Lawrence. *The Environmental Imagination: Thoreau, Nature Writing, and the Formation of American Culture*. Cambridge, Mass.: Harvard University Press, 1995.

Bushman, Richard L. *The Refinement of America: Persons, Houses, Cities*. New York: Alfred A. Knopf, 1992.

Chan, Alexandra A. *Slavery in the Age of Reason: Archaeology at a New England Farm*. Knoxville: University of Tennessee Press, 2007.

------. "The Slaves of Colonial New England: Discourses of Colonialism and Identity at the Isaac Royall House, Medford, Massachusetts, 1732–1775." Ph.D. diss, Boston University, 2003.

Cleary, Patricia. *Elizabeth Murray: A Woman's Pursuit of Independence in Eighteenth-Century America*. Amherst: University of Massachusetts Press, 2000.

Concord, Massachusetts, Births, Marriages, and Deaths, 1635–1850. Concord, Mass.: Town of Concord, 1895.

Coughtry, Jay. *The Notorious Triangle: Rhode Island and the African Slave Trade, 1700–1807*. Philadelphia: Temple University Press, 1981.

Deetz, James. *In Small Things Forgotten: The Archaeology of Early American Life*. Garden City, N.Y.: Anchor Press / Doubleday, 1977.

Dershowitz, Alan M. *America on Trial: Inside the Legal Battles That Transformed Our Nation; From the Salem Witches to the Guantanamo Detainees*. New York: Warner Books, 2004.

Dexter, Franklin Bowditch. "On Some Social Distinctions at Harvard and Yale Before the Revolution." *American Antiquarian Society Proceedings* 9 (1894): 34–59.

Dietz, Anthony G. "The Prisoner of War in the United States During the War of 1812." Ph.D. diss, American University, 1964.

Dobson, David. *Scots in New England, 1623 – 1873*. Baltimore: Genealogical Publishing Co., 2002.

Donahue, Brian. *The Great Meadow: Farmers and the Land in Colonial Concord*. New Haven, Conn.: Yale University Press, 2004.

Dwight, Timothy. *Travels in New-England and New-York*. 4 vols. 1821 – 22.

Elliott, Barbara K., and Janet W. Jones. *Concord: Its Black History, 1636 – 1860*. Concord, Mass.: Concord Public School System, 1976.

Emerson, Edward Waldo. *Emerson in Concord: A Memoir Written for the "Social Circle" in Concord, Massachusetts*. Boston: Houghton Mifflin, 1889.

Emerson, Ralph Waldo. *The Complete Works of Ralph Waldo Emerson*. Ed. Edward Waldo Emerson. 12 vols. Boston: Houghton Mifflin, 1918.

Emerson, William. *Diaries and Letters of William Emerson, 1743 – 1776*. Ed. Amelia Forbes Emerson. Boston: Thomas Todd Co., 1972.

Forbes, Anne McCarthy. *Survey of Historical and Architectural Resources, Concord, Massachusetts*. 6 vols. Concord, Mass.: Concord Historical Commission, 1994 – 95.

Foster, David R. *Thoreau's Country: Journey Through a Transformed Landscape*. Cambridge, Mass.: Harvard University Press, 1999.

Foster, Helen H., and William W. Streeter. *Only One Cummington*. Cummington, Mass.: Cummington Historical Commission, 1974.

Glass, Kerry, and Elizabeth A. Little. *Map of Lincoln as It Appeared in 1776*. Lincoln, Mass.: Lincoln Historical Commission, 1975.

Gomez, Michael A. *Exchanging Our Country Marks: The Transformation of African Indentities in the Colonial and Antebellum South*. Chapel Hill: University of North Carolina Press, 1998.

Goodell, Abner Cheney, Jr. *The Trial and Execution, for Petit Treason, of Mark and Phillis*. Cambridge, Mass.: John Wilson and Son, 1883.

Goodwin, Lorinda B. R. *An Archaeology of Manners: The Polite World of the Merchant Elite of Colonial Massachusetts*. New York: Kluwer Academic / Plenum Publishers, 1999.

Greene, Lorenzo J. *The Negro in Colonial New England, 1620 – 1776*. n.p.: Classic Textbooks, 1942. Rpt., Port Washington, N.Y.: Kennikat Press, 1966.

Gross, Robert. "The Biography of a Town: The Social Circle and Its Members." Presentation, February 15, 2005, Concord, Mass.

------. "Culture and Cultivation: Agriculture and Society in Thoreau's Concord." In *Material Life in America, 1600–1860*, ed. Robert Blair St. George, 519–33. Boston: Northeastern University Press, 1988.

------. "The Great Bean Field Hoax: Thoreau and the Agricultural Reformers." *Virginia Quarterly Review* (Summer 1985): 483–97.

------. *The Minutemen and Their World*. Twenty-fifth anniversary ed. New York: Hill and Wang, 2001.

------. "The Most Estimable Place in All the World: A Debate on Progress in Nineteenth-Century Concord." In *Studies in the American Renaissance*, ed. Joel Myerson, 1–15. Boston: Twayne, 1978.

------. "Squire Dickinson and Squire Hoar." *Proceedings of the Massachusetts Historical Society* 101 (1989): 1–23.

Gupta, Carol E. *Concord's Great Meadows: A Human History*. Victoria, B.C.: Trafford Publishing, 2004.

Hammond, Charles. "Concord's 'Factory Village': 1776–1862." *Old-Time New England* 61, nos. 1–2 (Summer–Fall 1975): 32–38.

Harding, Walter, ed. *Walden: An Annotated Edition*, by Henry David Thoreau. Boston: Houghton Mifflin, 1995.

Harris, Marc. "The People of Concord: A Demographic History, 1750–1850." In *Concord: The Social History of a New England Town, 1750–1850*, ed. David Hacket Fischer, 65–138. Waltham, Mass.: Brandeis University, 1983.

Hawthorne, Nathaniel. *Mosses from an Old Manse*. 1854. Boston: Houghton Mifflin, 1900.

------. *The Elixir of Life Manuscripts: "Septimius Felton," "Septimius Norton," and "The Dolliver Romance."* Columbus: Ohio State University Press, 1977.

Heath, Anita L. "Five Almshouses in Middlesex County, Massachusetts, and Their Records." M.A. thesis, University of Massachusetts, Boston. 1998.

Horton, James Oliver, and Lois E. Horton. *Black Bostonians: Family Life and Community Struggle in the Antebellum North*. Boston: Holmes & Meier, 1999.

Hunter, Phyllis Whitman. *Purchasing Identity in the Atlantic World: Massachusetts Merchants, 1670–1780*. Ithaca, N.Y.: Cornell University Press, 2001.

Jarvis, Edward. *Houses and People in Concord, 1810–1820*. Typed transcript annotated by Adams Toman, Concord, Mass., 1915.

------. *Traditions and Reminiscences of Concord, Massachusetts, 1779–1878*. Ed. Sarah Chapin. Amherst: University of Massachusetts Press, 1993.

Jefferson, Thomas. *Writings*. Ed. Merrill D. Peterson. New York: Library of America, 1984.

Lee, Felicia R. "Bench of Memory at Slavery's Gateway." *New York Times*, July 28, 2008.

Lee, William, compiler. *John Leigh of Agawam (Ipswich) Massachusetts 1634–1671 and His Descendants of the Name of Lee*. Albany, N.Y.: John Munsell's Sons, 1888.

Lemire, Elise. *"Miscegenation": Making Race in America*. Philadelphia: University of Pennsylvania Press, 2002.

------. Review of *To Set This World Right: The Antislavery Movement in Thoreau's Concord*, by Sandra Harbert Petrulionis. New England Quarterly 80 (June 2007): 338–40.

Lemire, Robert A. *Creative Land Development: Bridge to the Future*. Boston: Houghton Mifflin, 1979.

Lenney, Christopher J. *Sightseeking: Clues to the Landscape History of New England*. Hanover, N.H.: University Press of New England, 2003.

Litwack, Leon. *North of Slavery: The Negro in the Free States, 1790–1860*. Chicago: University of Chicago Press, 1965.

MacGaffey, Wyatt. "Complexity, Astonishment and Power: The Visual Vocabulary of Kongo Minkisi." *Journal of Southern African Studies* 14 (January 1988): 188–203.

MacLean, John C. *A Rich Harvest: The History, Buildings and People of Lincoln, Massachusetts*. Lincoln, Mass.: Lincoln Historical Society, 1987.

McManus, Edgar T. *Black Bondage in the North*. Syracuse, N.Y.: Syracuse University Press, 1973, 2001.

Main, Jackson Turner. *The Social Structure of Revolutionary America*. Princeton, N.J.: Princeton University Press, 1965.

Manoli-Skocay, Constance. "A Gentle Death: Tuberculosis in Nineteenth-Century Concord." *Concord Magazine* (Winter 2003).

Martin, John Frederick. *Profits in the Wilderness: Entrepreneurship and the Founding of New England Towns in the Seventeenth Century*. Chapel Hill: University of North Carolina Press, 1991.

Martin, Margaret Mutchler. *The Chambers-Russell-Codman House and Family in Lincoln, Massachusetts*. Lincoln, Mass.: Lincoln Historical Society, 1996.

Massachusetts Soldiers and Sailors of the Revolutionary War. 17 vols. Boston, 1904.

Maynard, W. Barksdale. *Walden Pond: A History*. New York: Oxford University Press, 2004.

Melish, Joanne Pope. *Disowning Slavery: Gradual Emancipation and "Race" in New England, 1780–1860*. Ithaca, N.Y.: Cornell University Press, 2000.

Morgan, Kenneth. *Bristol and the Atlantic Trade in the Eighteenth Century*. 1993. Cambridge: Cambridge University Press, 2004.

Morison, Samuel Eliot. "Precedence at Harvard College in the Seventeenth Century." *American Antiquarian Society Proceedings* 42 (1932): 371–431.

Morrell, J. B. "The University of Edinburgh in the Late Eighteenth Century: Its Scientific Eminence and Academic Structure." *Isis* 62, no. 2 (Summer 1971): 158–71.

Morrison, Toni, and Robert Richardson. "A Bench by the Road: *Beloved*." *The World* 3 (January–February 1989): 4, 5, 37–41.

Moss, Marcia, ed. *A Catalog of Thoreau's Surveys in the Concord Free Public Library*. Geneseo, N.Y.: Thoreau Society, 1976.

Munro, Wilfred Harold, et al. *Tales of an Old Sea Port: A General Sketch of the History of Bristol, Rhode Island*. Princeton, N.J.: Princeton University Press, 1917.

Nash, Gary. *The Forgotten Fifth: African Americans in the Age of Revolution*. Cambridge, Mass.: Harvard University Press, 2006.

Nelson, Liz. *Concord: Stories to Be Told*. Beverly, Mass.: Commonwealth Editions, 2002.

Parkman, Ebenezer. *The Diary of Ebenezer Parkman, 1703–1782. First Part: Three Volumes in One: 1719–1755*. Ed. Francis G. Walett. Worcester, Mass.: American Antiquarian Society, 1974.

Peragallo, Thomas. "Soils of the Walden Ecosystem." In *Thoreau's World and Ours: A Natural Legacy*, ed. Edmund A. Schofield et al., 254–59. Concord, Mass.: Thoreau Society, 1993.

Petrulionis, Sandra Harbert. *To Set This World Right: The Antislavery Movement in Thoreau's Concord*. Ithaca, N.Y.: Cornell University Press, 2006.

Phalen, Harold R. *History of the Town of Acton*. Acton, Mass., 1954.

Pierce, Frederick Clifton. *The Descendants of John Whitney, Who Came from London, England, to Watertown, Massachusetts, in 1635*. Chicago, 1895.

Pierson, William D. *Black Yankees: The Development of an Afro-American Subculture in Eighteenth-Century New England*. Amherst: University of Massachusetts Press, 1988.

Poe, Edgar Allan. "The Purloined Letter." In *Selected Tales*, 192–210. New York: Library of America, 1991.

Pruitt, Bettye Hobbs, ed. *Massachusetts Tax Valuation List of 1771*. Boston: G. K. Hall, 1978.

Quintal, George, Jr., ed. *Patriots of Color, "A Peculiar Beauty and Merit": African Americans and Native Americans at Battle Road and Bunker Hill*. Boston: Division of Cultural Resources, Boston National Historical Park, 2004.

Richardson, David. *Bristol, Africa, and the Eighteenth-Century Slave Trade to America*. 2 vols. Bristol, U.K.: Bristol Record Society, 1986–87.

Ring, Betty. *Girlhood Embroidery: American Samplers and Pictorial Needlework, 1650–1850*. 2 vols. New York: Alfred A. Knopf, 1993.

Ronsheim, Robert D. *The Wayside: Home of Authors*. Washington, D.C.: U.S. Department of the Interior, 1968.

Rothman, Joshua D. *Notorious in the Neighborhood: Sex and Families Across the Color Line in Virginia, 1787–1861*. Chapel Hill: University of North Carolina Press, 2003.

Rules and Statutes of the Professorships in the University at Cambridge. Cambridge, Mass.: Metcalf, 1846.

Sanborn, Franklin. *The Personality of Thoreau*. Boston: Charles E. Goodspeed, 1901.

Schneider, Richard J. Introduction to *Approaches to Teaching Thoreau's "Walden" and Other Works*, 1–4. New York: Modern Language Association, 1996.

Schofield, Edmund A. "The Ecology of Walden Woods." In *Thoreau's World and Ours: A Natural Legacy*, ed. Edmund A. Schofield, 155–70. Concord, Mass.: Thoreau Society, 1993.

Shattuck, Lemuel. *History of the Town of Concord*. 1835. Rpt., Salem, Mass.: Higginson Book Co., 2002.

Sheldon, Asa. *Yankee Drover: Being the Unpretending Life of Asa Sheldon, Farmer, Trader, and Working Man, 1788–1870*. Hanover, N.H.: University Press of New England, 1988.

Shipton, Clifford K. *Sibley's Harvard Graduates: Biographical Sketches of Those Who Attended Harvard College*. Boston: Massachusetts Historical Society, 1933–75.

------. "Ye Mystery of Ye Age Solved." *Harvard Alumni Bulletin* 57 (1954): 258–63.

Skaggs, Jimmy M. *Prime Cut: Livestock Raising and Meatpacking in the United States, 1607–1983*. College Station: Texas A&M University Press, 1986.

Smith, Venture. *A Narrative of the Life and Adventures of Venture, A Native of Africa But Resident Above Sixty Years in the United States of America*. 1798. Whitefish, Mont.: Kessinger Publishing, 2004.

Social Circle. *Memoirs of Members of the Social Circle in Concord*. 7 vols. Cambridge, Mass.: Riverside Press, 1888–.

Sokolow, Michael. " 'New Guinea at One End, and View of the Alms-house at the Other': The Decline of Black Salem, 1850–1920." *New England Quarterly* 71, no. 2 (June 1998): 204–28.

Sontag, Susan. *Illness as Metaphor*. New York: Vintage Books, 1979.

Stowe, Harriet Beecher. *Oldtown Folks*. 1869. New Brunswick, N.J.: Rutgers University Press, 1987.

Sweet, John Wood. *Bodies Politic: Negotiating Race in the American North, 1730–1830*. Baltimore: Johns Hopkins University Press, 2003.

Teele, John Whittemore. *The Meeting House on the Green: A History of the First Parish in Concord*. Concord, Mass.: First Parish in Concord, 1985.

Thompson, Robert Farris. *Flash of the Spirit: African and Afro-American Art and Philosophy*. New York: Random House, 1983.

Thoreau, Henry D. *Faith in a Seed: The Dispersion of Seeds and Other Late Natural History Writings*. Ed. Bradley P. Dean. Washington, D.C.: Island Press / Shearwater Books, 1993.

------. *The Journal of Henry D. Thoreau*. Ed. Bradford Torrey and Francis H. Allen. 14 vols. in 2. 1906. Rpt., New York: Dover, 1962.

------. *Journal*. Ed. John C. Broderick et al. 8 vols. Princeton, N.J.: Princeton University Press, 1981–.

------. *Walden: A Fully Annotated Edition*. Ed. Jeffrey S. Cramer. New Haven, Conn.: Yale University Press, 2004.

------. *Wild Fruits: Thoreau's Rediscovered Last Manuscript*. Ed. Bradley P. Dean. New York: W. W. Norton, 2000.

Thoreau, Henry D., and Ralph Waldo Emerson. *Nature and Walking.* Boston: Beacon Press, 1991.

Tolman, George. *John Jack, the Slave, and Daniel Bliss, the Tory.* Concord, Mass.: Concord Antiquarian Society, 1901–2.

Towner, Lawrence William. *A Good Master Well Served: Masters and Servants in Colonial Massachusetts, 1620–1750.* New York: Garland Publishing, 1998.

Trumbull, Joan. "Concord and the Negro." B.A. thesis, Vassar College, 1944.

Ulrich, Laurel Thatcher. *The Age of Homespun: Objects and Stories in the Creation of the American Myth.* New York: Alfred A. Knopf, 2001.

Vital Records of Acton, Massachusetts, to the Year 1850. Boston: New England Historic Genealogical Society, 1923.

Waters, Wilson. *History of Chelmsford, Massachusetts.* Lowell, Mass.: Courier-Citizen Co., 1917.

Watkins, Lura Woodside. *Early New England Potters and Their Wares.* Cambridge, Mass.: Harvard University Press, 1950. Rpt., Hamden, Conn.: Archon Books, 1968.

West, Michael. *Transcendental Wordplay: America's Romantic Punsters and the Search for the Language of Nature.* Athens: Ohio University Press, 2000.

West, Patricia. *Domesticating History: The Political Origins of America's House Museums.* Washington, D.C.: Smithsonian Institution Press, 1999.

Wheeler, Ruth. *Concord: Climate for Freedom.* Concord, Mass.: Concord Antiquarian Society, 1967. Rpt., Concord, Mass.: Concord Museum, 2000.

Whitney, Henry Austin. *Incidents in the Life of Samuel Whitney.* Boston, 1860.

Wiencek, Henry. *An Imperfect God: George Washington, His Slaves, and the Creation of America.* New York: Farrar, Straus and Giroux, 2003.

Wilkes, Laura. *Missing Pages in American History: Revealing the Services of Negroes in the Early Wars in the United States of America, 1641–1815.* Washington, D.C.: Press of R. L. Pendleton, 1919. Rpt., New York: AMS Press, 1973.

Wolverton, Nan. "Bottomed Out: Female Chair Seaters in Nineteenth-Century Rural New England." In *Rural New England Furniture: People, Place, and Production,* Ed. Peter Benes, 175–90. Dublin Seminar for New England Folklife. Annual Proceedings. Boston: Boston University, 1998.

------. "'A Precarious Living': Basket Making and Related Crafts Among New England Indians." In *Reinterpreting New England Indians and the Colonial Experience,* ed. Colon G. Colloway and Neal Salisbury, 341–68. Boston: Colonial Society of Massachusetts, 2003.

Wood, David F., ed. *The Concord Museum: Decorative Arts from a New England Collection*. Concord, Mass.: Concord Museum, 1996.

Wood, Frederic J. *The Turnpikes of New England and Evolution of the Same Through England, Virginia, and Maryland*. Boston: Marshall Jones Co., 1919.

Wyman, Thomas Bellows. *The Genealogies and Estates of Charlestown, Massachusetts, 1629–1818*. Boston: D. Clapp, 1879. Somersworth, N.H.: New England History Press, 1982.

Young, Alan. *Robert the Bruce's Rivals: The Comyns, 1212–1314*. East Linton, Scotland: Tuckwell Press, 1997.

Zilversmit, Arthur. *The First Emancipation: The Abolition of Slavery in the North*. Chicago: University of Chicago Press, 1967.

INDEX

Acton, Massachusetts, 32, 97, 105, 114, 121, 190 n19, 202 n5
Adams, Charles, 200 n12
Adams, John, 68, 70, 71
Adams, Joseph, 123
Africa, 17, 21, 23, 44, 47, 119, 141–145, 150, 170, 193 n 4, 202 n12
Alcott, Bronson, 84
Alcott, Louisa May, 6, 84
American Revolution, 1, 5, 9, 10, 65, 70–112, 151, 173, 177–182
Amy, 185–186 n13
"Angler's Repast, The," 83
Antigua. *See* West Indies
Arlington, Massachusetts, 98
Attucks, Crispus, 70

Baker, George Minott, 126
Baker, Joseph, 2, 126, 184 n1
Baker, Lavina Minot, 2, 126, 166
Ball, Boston, 118, 200 n12
Bannocks, Tuggie, 136
Barnes, Nathan, 165
Barnes, Violet, 46, 48, 117, 151, 177, 178, 186 n13
Barrett, Ann Maria, 203 n15
Barrett, George Minot, 206 n15
Barrett, Lieutenant Humphrey, 76, 120–121, 125, 147–148, 154, 157, 177, 185 n13, 187 n4

Barrett, Colonel James, 60, 88, 91, 117–118, 120, 187 n4, 194 n25
Barrett Esq., Joseph, 203 n15
Barrett, Peter, 60, 118
Barrett, Philip, 60, 117–118, 186 n13, 194 n25, 200 n12
Barrett, Sophia, 203 n15
Barrett, Stephen, 60, 118
Barron, Benjamin, 19, 46, 48, 177, 188 n6
Barron, Elizabeth Parris, 46–48, 177
Barron, Jack. *See* John Jack
Barron, Susanna, 46, 47, 48, 117, 151, 177
Barron, Violet. *See* Violet Barnes
Barrow. *See* Barrow/Maro Parkman
Basket-making, 132–133, 137, 141, 150. *See also* Zilpah White
Battle of Bunker Hill, 98, 100, 101, 103, 134, 149, 204 n19
Battle of Lexington and Concord, 1, 5, 65, 72, 78–79, 83, 91, 95–100, 106, 160–161, 170, 173
Bay Road. *See* Lexington Road
Bay, Rose. *See* Rose Bay Robbins
Beatton, Squire John, 29–30, 185 n13, 187 n4, 190 n21
Belinda. *See* Belinda Royall
Benson, Francis, 200 n12
Bentley, Reverend William, 109–110

Bill, Boston. *See* Boston Ball

Black Horse Tavern Church. *See* West
   Church

Bliss, Cate, 75, 76, 79, 80, 103, 106, 109,
   110, 128, 151, 178, 179, 185 n13

Bliss, Reverend Daniel, 34, 39, 59, 61, 62,
   73, 75, 77, 178, 179, 191 n27

Bliss Esq., Daniel, 75, 99, 102–103, 117,
   171, 178, 187 n4, 191 n27, n29

Bliss, Hannah, 75–76

Bliss, Phoebe Walker, 74–77, 79, 80, 178,
   179, 181. *See also* Phoebe Bliss
   Emerson Ripley

Bliss, Phyllis, 75–77, 79, 103, 106, 110,
   117, 178, 179, 202 n9. *See also* Phyllis
   Bliss Ingraham

Block House, 61, 75, 77, 110

Blood, Sambo/Samuel, 118, 200 n12

Blood, Phinihas, 185 n13, 187 n4

Boaz, Catherine. *See* Catherine Boaz
   Robbins

Bootin, Reuben, 186 n13

Boston. *See* Boston Ball; Boston Potter

Boston, Massachusetts, 2, 13, 17, 23, 24,
   32, 36, 39, 44, 47, 48, 50, 52, 53, 59,
   62, 66, 72, 84, 86, 91, 93, 95, 98, 99,
   101, 103, 119, 122, 139, 141, 145,
   149, 162, 173, 189 n8, n11; black
   neighborhoods in, 159–160; British
   occupation of, 10, 70, 84, 87, 99

Boston Massacre, 70–71, 84

Bradford Academy, 83

Brattle, Dick, 43

Brattle, William, 43

Breed, John, 162–163, 167

Brickett, General James, 105

Bridge, Reverend Ebenezer, 49–50, 57,
   62, 112, 195 n28

Bridge, Sally, 57

Bridge, Venus, 49, 50

Brighton Cattle Market, 138

Brister. *See* Sippio Brister; Brister
   Freeman

Brister (Freeman's) Hill, 13, 14, 154, 171,
   175–176

Brister, Sippio, 15–19, 39, 43, 45, 61, 76,
   107, 117, 170, 181, 186 n1

Brister's Spring, 14

Bristo. *See* Brister Freeman

Bristol. *See* Brister Freeman

Bristol, England , 17, 108, 186 n3

Bristol, Rhode Island, 17, 186–187 n3,
   202 n12

Brooks, Asa, 152

Brooks, Joshua, 193 n2

Brooks, Nathan, 171–173

Brooks, Peter, 193 n2

Brown, Jacob, 152

Bulkeley, Reverend Peter, 26, 27, 35, 46,
   189 n15, n16

Bulkeley Esq., Peter, 187 n4

Burden, Reuben, 126, 204 n23

Burgoyne, General John, 107, 108, 140

Burial Hill, Concord, 35–36, 65, 72, 91,
   102, 113, 119, 195 n33, 200 n13

Buttrick, Colonel John, 140

Caesar, 185 n13. *See also* Caesar
   Chambers; Caesar Kettle; Caesar
   Minot; Caesar Prescott; Caesar
   Robbins

Caesar's Woods, 14, 120, 147–148, 154,
   160. *See also* Caesar Robbins

Cambridge, Massachusetts, 16, 43, 44,
   50, 60, 100

Campbell, Elizabeth Murray. *See*
   Elizabeth Murray

Campbell, Thomas, 86. *See also*
   Elizabeth Murray

Case. *See* Case(y) Feen

Casey. *See* Case(y) Feen

Cate. *See* Catherine Bliss

Catherine, 185 n13

Cato, 42. *See also* Cato Ingraham; Cato
   Lee

Cato's Conspiracy. *See* Stono Rebellion

Chair seating, 133, 150

Chambers, Caesar, 27, 179

Chambers, Squire Charles, 26–30, 33, 41, 45–47, 49, 50, 68, 93, 94, 122, 179, 180, 189 n16

Chambers, Chloris, 27, 28, 45, 179

Chambers, Jack, 27, 45, 47, 179

Chambers, Lincoln, 27, 33–35, 179, 181, 191 n28

Chambers, Rebecca, 33

Chambers-Russell-Codman Estate, 10, 12, 13, 26, 33, 40, 41, 93, 94, 103, 122, 123, 131, 166–167, 169, 179, 180, 189 n16, 192 n30, 200 n14

Channing, William Ellery, 125, 186 n13

Charlestown, Massachusetts, 2, 13, 20, 23, 26, 28, 33, 41–44, 47, 48, 51–55, 59, 93–95, 122, 179, 180, 182, 210 n1. *See also all Codman entries*

Chelmsford, Massachusetts, 49, 57, 112

Cheshire, Massachusetts, 167

Chloris. *See* Chloris Chambers

Church Green, Concord, Massachusetts, 24, 25, 36, 65

Civil War, 18

Clarke, Doctor William, 43, 47, 51, 53, 182

Codman, Elizabeth, 49, 51, 53, 54

Codman, Captain John, 43, 45, 47, 49–52, 81, 91, 122, 180; murder of, 41, 42, 48–49, 51–54, 64, 69, 70, 94, 106, 167, 182, 194 n17

Codman, John III, 180

Codman, Mark, 42–49, 51–56, 59, 61, 122, 126, 170, 180, 182, 193 n4, n10, 194 n17

Codman, Mary, 49, 51, 53, 54

Codman, Parnell, 49, 51

Codman, Phoebe, 42, 47–55, 180, 182

Codman, Phyllis, 42, 47–56, 180, 182, 193 n10

Codman, Scipio, 180

Codman, Tom, 49, 51, 180, 194 n17

Codman estate. *See* Chambers-Russell-Codman estate

Cogswell, Emerson, 89

Cogswell, Eunice, 89

Comyn clan, 30–31, 105, 191 n23

Concord, Massachusetts; First and Second Division of, 25, 26; incorporation of, 24, 25; mortality rates in, 158

Concord Church; gifts to, 114; schisms in, 33–35, 39, 73, 77, 101, 182; segregated seating in, 20, 24–25; social status and pew location, 26

Concord Committee of Correspondence, Inspection, and Safety, 84, 88, 99, 107

Concord Female Charitable Society, 136, 160, 169

Concord Social Circle, 96, 140, 147, 159–162, 164–166, 183 n1, 188 n6, 195 n33, 199 n5, 206 n15

Connecticut, 49, 119, 131, 187 n4

Consumption. *See* Tuberculosis

Cook, Beulah, 122

Cook, Hephzibah, 122

Cook, Mary Russell, 122–125

Cook, Thomas, 122–123, 125, 203 n17

Copley, John Singleton, 21

Cuba, 17. *See also* Cuba Vassall

Cuming, Abigail Wesson, 19, 23, 35–37, 39, 41, 57, 61–66, 87, 104–107, 114, 180, 188 n5, 192 n36

Cuming, Alexander (John Cuming's brother), 24, 29, 30, 37, 57, 189 n11, 190 n22, 191 n27

Cuming, Alexander (John Cuming's uncle), 28, 46, 187 n4, 190 n19

Cuming, Amy, 28, 29, 33, 39, 60, 64, 85–87, 91, 93, 99, 100, 103, 107, 114, 180, 190 n19, 192 n36, 197 n22

Cuming, Anne, 19, 46, 60, 188 n6, 190 n19, 193 n8, 202 n5

Cuming, Brister. *See* Brister Freeman

Cuming, Elizabeth (Betsy), 28, 29, 33,

Cuming, Elizabeth (continued)
   39, 60, 64, 85–87, 91, 93, 99, 100, 103,
   107, 112, 114, 180, 190 n19, n22, 192
   n36, 197 n22
Cuming, Helen (John Cuming's
   mother), 23, 24, 28, 64, 85, 189 n10,
   192 n36, 197 n22
Cuming, Helen (John Cuming's daughter), 57, 59–65, 68, 69, 81, 91, 104,
   105, 113, 180
Cuming, Isabella. *See* Isabella Cuming
   Nevins
Cuming, James, 28, 29, 86, 190 n19, n22,
   197 n22
Cuming, Jem, 41, 61, 62, 64, 66, 69, 78,
   107, 118, 126–127, 180, 185 n13, 192
   n1, 201 n22
Cuming, Colonel John, 9, 13, 28, 30, 35,
   42, 49, 57, 77, 89, 91, 94, 106, 109,
   170, 171, 180, 190 n19, n20, n22, 191
   n27, 192 n36, 200 n13, 201 n22, 209
   n19, 210 n1; acquires Brister Freeman,
   19–21, 23, 42, 181, 192 n30; and Abigail Wesson Cuming, 35–36, 39, 41,
   57; captivity by Indians, 61, 62, 63,
   104, 195 n28; civil service performed,
   67–70, 73, 95, 99–100; death of, 112–
   113, 115–116, 201 n2; desk of, 21, 22,
   188–189 n8, 192 n35; education, 31,
   32, 35, 36, 39, 69, 115, 191 n25; gifts
   and bequests made, 68–69, 114–116,
   126–127, 150–152, 195 n38, 202 n5;
   land speculation, 66–67, 69; link between his status and slaveholding, 12,
   19, 39, 41, 69, 90; loss of daughter
   Helen Cuming, 62–65, 69; military
   service of, 55, 57, 59, 103–105, 194
   n22, 195 n34; ownership of slaves in
   addition to Brister Freeman, 41, 43,
   64, 116, 118, 137, 185 n13, 187 n4,
   188 n5, 192 n1; mansion house of, 13,
   37, 38, 40, 66, 69, 77, 78, 104, 161,
   192 n35; political struggles during the
   Revolution, 85, 87–88, 99–100, 103;
   property in Concord, 33, 120–121,
   124; treatment of slaves, 60–61, 64,
   69, 90, 107–108, 203 n17
Cuming, Robert (John's brother), 28, 57,
   190 n19
Cuming, Robert (John Cuming's father),
   20, 21, 23, 24, 26, 28–30, 35–37, 39,
   57, 65, 66, 69, 85, 89, 104, 116, 180,
   187 n4, 189 n10, n11, 190 n19, n20,
   n21, 191 n23, 192 n36
Cummington, Massachusetts, 66–67, 69

Darby. *See* Darby Vassall
Darby, Eunice, 126
Davis, Charles, 89
Day, Jannette, 86
Declaration of Independence, 71, 103
Deerfield, Massachusetts, 66
Dick. *See* Dick Brattle
Doolittle, Amos: *A View of the Town of
   Concord*, 92
Dorchester, Massachusetts, 3, 145, 184
   n3
Dugan Trail, 129
Dugan, Catherine Porter, 128, 180
Dugan, Elisha, 128–129, 159, 180
Dugan, Elsea, 128, 129, 159, 180
Dugan, Jennie Parker, 128, 129, 158, 180,
   206 n16
Dugan, Thomas, 11, 128, 129, 151–153,
   157, 180, 205 n1
Dustan, Hannah Emerson, 61–62
Dwight, Timothy, 139

Edes, Charlestown, 124, 126, 138–139,
   152–154, 156, 204 n19, 207 n2
Edes, Isaiah, 124, 204 n19
Emerson, Edward W., 135, 183 n1
Emerson, Frank, 72, 79, 81, 83, 89, 97–
   98, 103, 105–107, 118, 178, 179, 185
   n13
Emerson, Hannah, 80, 104

Emerson, Mary Moody, 75

Emerson, Phoebe Bliss. *See* Phoebe Bliss Emerson Ripley

Emerson, Phoebe (William Emerson's daughter), 80, 104

Emerson, Ralph Waldo, 2, 5, 7, 13, 75, 81, 129, 135, 138, 148, 156, 157, 159, 163, 173, 178, 183 n5, 186 n15, 203 n16, 206 n13

Emerson's Cliff, 4, 14

Emerson, Rebecca, 104

Emerson, Waldo, 159

Emerson, Reverend William, 5, 6, 59, 62–63, 73–75, 77, 78, 101, 103–107, 119, 156, 178; and slavery, 72, 75, 76, 79–83, 89–90, 97, 103, 105–107, 118, 178–179, 185 n13, 187 n4, 202 n9; military service, 72, 91, 104–106. *See also* Old Manse

Emerson, William (the Reverend William Emerson's son Billy), 79–81, 104, 126, 156

Estabrook Woods, 186 n15, 203 n16

Feen, Case(y), 146, 182; enslavement to Samuel Whitney, 84, 85, 98–99, 182, 185 n13, 197 n20; living situation after slavery, 149–150; military service, 89, 149, 198 n28, 200 n12; rebellion against slavery, 84, 88–89, 100, 102, 107, 182; ties to Africa, 142–145; use of *nkisi*, 143–145, 150

Female Charitable Society. *See* Concord Female Charitable Society

Fenda. *See* Fenda Freeman

Fillis, William, 123

A Fishing Party. See Lydia Hosmer

Flint, Edward, 193 n8

Flint's Pond, 14

Former slaves, 12, 177–180; access to fuel and timber, 146–148; African beliefs of, 141–145, 150; and Thoreau, 1, 8, 9, 11, 14; continued management of by area whites, 127, 147–150; diet, 134–136, 138–140, 142, 145–146, 148, 153, 155–158, 171; forced to squat on infertile land, 10–11, 118–119, 150; forgotten by history, 5, 7, 9, 175–176, 195 n33; harassment of, 160, 162, 164–168; idealized in later years by locals, 171–173; jobs performed by, 131–134; lack of local marriage prospects, 159–160; mortality rates, 158–159; naming practices and, 14, 102, 107, 123, 136, 142–143, 171; no change in situation of, 10, 128, 137, 138; required to be single and childless, 138. See also Basket-making; Chair seating; Case(y) Feen; Brister Freeman; Great Field, Cato Ingraham, Pulling wool; Slaves; Spinning; Walden Woods; Warning-out system; Zilpah White

Fort Ticonderoga, 81, 83, 105, 106

Fortune Telling 3, 9, 140, 150, 181. *See also* Fenda Freeman

Framingham, Massachusetts, 134, 202 n9

Frank. *See* Frank Emerson

Freeman, Amos, 125, 154, 156, 157, 181, 210 n32

Freeman, Brister, 8, 12, 13, 45, 94, 111, 116, 118, 122, 128, 156–157, 179–181, 188 n6, n7, 191 n28; birth of, 12, 33, 192 n30; confused or conflated with Sippio Brister, 170, 181; death and burial of, 169–171, 188 n7; diet of, 138–140, 145–146, 153, 171; enslavement to John Cuming, 12, 19–21, 23, 37, 39–40, 41, 43, 59–62, 64, 66, 69, 78, 81, 124, 185 n13, 203 n17; enslavement to Timothy Wesson, 18, 19, 35, 37, 39, 42, 192 n30; harassment of, 145, 151–154, 160, 162, 164–166, 168; John Cuming's bequest to, 150, 151, 152; military service of, 107–108, 119–120, 124, 200 n12, 204 n19;

Freeman, Brister (continued)
  pulls wool, 139, 160; Rachel Le Grosse
  and, 162–164, 169–170; takes his
  freedom, 107–109; takes the last name
  of Freeman, 12, 108, 109, 116, 138,
  201 n22; and Walden Woods, 12,
  123–126, 137–141, 148, 151–158,
  163–164, 170, 175–176, 191 n28,
  192 n30, 204 n23, 209 n19; *See also*
  Brister (Freeman's) Hill
Freeman, Edward, 125, 153, 181
Freeman, Fenda, 8, 9, 125, 126, 138, 140,
  153, 154, 156, 162, 163, 181, 185 n13,
  206 n16,
Freeman, Jacob (Brister Freeman's son-in-
  law), 154, 156–157
Freeman, Jacob (Brister Freeman's grandson), 154, 156
Freeman, John, 157, 169, 171, 181
Freeman, Love Oliver, 154, 157, 162,
  169, 171, 181
Freeman, Nancy, 125–126, 154, 156–
  157, 181, 210 n32
French and Indian War, 56–57, 59, 61,
  62, 64, 66, 70, 104

Gage, General Thomas, 84, 98, 99
Gandhi, Mahatma, 175
Garfield, Daniel, 128, 129
Garfield, Elizabeth, 128, 129
Garfield, Louisa, 128, 129
Garrison, Jack, 121, 157, 158, 160, 171–
  173, 172, 177, 202–203 n15
Garrison, John, 157–159, 173, 177
Garrison, Elizabeth, 173
Garrison, Ellen, 159, 160
Garrison, Lewis, 158
Garrison, Susan (John Garrison's wife),
  157, 159
Garrison, Susan Robbins (Jack Garrison's
  wife), 121, 157, 158, 202–203 n15
Garrison House. *See* Block House
Georgia, 142

Gibbet, 55, 56
Gigger, Simon, 133
Gleason, Herbert Wendell, 4, 203 n16
Gloucester, Massachusetts, 118
Goose Pond, 125
Grant, President Ulysses S., 173
Great County Road. *See* Walden Street
Great Field, 10, 11, 19, 24, 25, 46, 88,
  154, 168, 186 n15; former slave com-
  munity there, 47, 119–121, 136, 138–
  140, 147, 151, 157–160, 177, 178
Great Meadows, 24, 25, 88, 119, 120,
  145, 161, 189 n12
Groton, Massachusetts, 124, 190 n 19,
  204 n19

Hancock, John, 21
Harris, John, 52, 53, 194 n17
Harvard College, 29, 31, 32, 39, 50, 57,
  68–69, 73, 74, 93, 100, 109, 113–115,
  151, 191 n24, n25, 195–196 n38
Hawthorne, Nathaniel, 5, 6, 84, 97, 119,
  138, 206 n13
Hendricks, Bets, 133
Heywood, Abiel, 195 n33
Heywood, Jonas, 186 n13
Heywood's Meadow, 14
Hoar, Brister. *See* Sippio Brister
Hoar, Elizabeth, 15–20, 39, 107, 170,
  181, 186 n1
Hoar, John, 15–20, 39, 43, 107, 170,
  181, 186 n1
Hoar Esq., John, 61, 187 n4
Hoar, Sarah, 16
Hoar, Timothy, 185 n13, 187 n4
Hobby, Richard, 200 n12
Hodon, Charleston, 200 n12
Hosmer, Lydia: *A Fishing Party*, 82, 83,
  133–134
How, Estes and Rachel, 162
Hubbard, Peter, 42
Hunt, Ruth, 80
Hunt, Deacon Simon, 185 n13, 187 n4

Hutchinson, Ann Maria, 203 n15
Hutchinson, Nancy, 121, 140, 159
Hutchinson, Peter, 120, 121, 140, 157–159, 203 n15, 206 n15
Hutchinson, Governor Thomas, 100

Inches, Henderson, 200 n14
Indians. *See* Native Americans
Ingraham, Cato, 8, 119, 138, 147, 181, 186 n13, 199 n5, 204 n23; abandonment by Duncan Ingraham, 110–111, 125, 146, 148–149, 155, 204 n22; death of, 155–156; diet of, 139–140, 146, 148, 155; rebellion against slavery, 96, 134; and Walden Woods, 125, 126, 141, 148–149, 156, 158. *See also* Captain Duncan Ingraham
Ingraham, Captain Duncan, 8, 91–93, 95–97, 99, 110, 124, 134, 141, 152, 154, 181, 186 n13, 187 n4, 199 n5, 202 n5. *See also* Cato Ingraham
Ingraham, Mary, 202 n5
Ingraham, Nancy, 110, 125–126, 149, 156, 181
Ingraham, Phyllis Bliss, 77, 80, 81, 110, 111, 121, 125, 126, 149, 155, 177–179, 181, 185 n13. *See also* Cato Ingraham
Inman, Elizabeth Campbell Smith. *See* Elizabeth Murray
Inman, Job, 100–101
Inman, Ralph, 100–101
Isaacs, David, 164

Jack. *See* Jack Chambers; John Jack
Jack, John, 19, 46–48, 102–103, 107, 117, 120, 151, 171, 177, 178, 180, 188 n6, 193 n8, n9, 200 n13
Jane, 185–186 n13
Jarvis, Edward, 135, 145, 146, 184 n1, 202–203 n15, 204 n21
Jefferson, Thomas, 49, 71, 103
Jem. *See* Jem Cuming

Jennie Dugan's Brook, 205 n1, 208 n9
Jennie Dugan's Spring, 208 n9
Jennings, Ginna, 131
Jennings, Mary, 131
Job. *See* Job Inman
John Cuming Medical Building, 13
Johnson, Samuel, 103
Jube, Cate, 186 n13
Jude, 141. *See also* Fortune telling

Kennedy, President John F., 175
Kettle, Caesar, 118, 200 n12
King, Martin Luther, 175
King Philip's War. *See* Metacom's War

Lancaster, Massachusetts, 198 n28
Lee, Cato, 101–102, 107, 110, 111, 118, 137–138, 182, 185 n13, 200 n12
Lee, John, 101
Lee, Jonas, 101–102, 200 n12
Lee, Dr. Joseph, 73, 77, 93, 98, 101–102, 107, 110, 117, 120, 137, 182, 187 n4, 200 n12
Lee, Pegge, 101
Le Grosse, Francis, 162, 163, 203 n17, 209 n18
Le Grosse, Rachel Harrington, 162, 163–164, 168, 169–170, 209 n18
Lexington Road, 2, 35, 67, 72, 122, 149, 182
Lexington, Massachusetts, 34, 72, 96, 122
Lincoln. *See* Lincoln Chambers
Lincoln, Massachusetts, 2, 3, 5, 6, 13, 15, 18–20, 26, 33–35, 73, 93–95, 107, 117, 123, 126, 145, 154, 161, 162, 167, 170, 179, 180, 187 n4, 188 n7, 191 n29, 193 n2. *See also* Chambers-Russell-Codman estate
Littleton, Massachusetts, 24, 29, 189 n11, 190 n19
London, England, 13, 17, 27, 30, 36, 39, 86, 87, 93

Lothrop, Margaret, 84
Lowell, James Russell, 173
Loyalists, 93–95, 98, 100–103, 199 n10
Luck. *See* Luck Russell

Maine, 134, 140
Malcolm X, 210 n1
Malden, Massachusetts, 73, 74, 118
Manse. *See* Old Manse
Mark. *See* Mark Codman
Maro. *See* Barrow/Maro Parkman
Mascarene, Margaret, 195–196 n38
Massachusetts Constitution, 108
Massachusetts Department of Conservation and Recreation, 6–7
Mather, Reverend Cotton, 20, 51, 188 n7
Medford, Massachusetts, 74, 78, 110, 125, 146, 148, 182. *See also* Royall Estate
Melvin, Sarah, 42, 186 n13
Menotomy. *See* Arlington, Massachusetts
Merrick, Mary, 91
Metacom's War, 61
Mexican-American War, 6, 152
Middlesex, Catherine, 117
Middlesex, Perkins, 117
Middlesex, Salem, 117, 124, 202 n9
Milton, Massachusetts, 100
Minkisi. See Case(y) Feen
Minot, Caesar, 118, 200 n12
Minot, Ephraim, 1, 148
Minot, George, 1–3, 5, 9, 28, 84, 89, 126, 135, 142, 145–147, 149, 150, 158, 183–184 n1
Minot, Captain George, 185 n13, 187 n4
Minot, Captain John, 205 n1
Minot, Mary, 1–3, 5, 7, 11, 28, 135, 145, 147, 148, 150, 153, 166, 183–184 n1, 184 n2
Minot, Rose, 32, 151, 186 n13
Minot, Master Timothy, 29, 32, 151, 191 n26

Minot, Dr. Timothy, 32, 186 n13, 187 n4
Minuteman Statue, 5–7, 13, 173, 175
Moore, Francis, 60, 194 n25
Morrison, Toni, 175–176
Munroe, Nathaniel, 162
Murray, Elizabeth, 85–87, 100, 190 n19, n22, 197 n22

Nancy, 42, 186 n13
Natick, Massachusetts, 71–73, 116, 118–119, 202 n8
Native Americans, 133, 135–137, 189 n12
Nedson Family, 133
Nero, 186 n13
Nevin, Isabella Cuming, 24, 29, 114, 189 n11, 190 n21, 191 n27
Nevin, James, 29, 190 n21
New Bedford, Massachusetts, 119
New Guinea, as name of black enclaves, 119
New Hampshire, 121
New Jersey, 121, 173
New York, 54, 55, 108, 116, 119, 140, 155
Nichols, Thomas, 71–72
Nkisi. See Case(y) Feen
North Bridge, 1, 5, 72, 91, 96, 97, 101
Nova Scotia, 32, 36–37, 39, 43, 99, 112
Nutting, Nathaniel, 203 n17
Nutting, Stephen, 162

Old Manse, 5, 6, 72, 77–79, 97, 104, 105, 161, 196–197 n13
Old Marlborough Road, 11, 128, 180, 186 n15. *See also all Dugan entries*
Old North Bridge. *See* North Bridge
Oliver, Almira, 121, 177, 181
Oliver, Elizabeth, 123
Oliver, Fatima. *See* Fatima Oliver Robbins
Oliver, Love. *See* Love Oliver Freeman

Oliver, Lucy, 123
Oliver, Robert, 123
Orchard House, 6
Otis, James, 68

Park, William, 65
Parker, Jennie. *See* Jennie Parker Dugan
Parkman, Barrow/Maro, 50–51, 188 n5
Parkman, Reverend Ebenezer, 41, 50–51, 55, 63, 79, 188 n5
Parris, Reverend Samuel, 46, 178
Pegge. *See* Pegge Lee
Peter's Field, 14. *See also* Peter Hutchinson; Peter Robbins
Peter's Pasture, 160
Peter's Path, 14, 120. *See also* Peter Hutchinson; Peter Robbins
Peter's Spring, 14, 120. *See also* Peter Hutchinson; Peter Robbins
Philadelphia, Pennsylvania, 119
Philip. *See* Philip Barrett
Phoebe. *See* Phoebe Codman
Phyllis, 123. *See also* Phyllis Bliss; Phyllis Codman
Pintard, John, 155
Piper, Lucy, 101
Pitcairn, Marine Major John, 91, 93, 95–97, 134
Plymouth, Massachusetts, 118, 119, 141–142, 206–207 n17
Poe, Edgar Allan, 143–144
Poor List, 28, 45, 118, 123, 125, 127, 143, 147, 148, 150, 152
Pope, Alexander, 143
Potter, Boston, 76, 80, 109–111, 118, 124, 138, 151, 179, 185 n13, 200 n12
Potter, Elizabeth, 1, 2, 183 n 1
Potter, Jacob, 124, 138, 154
Potter, Samuel, 76, 109–110, 185 n13, 187 n4
Powers, Essex, 194 n17
Powers, Thomas, 194 n17
Prescott, Dr. Abel, 149–150, 162

Prescott, Benjamin, 31–32, 191 n25
Prescott, Caesar, 117, 118
Prescott, Colonel Charles, 117, 118, 185 n13, 187 n4, 202 n10
Prescott, John, 32, 35
Prescott, Jonathan, 32
Prescott, Peter, 32, 35
Preston, Captain Thomas, 70
Pulling wool, 139, 160

Quaco, Caesar, 200 n12
Quoil, Hugh, 163

Reed, George, 193 n5
Revere, Paul, 21, 59, 71
Rhode Island, 136, 159
Richardson, John, 148–149, 152, 154, 156, 162
Riethmuller, C. J., 75
Ripley, Reverend Ezra, 6, 112, 119, 126, 178
Ripley, Phoebe Bliss Emerson, 58, 59–60, 72, 74–79, 81, 83, 89, 96, 99, 101, 103–106, 119, 126, 178, 181
Robbins, Adaline, 159–160
Robbins, Ann Maria, 159, 203 n15
Robbins, Caesar, 76, 77, 117, 120, 121, 151, 154, 157, 158, 177, 181, 185 n13, 202 n9, n14. *See also* Caesar's Woods
Robbins, Catherine Boaz, 117, 157, 202 n14
Robbins, Charlotte, 159–160
Robbins, Fatima Oliver, 121, 123, 177, 181, 203 n15
Robbins, Peter, 120, 121, 151, 157–160, 177, 202–203 n15
Robbins, Rose Bay, 117
Robin. *See* Robin Vassall
Rose. *See* Rose Minot
Route 126. *See* Walden Road
Rowlandson, Mary, 61
Roxbury, Massachusetts, 2, 23–24, 122
Royall, Abba, 44, 193 n193

Royall, Belinda, 44–45
Royall, Elizabeth, 74
Royall Estate, Medford, Massachusetts, 20–21, 44, 74, 77, 78, 131, 188
Royall, Squire Isaac, 20–21, 31, 44, 54, 68, 94, 123, 182, 188 n7
Royall, Squire Isaac Jr., 20, 21, 31, 44, 54, 68, 74, 103, 115, 182, 191 n23
Royall, Mary, 74
Royall, Penelope. See Penelope Royall Vassall
Russell, Betty, 122–123, 203 n17
Russell, Bilhah, 33, 179, 191 n28
Russell, Squire Chambers, 18, 33–35, 41, 42, 50, 55, 68, 93, 94, 108, 122, 179, 181, 187 n4, 192 n30, 193 n5, 198 n3
Russell, Dr. Charles, 93–94, 103, 123, 124, 128, 131, 169, 179, 182, 193 n5, 200 n14
Russell, Daniel, 33, 179
Russell, Elizabeth Vassall, 94, 103, 179, 182, 193 n5, 198 n3
Russell, Ishmael, 33, 179
Russell, James, 93, 103
Russell, Luck, 94–95, 100, 102, 103, 179
Russell, Peter, 33, 61, 94, 103, 122, 168, 179, 191 n28, 203 n17
Russell, Zilpah, 33, 35, 179, 181, 191 n28
Rutland, Vermont, 106, 107

Salem. See Salem Middlesex
Salem, Peter, 134, 202 n9
Salem, Massachusetts, 46, 116, 119, 141, 178
Salmon, John, 48
Sambo. See Sambo Blood
Savage, Jube, 123, 124
Scipio Africanus, 170
Scotland, 23, 28–31, 35, 36, 39, 93, 105
Shattuck, Daniel, 203 n15
Sidney, Margaret. See Margaret Lothrop
Slaveholders, and titles, 18, 187 n4; names they gave their slaves, 14, 17, 18,

27, 33, 34, 42, 50, 76, 85, 125, 197 n20; provisions in their wills for slaves, 60, 94, 110, 118, 126–127, 137; why they owned slaves, 16, 17–18, 23, 35, 41, 50, 61, 66, 69, 79, 83, 187 n4
Slaves; baptism of, 19–20, 46, 51, 188 n7; continued enslavement after the Revolution, 109–111, 117, 128–129, 137–138, 151; given and received as gifts, 15–16, 18, 19, 20, 21; emancipation of, 10, 18, 27–28; forcing their owners to abandon them, 10, 45–49, 88–89, 95, 99, 100–102, 106–109; labor performed by, 18, 19, 27–29, 32, 37, 52, 66, 69, 78, 79, 81–84, 89, 97, 102, 137; military service of, 102, 107–108, 110, 116–118; monetary value of, 19, 204–205 n25; number of in Concord, 9, 185–186 n13; punishments of, 54–55, 88; separation of families, 15, 16, 18, 40, 42–48, 64, 76, 94, 126, 138, 186 n2; treatment of, 9–10, 17, 49–52, 59–61, 69, 78, 80–81, 88–90, 195 n33. See also Former slaves
Slave insurrections, 54, 55, 84, 88–90, 94; fears of, 70–73, 96–98, 106
Smith, Elizabeth Murray Campbell. See Elizabeth Murray
Smith, James, 87. See also Elizabeth Murray
Smith, Lieutenant Colonel Francis, 91
Smith, Venture, 49, 188 n6
Social Circle. See Concord Social Circle
Southbridge, Massachusetts, 133
South Carolina, 54, 176
Spinning, 131–132, 137, 150, 169. See also Zilpah White
Sprague, Sarah Brown, 133
Spring, Henry, 42
Springfield, Massachusetts, 76
Staples, Samuel, 6, 159–160
Stone, Martha, servant of, 186 n13
Stono Rebellion, 54

Stow, Massachusetts, 47
Stowe, Harriet Beecher, 116, 118
Stratton, John, 124
Stratton's Hill, 122, 124, 154. *See also*
Brister's Hill
Sudbury, Massachusetts, 46, 71, 190 n19

Thoreau, Henry David, 1, 2, 6–9, 11, 14,
35, 152, 153, 156, 159, 163, 169, 175,
184 n4, 186 n15, 203 n16; journals of,
2, 3, 9, 84, 88, 89, 125, 137, 140, 142,
146–148, 157–158, 183–184 n1, 184
n2, n3, 197 n20, 189 n28, 204 n22;
"Walking," 128–129; Walden, 1, 3, 6–
9, 11, 13, 14, 119, 122, 123, 125, 126,
129–135, 130, 138–141, 148, 150,
156, 157, 162, 163, 166, 167, 170,
171, 175, 181, 184 n4, 185 n6, 204
n21, 206 n16, 209 n19
Thoreau, John, 184 n4
Thoreau's Path at Brister's Hill, 175–176
Thoreau Street, 14
Titus, 186 n13
Tom. *See* Tom Codman
Tony. *See* Tony Vassall
Twain, Mark, 173

Vassall, Abba, 44, 193 n5
Vassall, Colonel Henry, 43, 44, 54, 94,
179, 182, 193 n5, 198 n3
Vassall, Cuba, 193 n5
Vassall, Darby, 193 n5
Vassall, Elizabeth. *See* Elizabeth Vassall
Russell
Vassall, John, 193 n5
Vassall, Penelope Royall, 44, 94, 103,
179, 182, 193 n5
Vassall, Robin, 43–45, 47, 52, 53, 55,
123, 182, 193 n5
Vassall, Tony, 193 n5
Venus. *See* Venus Bridge
A View of the Town of Concord. See Amos
Doolittle

Violet. See Violet Barnes
Virgil, 50
Virginia, 128, 164, 180

Walden; or, Life in the Woods. See Henry
David Thoreau
Walden Pond, 1, 4, 5, 6, 14, 25, 121, 122,
124, 162, 175, 176, 184 n4, 185 n12
Walden Pond State Reservation, 6, 175–
176
Walden Road. *See* Walden Street
Walden Street, 2, 3, 67, 121–122, 176
Walden Woods, 1–3, 5, 8, 10–14, 25, 26,
81, 91, 186 n15, 189 n14, 203 n16;
black enclave in, 1, 3, 8–11, 121–127,
129–150, 152, 158, 162–163, 179,
181, 185 n12
Walden Woods Project, 175–176, 184
n1
War of 1812, 160, 167–168
Warning-out system, 10, 44, 45, 47, 107,
116–117, 149, 204 n19
Washington, George, 93
Watertown, Massachusetts, 16
Watertown Road, 16. *See also* Walden
Street
Wayside, 6, 84, 85, 88, 89, 197 n20. *See
also* Samuel Whitney
Webster, Massachusetts, 133
Wesson, Abigail. *See* Abigail Cuming
Wesson, Brister. *See* Brister Freeman
Wesson, Mr. Timothy, 18, 19, 20, 23,
33–36, 42, 69, 179–181, 187 n4, 188
n5, 188 n7, 192 n30
West (Concord) Church. *See* Black
Horse Tavern Church
West, Nancy, 164
Westborough, Massachusetts, 41, 50, 63,
133
West Church, Concord, Massachusetts,
34
West Indies, 17, 20, 21, 23, 24, 27, 32,
36, 46, 54, 55, 103, 131, 139, 180,

West Indies (continued)
    182, 193 n4

Weston, Massachusetts, 34, 117, 123,
    170, 202 n9

West Point, New York, 116

Wheeler, Peter, 139–140, 161, 163, 168–
    169, 188 n6; harrassment of Brister
    Freeman, 160, 164–166, 168

Wheeler, Phoebe (Peter Wheeler's
    daughter), 169

Wheeler, Phoebe Brooks (Peter
    Wheeler's wife), 161, 168

Wheeler, Captain Timothy, 160–161

White, Ammi, 97

White, John, 136

White, Zilpah, 9, 33, 61, 94, 103, 122,
    124, 125, 128–138, 141, 142, 148,
    150, 166–169, 179, 191 n28, 204 n21,
    206 n16, 209–210 n29; and spinning,
    131–132, 150, 169, 179. *See also* Bas-
    ket-making; Chair seating; Spinning

Whitefield, George, 34

White Pond, Concord, 129

Whitney, Abigail (blood relation of
    Samuel Whitney), 84, 85

Whitney, Abigail (wife of Samuel
    Whitney), 85, 98, 149

Whitney, Casey. *See* Case(y) Feen

Whitney, Samuel, 84–85, 88, 98–99,
    102, 142, 149, 182, 185 n13, 187 n4,
    198 n28

Williamstown, Massachusetts, 134

Wilson, William, 42

Woburn, Massachusetts, 118

Wood, Ephraim, 88, 99, 148–149, 152

Wyman, John, 162–163

Wyman, Thomas, 163, 184 n4

Zilpah. *See* Zilpah Russell; Zilpah White

ACKNOWLEDGMENTS

Black Walden is a sequel to my father's book, *Creative Land Development: Bridge to the Future* (1979), a guide to preserving green spaces, which grew out of the practices he developed as chairman of the Lincoln Conservation Commission from 1966 to 1981. My book attempts to reveal how much of the conservation land in and around Lincoln, particularly in the neighboring town of Concord, was indelibly shaped by local slavery.

Both of my parents planted the seeds for this book in ways they could not have anticipated. They raised me on land that formerly belonged to the Chambers-Russell-Codman estate, where by all appearances Brister Freeman was born, and they had me christened in the same church he was. On my sixteenth birthday, my mother took me to get my ears pierced at the John Cuming Medical Building. I was so focused on the prospect of finally being able to wear earrings, I only recently bothered to ask who John Cuming was. This account of his and Brister Freeman's lives is dedicated to both of my parents, a small token of thanks for their support over the past forty-something years. It is also for Jim Taylor and Eli Taylor-Lemire, each a co-author of this book in his own way.

The writing of *Black Walden* was made possible by a fellowship from the National Endowment for the Humanities and a sabbatical from Purchase College. I am grateful to both institutions for providing me with release time.

I am also indebted to the many colleagues, archivists, and friends who helped shape *Black Walden*, among them Neil Bernstein, Walter Brain, Marie-Therese Brincard, Jane Buchan, Larry Buell, Claudia Carlson, Laura Chmielewski, Frank Farrell, Bob Gross, Carol Haines, Emma Kaplan, Paul Kaplan, Jane Kromm, Jane Langton, Jonathan Levin, Catherine Lewis, Lynn Mahoney, Conni Manoli-Skocay, Noreen O'Connor-Abel, Linda Orton, Charlie Ponce de Leon, Werner Sollors, Michelle Stewart, Wayne TeBrake, Leslie Wilson, David Wood, and Louise Yelin. Special thanks to Jerry Singerman at Penn Press for shepherding me once again through the revision and publishing process and to my friend and writing partner Audrey Fisch for her unflagging patience and support.